AF624419

KṢEMENDRA STUDIES

OF

DR. SURYAKANTA

Text with English Translation

Edited by:

Prof. R.K.Panda

BHARATIYA KALA PRAKASHAN

DELHI (INDIA)

First Published : 2010
Revised Edition : 2024

© **BHARATIYA KALA PRAKASHAN**

All right reserved, no part of this Publication may be reproduced in any form or by any means without permission of the publisher.

Published by C.P. Gautam *for*
BHARATIYA KALA PRAKASHAN
3480/1, IInd Floor, Narang Colony, Tri Nagar,
Delhi - 110035, Ph. 011 71522860, Mob.: 9811642997, 8595139625
E-mail : info@bkpbooks.com; sales.bkpbooks@gmail.com
Website: www.bkpbooks.com

ISBN : 978-81-8090-253-6

Laser Type Setting by
A-ONE GRAPHICS

Printed by :
G.S. Offset Printer
Delhi

Contents

Editor's Foreword

We have hereby great pleasure to present Dr. Sūryakānta's *Kṣemendra Studies,* as volume 91 of the Poona Oriental Series. This work provides for the first time in the English language, together with a translation, a study of Kṣemendra's works in general and, in particular, a detailed study of his three manuals on Literature and Criticism, viz. *Kavikaṇṭhābharaṇa, Aucityavicāracarcā* and *Suvṛttatilaka.*

Kṣemendra, the Kashmirian poymath of the eleventh century A.D., holds a distinct place in the galaxy of Sanskrit poets. Most of his works are available in print, some are still in manuscript and some more have to be unearthed. Critical editions, even of published works, are yet a desideratum. Kṣemendra is widely known but his works are not as widely studied. They deal with diverse subjects, and provide rich material for study from the sociological, as well as literary, point of view.

A word may be said with regard to the mauals under reference. The *Kavikaṇṭhābharaṇa* deals with the making of the poet, the *Suvṛttatilaka* with the proper use of metres and the *Aucityavicāracarcā* seeks to establish *propriety* as the *soul* of poetry. It is true that *propriety* (aucitya) did not hold ground and was indeed swept away by the overwhelming flood of *suggestion* (dhvani). The Dhvani doctrine of Ānandavardhana was the topic of the day as it were. Mahimabhaṭṭa criticised it; but the great Ācārya Abhinavagupta upheld it. Kṣemendra, Abhinavagupta's own pupil, however, ventured to put some new thought into the whole problem and enunciate propriety *(aucitya)* as a distinct concept constituting the soul of poetry. Perhpas it was little too much. *Aucitya,* at all events, is a potent factor with which poetry—or anything for the matter of that—must be judged. But is lacks the all-absorbing appeal of *dhvani* which marks the ineffable *lāvaṇya* or charm of the Muse of Poetry.* The attempt, however, the analyse and dissect the delicate yet exquisite beauty and peculiar appeal of *dhvani* was not wise, though correct in theory. The numerous divisions and sub-divisions have made *dhavni* too ponderous to conceive and too lybyrinthine to negotiate. It were nice if the sastra was there to stimulte and help critical appreciation but not throttle genius by means of hair-splitting rules and injunctions. The growing dialectic about *rasa* and *alaṅkāra* sharpened the faculty to reason rather than inspire the faculty to create.It is natural therefore that the less abstract and less equivocal principle of propreity would attract the eye of the longing critic. Though not a big work, the *Disccourse on Propriety* is provoking enough. The numerous examples are illuminating. Nowadays when the knowledge of literary criticism is enriched by contributions from other literature, it is hoped that Kṣemendra will prove a welcome thinker in the field for many an enthusiastic scholar to emulate.

Dr. Sūryakānta, Mayūrbhanj Professor of Sanskrit, Banaras Hindu University, deserves the gratitude of scholars for having made this important contribution for the advancement of Learning.

R.K. Panda

---

*. Compare : Dhvanyāloka I, 4—
प्रतीयमानं पुनरन्यदेव वस्त्वस्ति वाणीषु महाकवीनाम्।
यत्तत्प्रसिद्धावयवातिरिक्तमाभाति लावण्यमिवाङ्गनासु।।

Preface

The present volume is composed, with a few additions and alterations, of the series of lectures I read at the Lahore University in 1943-44. Though produced under such a learned auspices, it can make no claims to learning. It contains the expressions of an ordinary reader concerning the great Kāsmiran poet, who might furnish matter enough for study during one's life-time. I am no specialist in the study of Kṣemendra, nor a scholar of the bewildering variety of subjects he chose to treat in his works. I can report no facts and propose no hypotheses about him which are not at hand in his own informative works; and perhaps it is his intellectual vision of the world that the poet himself in particular wishes to hand down to us, and not the shabby incidents that preceded that vision in his own person. My excuse for writing about him, notwithstanding, is, therefore, merely the common excuse for writing about the spring or the moon or a maiden. Kṣemendra has attracted me; he has moved me to reflection; he has revealed to me certain aspects of Indian life, literature and philosophy, which I am prompted to express, together with recording a few contributions of fact and opinion that are likely to throw light on the many facest of his complex personality, his works, his enviroment, his faith, his fancy that fed on the study of real things and the vision into which he poured his faculties. What I am offering to the benevolent reader is, thus, a piece of literary criticis, illustrated with an English translation of three of his works; and I hope that even this, necessarily brief, attempt will attract attention of scholars to the intensive study of one, who represents the Kāsmīrian spirit in its best form, and is the one versatile author in whom poetry and wisdom were intimately fused; for Kṣemendra's poetry and prose, in their infinite variety, blended with the meditation and a virile practical intelligence by which he sought to penetrate into the springs of life. In him creative emotion and reasoned thought were locked together to a degree rearely attained in India; and it is this human synthesis, coupled with the alert awareness of the activities of his day, that has appealed to me so much that it seemed to be permissible to signalize Kṣemendra's achievements and supplement them with a few such observations as seemed relevant. In view of some tendency towards a 'general opinion' a new objectively elaborated interpretation has a colam to careful consideration; and I hope this little work, may be instrumental in linking anew the Indian mind with Kāsmīra, that has contributed so infinitely and so vitally to our culture and literature, but whoe original spirit and tradition are now seriously menaced by exotic contaminations. I, as a member of the Panjab Legislature, think no task more important than to ensure that the bonds of Indo-Kāśmīrian Scholarship remain firm.

I owe thanks to Dr. H. L. HARIYAPPA for help generously given. It was at his suggestion that I gave this work to Dr. R. N. SARDESAI, the proprietro of the meritorious Poona Orientl series for publication; and I also owe a great debt to him and to my old pupil Mr. Jnān Cand for their acute scrutiny of my manuscript and its proofs. For such errors and omissions as remain, I alone am responsible.

Suryakānta

Introduction

KASHMIR, the ancient land of learning produced in the eleventh century of the Christian era a writer of great eminence, the polymath Kṣemendra. He is a writer of indomitable zeal and inexhaustible resources. His writings cover a very wide range of subjects. He is a versatile genius; his works include treatises on poetics and prosody. He wrote Kāvyas and Mahākāvyas, a drama, many didactic poems, poetical epitomes of the Rāmāyaṇa, the Mahābhārata, and of Guṇāḍhya's Bṛhatkathā, a chroinicle of Kings of Kashmir and a lexicon. Most of his works, numbering about thirty-two, have been published while some are yet in their manuscript form. In the whole range of Sanskrit literature few indeed have tried their hand on such a variety of subjects and with such success. Kṣemendra's comprehensive style, his clarity of expression, his power to use satire to the best advantage and his critical insight into literature have earned for him a place among the masters of Indian literary traditon.

In the present work an attempt has been made to deal with several aspects of Kṣemendra's life and works, his language and style, his contribution to Sanskrit literature, and his eminence as a critic of the theory and practice of poetry.

In his Kavikaṇṭhābharaṇa (which may be rightly called kaviśikṣā) besides discussing possibilities of becoming a poet, of borrowing and adopting from masters of poetic art the poetic charm and its illustration in its ten aspects, merits and demerits with regard to sense, sound and sentiment, Kṣemendra gives a hundred pieces of sound advice to the budding poets. Eminent writers on Sanskrit poetics like Daṇḍin, Rudraṭa, Vāmana, Vāgbhaṭa, Rājaśekhara,

Bhoja and Hemacandra have developed this subject in their treatises, but Kṣemendra appears to be quite original in his treatment.

A study of Kṣemendra's works reveals that they were written in accordance with the doctrines propounded in his Kavikaṇṭhābharaṇa. For instance, his didactic poems, the Samayamātṛkā, the Kalāvilāsa, the Darpadalana, the Sevyasevakopadeśa, and the Cārucaryāṣataka illustrate his *lokācāraparijñāna* (Kavi. II 6) i.e., 'familiarity with the ways of the world', and *upadeśaviśeṣokti* (Kavi II 16) i.e., 'special didacitc skill'. His epitomes of the Epics and the Nṛpāvali bear testimony to the fact that he was pursuing the principle of *itihāsānusaraṇam* (Kavi II 6) i.e., 'accordance with history'. In his Daśāvatāracarita he illustrates his *sāmyaṁ sarvasurastutau* (Kavi II 19) i.e., 'impartiality in the priase of all deities'; in the Padyakādambarī his *viviktākhyāykārasa* (Kavi II 6) i.e., 'sparkling interest in romances'; in the Citrabhāratanāṭaka his *nāṭakābhinayaprekṣā* (Kavi II 15) i.e., 'fondness for dramatic performances', and in his works on poetics *kāvyāṅgavidyādhigama* (kavi II 3) i.e., 'a knowlege of ancillary disciplines'. Since all his works are complete, one might say that he follows faithfully *prārabdhakāvyanirvāha* (Kavi II 22) i.e., 'seeing a poem to its finish'. In fact all the one hundred instructions to the poet are amply illustrated in his works, and it may be concluded that the Kavikaṇṭhābharaṇa was a product of his mature genius.

In his Aucityavicāracarcā, Kṣemendra has developed the theme of PROPRIETY as essentail to poetry. He has illustrated under twenty-eight headings how propriety can either be displayed or violated. His forceful arguments and discussions and his clear enuncitation of principles in defence of what he believes to be poetry, point to his remarkable conception of poetic art and its practice. His Aucityavicāracarcā, like his Kavikaṇṭhābharaṇa, is a mine of quotations from his contemporaries as well as predecessors and fully illustrates his contention *vyutpattyai sarvaśiṣyatā* (Kavi II 14) i.e., 'readiness to become other's disciple for poetic culture'; *paronmeṣajigīṣā* (Kavi II 14) i.e., 'eagerness to emulate or excel others' poetic genius'; *mahākāvyārthacarvaṇam* (Kavi II 14) i.e., 'ruminating upon the contents of great poems'; *sahavāsaḥ (kavivaraiḥ* Kavi II 14) i.e., 'contact or association with eminent poets'; and *pāṭhaḥ parakṛtasya* (Kavi II 3) i.e., 'study of others' compositions'.

Kṣemendra, to some, might appear in his Aucityvicāracarcā as a better critic than a poet. But this is a matter of opinion. At any rate, he is to be counted among the great literary critics like Daṇḍin, Vāmana and Ānandavardhana.

The well-known doctrines of Rasa, Alaṅkāra and Dhvani, held the ground when Kṣemendra propounded his theory of Aucitya. One might say that the concept of *propriety* had been felt by the elders but it was given to Kṣmendra to develop it into a system and declare that *Aucitya* is the *Soul* of poetry. Long ago Ānandavardhana realised that nothing spoils Rasa as *Anaucitya* or Impropriety. On the other hand, a composition based on the well-known (*prasiddha*) and the proper (ucita), constitutes the very secret of Rasa.

अनौचित्याद्दृते नान्यद्रसभङ्गस्य कारणम्।
प्रसिद्धौचित्यबन्धस्तु रसस्योपनिषत्परा।।–Dhvan. III

Aucitya is Harmony, Adaption, Proportion, Appropriateness, or Propriety. It presupposes Rasa and Dhvani. Professor S. Kuppuswami SASTRI has given a very interesting kārikā on the position of Aucitya among these concepts, viz.

औचितीमनुधावन्ति सर्वे ध्वनिरसोन्नयाः।
गुणालङ्कृतिरीतीनां नयाश्चानृजुवाङ्मयाः।।

Kṣemendra has reproduced faithfully the original epics in his Bhārata and Rāmāyaṇa *Majñjarīs.* His fondness for Vyāsa is clear since he added the appellation Vyāsadāsa (a follower of Vyāsa) to his name; for Vyāsa, according to him, is *bhuvanopajīvya* 'world-sustainer'. The lost Bṛhatkathā of Guṇaḍhya finds an echo in his *Bṛhatkathā mañjarī.* His abridgement of the KATHĀ may be considered to be quite faithful as it easily bears comparison with other extant abridgement.

In his reflections on the world and its vanities, there is sharpenss tones up with good humour and realism. His redicule of the bards and singers, goldsmiths, quacks, astrologers and vendors of patent medicines is frequent and poignant. His *Darpadalana* is intended to show the folly of pride, while the *Sevyasevakopadeśa* aims at issuing instructions for servants and their masters. The *Caturvargasaṅgraha* describes the four ends of life, and the *Cārucaryāśataka* prescribes the rules of conduct. Almost all his works are interspersed with moral maxims and didactic sayings.

Kṣemendra's treatment of Prosody is remarkable in more than one respect. Being an exponent of the Aucitya school he had said at the end of his Aucityavicārcarcā that innumerable facets of Aucitya could be discerned and elaborated besides the twenty-seven discussed by him. Eventually in his Suvṛttatilaka he seems to have taken up *vṛttaucitya* i.e. 'propriety of metre'.

Illustrations of different metres are from his own pen. He aims at originality with a vengeance as it were. Excellences and blemished of metres are brought out prominently. Further, there is a discussion on the characteristics of certain metres which makes them luminous and forceful. The appropriateness of ceratin metres to certain subjects, moods and situations is very instructive. Poets should employ a variety of metres. The favourite metres of Abhinanda, Pāṇini, Kālidāsa, Bhāravi and Bhavabhūti are remembered. Kṣemendra appears to be the only wrtier on Prosody who has dealt with this latter aspect of the subject.

A word on the text of the three treatises translated here : These are published in the Kāvyamālā series No. 1, 2 and 4, and also in the Haridāsa Saṁskṛta Granthamālā No. 24, 25, 26 also known as the Chowkhambā Sanskrit Series. The latter edition, though giving all the three at one place, is unfortunately defective.

With regard to the translation of the Kavikaṇṭhabharaṇa, the Aucityavicāracarcā and the Suvṛttatilaka, I may add that to render them into English has been by no means an easy task. Every translator has his limitations depending on the nature of the work he translates. As a matter of fact no translation can adequately reflect the original author's mind. Translation is at best a 'shadow'. Rhythm, word order, figures of speech, compactness or diffuseness of expression, these cannot be reproduced from one language into another. A miniature Sanskrit poem is like a little picture drawn by a master hand, complete alike in its nature and in its art, coloured with all the richness which a copious and flexible language like Sanskrit could impart.

Kṣemendra's works on poetics abound in vivid pictures in the fewest possible words; they defy translation. The ideas may be reproduced, but not their origianl excellence regarding situation, rhyme or rhythm. The difficulty of the task is aggravated by the highly technical nature of the subject and the complicated and critical prose of the author. Absence of any commentary on these treatises is perhaps another handicap.

While translation, however, the well-known dictum of Mallinātha has been trictly followed : neither make an unfounded statement nor say anything unwanted.

नामूलं लिख्यते किञ्चिन्नानपेक्षितमुच्यते।

Kṣemendra is, undoubtedly, a great luminary in the firmament of Poetry. He is trulyan inspirer like Vālmīki and Vyāsa who were his own mentors. His was 'a vow to perpetuate learning' in a selfless spirit, viz., *Vrtaṃ sārasvato yāgaḥ* (Kavi II 2). All praise be to him. He was

कविरविरविलुप्तव्याप्तिभिः सूक्तपादैर्नयति नवनवत्वं भावभावस्वभावम्।

—Kavi II 23

'The poet like the sun with his rays of poetry reaching every region reveals in fresh colours the sentiments, feelings and emotions of all beings.'

Chapter I

Kṣemendra's Life and Works

Like most Sanskrit witers Kṣemendra has not left for posterity any regular biographical account of himself. But this does not mean that we know nothing whatsoever about his life. He was not a mean to hide his light under the bushel. The concluding verses in his own works are informative. Some external evidence could be gatherd from Somendra's introduction to the Avadānakalpalatā and Kalhaṇa's Rājataraṅgiṇi. With the help of these it is possible to sketch the biography of Kṣemendra, though not in much detail. At any rate, his date, genealogy, private life, religion and identity, can be traced as follows.

Kṣemendra gives the name of the ruling king in all his works. In the Bṛhatrkathāmañjarī,[1] the Samayamātṛkā,[2] and the Daśāvatāracarita,[3] he gives the date on which each of the works was finished in the Laukika era. The centuries are omitted. We know from Kalhaṇa's Rājataraṅginī that the ear had its spoch in 3074-5 B.C. This enables us to determine Kṣemendra's date with some exactitude.

The omission of centuries is a serious handicap, but the name of the ruling king makes up for this. The sovereign mentioned in most of his works[4] is king ANANTA. Kalhaṇa's Rājataraṅgiṇī tells

---

1. कदाचिदेव व्रिपेण स द्वादश्यामुपोषितः।
   प्राथितो रामयशसाः सरसः स्वच्छचेतसा।। बृहत्कथामञ्जरी XIX 39
2. संवत्सेर पञ्चविंशे पौषशुक्लादिवासरे।
   श्रीमता भूतिरक्षायै रचितोऽयं स्मितोत्सवः।। समयमातृका App. 2
3. एकाधिकेऽब्दे विहितचत्वारिशं सकार्त्तिके।
   राज्ये कलशभूभर्तुः काश्मीरेष्वच्युतस्तवः।। दशावतारचरित App. 5
4. See colophons to the various works.

us that king Ananta ruled during the forty-second century of the Laukika era, which corresponds to 1028-63 A.D. This helps us in adding the missing centuries to the dates which Kṣemendra mentions. Counted in terms of the Christian era, we find that the Bṛhatkathāmañjarī was finished in 1037 A.D., the Samayamātṛkā in 1050 A.D., and the Daśāvatāracarita in 1066 A.D. during the reign of king Kalaśa, son and successor to king Ananta.

Kṣemendra's son Somendra, in his introduction to his father's Avadānakalpalatā, writes that the work was finished in the twenty-seventh year[1] at the rise of Vaiśākha. This means that the work was finished in 1052 A.D. under king Ananta.

It is clear therefore that the earliest date in Kṣemendra's works is 1037 A.D. (the Bṛhatkathāmañjarī) and the latest 1066 A.D. (the Daśāvatāracarita). As will be shown later on, the Bṛhatkathāmañjarī is one of the poet's earliest works, and we find no extant work other than the Daśāvatāracarita, which he wrote under king Kalaśa. This means that the period of his literary activity falls roughly between 1037 and 1066 A.D.

Kṣemendra does not mention the date of his birth anywhere, nor do we know it from any other source. We, however, can make a fair surmise. In the Bṛhatkathāmañjarī he writes that he studied rhetoric under Abhinavagupta, author of the Vidyāvivṛti or the Pratyabhijñāvṛhatī-vimarśinī.

श्रुत्वाभिनवगुप्तारव्यात्साहित्यं बोधवारिधेः।
आचार्यशेखरमणेर्विद्याविवृतिकारिणः ॥

–बृहत्कथामञ्जरी XIX 37

Abhinavagupta, we know, wrote his commentary on the Pratyabhijñā-Darśana in 1014 A.D. This means that Kṣemendra studied under Abhinavagupta after or about 1014 A.D. and long before his Bṛhatkathāmañjari was written, because, we shall see later on, this was his third work. To allow a period long enough for

1. संवत्सरे सप्तविंशे वैशाखस्य सितोदये।
कृतेयं कल्पलतिका जिनजन्ममहोत्सवे॥
Somendra's introduction to the Baudhāvadānakalpalatā, 16.

the poet to be able to study rhetoric and have general acquaintance with the existing literature, we may, with Mr. Madhusūdan KAUL, say that he was nearly twenty-five years of age,[1] when he wrote the Bṛhatkathāmañjari. This should fix the date of his birth somewhere between 990 A.D. and 1010 A.D.

The date of Kṣemendra's death also, is not certain. He wrote the Daśāvatāracarita in 1065-6 A.D. This seems to have been his last work. He might, therefore, have died shortly after 1065-6 A.D. and it may not be wrong to place the date at about 1070 A.D.

Kṣemenda's span of life may have, thus, coverd the first three quarters of the elventh century, while his literary activity is limited to the second and third quarters of the same. Two points support this view. He was a pupil of Abhinavagupta, author of the Vidyāvivṛti. The latter's period of literary activity falls between 991 A.D. (corresponding to the year 66 mentioned in his Kramastotra) and 1015 A.D. (= Laukika year 90 in which he finished his Vidyāvivṛti). Thus the periods of literary activity of Abhinavagupta, the teacher, and Kṣemendra, the pupil, are separated by an interval of a couple of decades. In view of this fact it may be noticed that the passage in the Daśarūpāvaloka by Dhanika, in which a quotation from the Bṛhatkathāmañjarī is cited, is a later interpolation.

In his Aucityavicāracarcā, Kṣemendra quotes two verses (11, i; 16, viii) from PARIMALA. In the Suvṛttatilaka he quotes another verse, II, 21, (i) from the same author. Parimala, we know, is the same as Padmagupta, the author of the Navasāhasāṅkacarita. Padmagupta himself tells us that he was the court-poet of Vākpatirāja, king of Mālava, and his successor Sindhurāja, alias Navasāhasāṅka. The period during which these two kings ruled, as ascertained from inscriptions, falls roughly between 1074 A.D., and 1010 A.D. It follows therefrom, that the literary career of Padmagupta, alias Parimala, also falls within the same period, i.e, the last quarter of the tenth century and the first quarter of the eleventh. This conclusion is consistent with the results that have been established from the evidence of Kṣemendra's own works.

1. The Deśopadeśa and the Narmamālā by Madhusūdan KAUL.

There is a short account of the poet's genealogy at the end of the Daśāvatāracarita. Here he says that his father was Prakāśendra, while his grandfather was called Sindhu. He gives the name as Sindhu in his Rāmāyaṇamañjarī, and this seems to be the correct form of the name. In the Kavikaṇṭhābharaṇa, he mentions Cakrapāla as his brother.

Kṣemendra's son Somendra in his introduction to the Avadānakalpalatā gives a more detailed account of his parentage. He says that in the dynasty of Narendra, a minister to king Jayāpīḍa, was born Bhogendra, whose son was named Sindhu, while Sindhu's son was Prakāśendra. Kṣemendra, Somendra's father, was Prakāśendra's son.

As regards the identification of these names we have to turn to Kalhaṇa's Rājataraṅgiṇī, which mentions two kings of the name of Jayāpīḍa. One ruled over Kashmir in the latter half of the eighth century while the other lived under king Jayasiṁha (1128-49 A.D.). King Jayāpīḍa (8th century A.D.) had numerous ministers but none of the name Narendra. We may therefore conclude that Narendra held some unimportant office, and was perhaps one of the many ministers.

Coming to Bhogendra we find that no person of this name suiting our choronology is mentioned in the Rājataraṅgiṇī. One Bhogasena is mentioned under king Uccala (1101-11 A.D.) but for chronological reasons, he cannot be identified with Bhogendra of Narendra's family.

The Rājaṭaraṅgiṇī mentions one Sindhu, a treasurer to queen Diḍḍa (958-1003 A.D.) He is painted very black, and is shown as a foil to his younger brother Bhuyya, who was a city-prefect. The identification of the two names—Sindhu of the Rājataraṅgiṇī, and Sindhu of Kṣemendra—is tempting. The chronology also supports this. But there are grave objections to this. The Rājataraṅgiṇī shows Sindhu as an extremely wicked man, while Kṣemendra praises his grandfather for his charity and devotion to Śiva. Again Sindhu of the Rājataraṅgiṇī had a son Mataṅga, who was also a treasurer to Saṅgrāmarāja (1003-28 A.D.). We find no mention of Maṭaṅga in

Kṣemendra's writings. The objection, which explodes the identification, is that according to the Rājataraṅgiṇī, Sindhu's father was a litter-carrier Kuyya. Somendra says that Sindhu's father was Bhogendra. We have no justifiable grounds for indentifying 'Kuyya' with Bhogendra. There is no mention of Sindhu's son or grandson in the Rājataraṅgiṇī. Nor is there any mention of Prakāśendra. It speaks of Kṣemendra only as the author of Nṛpāvali.

We may conclude from all this that neither Kṣemendra nor any of his fore-fathers played any important role in the political history of Kashmir. Had they done so their names must have found place in the Rājatarṅgiṇī. The question whether they enjoyed royal patronage is equally hard to decide.

Supplementing Kṣemendra's account of his genealogy with that of Somendra, following would be the family-tree :

Narendra
(Minister to King Jayāpīḍa)
|
Bhogendra
|
Sindhu
|
Prakāśendra
|
Kṣemendra — Cakrapāla
|
Somendra

Nothing is known about Kṣemendra's private life. Neither he nor his son gives us any detailed information on this point. A few conjectures may, however, be made. When mentioning his father Prakāśendra,[1] Kṣemendra invariably speaks of his immense

1. सूर्यग्रहे त्रिभिर्लक्षैर्दत्वा कृष्णाजिनत्रयम्।
अल्पप्रदोऽस्मीत्यभवत्स लज्जानतकंधरः।।
स्वयंभूनिलये श्रीमान्यः प्रतिष्ठाप्य देवताः।
दत्वा कोटिचतुर्भागं देवद्विजमठादिषु।।
पूजयित्वा स्वयं शंभुं प्रसरद्बाष्पनिर्भरः।

wealth and charity. He says that Prakāśendra was a philanthrope and a great patron of the Brāhmaṇas whom he constantly fed in large numbers in his own house. Prakāśendra spent three crores (of what, is not mentioned) on the gods, Brāhamaṇas, and 'maṭhas'. He set up images of deities in Śiva's temple. On the occasion of the solar eclipse, he gave in charity three black-buck skins to Brāhmaṇas with three lacs each. He was a fervent worshipper of Śiva and died when embracing the image of his honoured god. From this it is clear that Prakāśendra was a very rich man. This means that Kṣemendra must have been brought up like a prince. His childhood, therefore, was without any suffering.

As regards his career as a student, Kṣemendra gives meagre information. He mentions the names of three of his teachers—Abhinavagupta, the author of the Vidyāvivṛti; Gaṅgakal; and Somapāda, a believer in the Bhāgavata faith. The Bṛhatkathāmañjarī tells us that he studied rhetoric under Abhinavagupta.

In his Aucityavicāracarcā, the author calls himself, "sarvamanīṣiśiṣyaḥ". Whether he says this out of sheer humility or he really means it is hard to decide. As he mentions three of his teachers, we may conjecture that he had studied with other teachers too. It is probable that he studied different brachnes of literature with different teachers who were specialists in them. The prolific nature of Kṣemendra's works supports this view.

The Kavikaṇṭhābharaṇa, the Aucityavicāracarcā and the Suvṛttatilaka, are manuals for earnest beginners. Possibly, he himself had a large number of pupils for whose edification he wrote them and other short poems which relate to daily life and conduct. Thus Kṣemendra, himself a diligent student, was perhaps earnest about the proper training of his pupils as well. And he may very well have practised his own tenets expounded in the

---

गाढं दोर्भ्यां समालिङ्ग्य यस्तत्रैव व्यपद्यत ।। बृहत्कथामञ्जरी । (XIX 33-35)

आसीत्प्रकाशेन्द्र इति प्रकाशः काश्मीरदेशे त्रिदेशश्वरश्रश्रीः ।

अभूद्गृहे यस्य पवित्रसत्रमच्छिन्नमग्रासनमग्रजानाम् ।।

यः श्रीस्वयम्भूभवने विचित्रे लेप्यप्रतिष्ठापितमातृचक्रः ।

गोभूमिकृष्णाजिनवेश्मदाता तत्रैव काले तनुमुत्ससर्ज ।। औचित्यविचारचर्चा

Kavikaṇṭhābharaṇa. He may also have been influenced by the Kāvyamīmāṁsā of Rājaśekhara.

A study of the works will indeed reveal the poet's personality. Judged by style and language, the Deśopadeśa and the Narmamālā were two of his earliest original compositions. Even a cursory reading of these two works would betray the sensuous youth that perhaps Kṣemedra was. He descends to low vulgarity in these works.[1] One can hardly appreciate the minute details in which he indulges, and everything points to the author's low taste. We then come to works like the Kalāvilāsa, the Samayamātṛkā and others. In these the poet, though not guilty of vulgarity, shows an intimate knowledge of the ways and habits of courtesans. Not even Bāṇa[2] gives such a vivid description of harlots as Kṣemendra does. Being the son of a fabulously rich father, he was perhaps given to youthful luxuries and possessed a conduct far from honourable.

After this there is a remarkable change in the spirit of his works. From the vulgarity of the Deśopadeśa and the sensuous character of the Samayamātṛkā, he rises to sublime heights in the Avadānakalpalatā, the Kavikaṇṭhābharaṇa, the Aucityavicāracarcā the Suvṛttatilaka, and the Daśāvatāracarita. What possibly could be the cause of such a change in the poet's outlook on life? Was it a sad event—say the death of his father? or was it just sobriety which advanced age not unoften brings in its train? Much can be said on both sides. One might argue that his father's or wife's death brought about that change. Such cases are met with not infrequently, e.g., the famous poet Tulasīdāsa began writing poetry after he had heard taunting remarks from his wife. It might also be argued that when the enthusiasm of youth cools down, and when a man leaves his thirties and enters his forties he grows sober. Then his judgement becomes ripe and he sees things in their proper perspective. Another

1. Though these two works are didactic in purpose, yet when compared witht he Kalāvilāsa and the Samayamātṛkā, they clearly show the author's tendency to include vulgar matters in his description. Even if we look at the narration as realistic, we cannot but chareg the author with low taste.
2. Cf. Rājakulavarṇanam in the Kādambarī.

view may be that too much indulgence itself brings about a reaction and the man is suddenly awakened as it were. He sees his msitakes and is remorseful for his past. This feeling brings about a refrom and is by itself capable of changing the outlook on life. Whatever the real cause of this change, there it was, a change for the better. It awakened the poet and the critic. The works written in this period have made him immortal both as a poet and a critic.

Kṣemendra mentions a number of his friends, teachers and pupils. Somendra supplements this number. Those mentioned are Gaṅgaka, Abhinavagupta, Rāmayaśas, Cakarapāla, Nakka, Sajjanānanda, Sūryaśrī, Vīryabhadra, Ratnasiṁha, Udayasiṁha, Lakṣmaṇāditya, Somapāda and Devdhara. Some of these may be identified with the help of Kalhaṇa's Rājataraṅgiṇī.

The identification of Abhinavagupta, the author of the Vidyāvivṛti, and the teacher with whom Kṣemendra studied rhetorics is obvious. He is the same person who wrote the *locana* commentary on the Dhvanyāloka of Ānandavardhana.

Kṣemendra mentions Gaṅgaka as one of his teachers.[1] We find no man of exactly the same name in the Rājataraṅgiṇī. However, one Gaṅga is mentioned as a friend of king Saṅgrāmarāja who ruled during 1003-28 A.D. He died soon after his friend's accession. The identification is open to no serious objection.

Kṣemendra mentions one Rāmayaśas[2] at whose request, he wrote several works. There are thre men of the name 'Rāma' in the Rājataraṅgiṇī, but it is unsafe to identify Rāmayaśas with any of these.

In the Kavikaṇṭhābharaṇa, Kṣemendra mentions Cakrapāla as his brother. We find no man of that name in Kalhaṇa's Rājataraṅgiṇī. The name of a village is given as Cakrapura in the same work, but this has nothing to do with Cakrapāla, because it was founded under king Lalitāditya long before Kṣemendra.

In his introduction to the Avadānakalpalatā Somendra calls

1. In the Aucityavicāracarcā.
2. In the Bṛhatkathāmañjarī and the Bhāratamañjarī.

Nakka his father's dear friend. We can find no person of that name in the Rājataraṅgiṇī. He may, therefore, have been only one of the admirers of Kṣemendra, though a person of no great significance in the history of Kashmir.

Somendra mentions Sajjanānanda also as a friend of his father. It is he who first requests him to compose the Avadānakalpalatā. In the Rājataraṅgiṇī no man of that name is found. One Sajjana is mentioned as a cavalier under king Jayasiṁha (1128-49 A.D.). He was killed in the battle at Padmapura. The identification of the two—Sajjana and Sajjanānanda—is tempting. But there is one objection. Sajjanānada requested Kṣemendra to compose the Avadānakalpalatā before 1052 A.D. (the year in which the work was finished). He must have been in the latter half of his twenties or the beginning of his thirties—if not of a riper age—at that time. That Sajjanānanda lived long enough to srve under Jayasiṁha as an active cavalier does not appear acceptable.

Somendra mentions Sūryaśrī as Kṣemendra's scribe. He praises him for his knowlege. We know nothing more about him from any other sources.

Vīryabhadra appears in Somendra's introduction to the Avadānakalpalatā only as an authority on Buddhistic texts. Obviously he held no high office either in the royal circles or at the vihāras, otherwise Somendra must have mentioned his office. The Rājataraṅgiṇi also ignores Vīryabhadra.

In his Aucityavicāracarcā, Kṣemendra mentions Ratnasiṁha as his friend, and Udayasiṁha's father. For chronological reasons he cannot be identified with Ratna, minister to king Utpalāpīḍa, who rules in the middle of the ninth century A.D.

Further, the poet states that he worte it for Bhaṭṭa Udayasimha, the son of Ratnasiṁha, Kalhaṇa's Rājataraṅgiṇī mentions a man called Udayasiṁha, as an officer of king Kalaśa on and successor of king Ananta. He is also shown as serving king Harṣa (1089-1101 A./d.), as in charge of the Lohara territory, His name also occurs as Udayasīmha. The identification of Bhaṭṭa Udayasiṁha,

Kṣemendra's pupil with Bhaṭṭa Udayasiṁha of the Rājataraṅgiṇī is temtping, and from chronological evidence even plausible.

Coming to Lakṣmaṇāditya,[1] we find that no man of exactly the same name is mentioned in the Rājataraṅgiṇī. However, one Lakṣmaka plays quite an important role in Kashmir history. He was a chamberlain under king Bhikṣācara (1120-21) A.D. and is mentioned as 'old Lakṣmaka' under jayasiṁha (1128-49 A.D.) during whose reign he died. He was Jayasiṁha's prime minister for some time, mentioned also as rājaputra. The only reason that militates against such an identification is the improbability of a rājaputra being appointed as chamberlain.

Kṣemendra mentions one Devadhara.[2] It was at his order that he composed the Bṛhatkathāmañjarī. Devadhara held the office of 'Dvijarāja' or 'King of Brāhmaṇas'. Since Kṣemendra calls him 'Sarvajña', he must have been a great scholar. It is probable that he was his teacher.

Kṣemendra speaks very highly of Somapāda,[3] who was a Vaiṣṇava. It was he who converted him to Vaiṣṇavism. For his father Prakāśnedra was a devout Śaiva, who set up many idols of Śiva and died actually embracing the image of his beloved god. Thus a born Śaiva though, and taught by Śaivite stalwarts like Abhinavagupta though, Kṣemendra became a Vaiṣṇava under the influence of Somapāda. Witness the riducule of Śaivism in his Deśopadeśa and the Narmamālā. As the Daśāvatāracarita is writeen in the spirit of a Vaiṣṇava, and as it is the last extant work of Kṣemendra, it may be said that he remained a Vaiṣṇava for the rest of his life.

Buddhism also exerted some influence on the poet. He must have studied the Buddhist religion very deeply as a result of which he wrote the Avadānakalpalatā. He was so much impressed by Buddhism that he included the Buddha among the ten incarnations of Viṣṇu.[4] As Buhler points out, the idea of the Buddha as an

1. Mentioned in the Kavikaṇṭhābharaṇa.
2. Mentioned in the Bṛhatkahāmañjarī.
3. Mentioned in the Bṛhatkathāmañjarī.
4. See the Dasśāvatāracatira, IX canto.

incarnation of Viṣṇu was long present among the people, but Kṣemendra is the first author to our knowledge who propagated that view and produced a work of literary merit to that end.

Regarding Kṣemendra's identity it was Peterson who first of all confused Kṣemendra Vyāsadāsa with Kṣemarāja,[1] a great commentator on philosophic treatises. Prof. Peterson repeated the mistake, but he soon revised his opinion concluding that it was extremely difficult to identify Kṣemendra Vyāsadāsa with Kṣemarāja.

The cause of the confusion is that both Kṣemendra Vyāsadāsa and Kṣemaraja were pupils of Abhinavagupta. Further, Kṣemarāja is mentioned as Kṣemendra in some manuscripts like the Spandasandoha. But this supposed identity may be set aside easily. While Kṣemendra Vyāsadāsa provides considerable information about his parentage, friends etc., Kṣemarāja is absolutely silent. He tells us nothing about his father, while it is almost a mannerism with Kṣemendra to praise his father for his generosity and religious bent of mind, Secondly, it is noticeable that Kṣemendra invariably styles himself Vyāsadāsa in all his works whereas Kṣemarāja avoids all appellations.

Moreover, while Kṣemendra Vyāsadāsa has mostly written light poetry and treatises on criticism. Kṣemarāja confines his activities to philosophical works. It is safe however to let the question remain open.

The extent and nature of Kṣemendra's literary output may now be discussed. Indeed, Kṣemendra is a prolific writer. His extant works fall into four divisions :—

I. *Poetical Epitomes*—Rāmāyaṇamañjarī or Rāmāyaṇakathāsāra, Bhāratamañjarī, Bṛhatakathāmañjarī, Daśāvatāracarita, and Bauddhāvadānakalpalatā or simply Avadānakalpalatā.

II. *Didactic Poems*—Kalāvilāsa, Samayamātṛka, Cārucaryās-

---

1. See the Journal of the Bombay Branch of the Royal Asiatic Society, Vol. XVI.

śataka, Sevyasevakopadeśa, Darpadalana, Deśopadeśa, Narmamālā and Caturvargasaṅgraha.

III. *Poetics and Metrics*—Kavikaṇthābharaṇa, Aucityavicāra-carcā and Suvṛttatilaka.

IV. *Miscellaneous*—Lokaprakāśakośa, Nītikalpataru and Vyāsāṣṭaka.

Other works atrribted to Kṣemendra are known in name only. For the present, however, let us confine ourselves to extant works.

1. *Ṛamāyaṇamañjarī.* This is a summary of Vālmiki's Rāmāyaṇa. The work is important in that it shows the condition of the text of Vālmiki's Rāmāyaṇa in the eleventh century. We find little genuine poetry and the work is full of obscure passages. The style is terse on account of studied brevity. The work has been edited in the Kāvyamālā series NO. 83.

2. *Bhāratamañjarī.* This is a summary of the Great Epic, the Mahābhārata of Vyāsa. The work proved a great success and elevated Kṣmendra to a high place among the poets of the day so much so that he assumed the little 'Vyāsadāsa'. The last verse of this work proclaims—

एव विष्णुकथातीर्थपुण्यवत्सलिलोक्षितः ।
प्राप्तः सामान्यजल्पोऽपि क्षेमेन्द्रोऽद्य कवीन्द्रताम् ।।

Bühler in his Kashmir Report writes that his manuscript of the Bhāratamañjarī bears the date 93 rd year of Saptarṣi era. Now it is highly improbable that Kṣemendra wrote his work in that year of the forty-second century of the Laukika era, as it is one of his earliest compositions. Moreover, Kṣemendra did not live long after 1070 A.D. Thus the date may refer to the date of the manusript itself. This is plausible as the century of the year is omitted.

This work has little literary merit or poetic value. Though a good summary, it is characteristically barren and lifeless. In his eagerness to compress as much matter as possible in a short space, the peot often makes his narrative obscure. The work is, however, important for the student of the history of Sanskrit literature. Kṣemendra mentions even unimportant incidents and episodes, be it by a single pharse or a single sentence. This helps us to determine the exact condition of the text of the Mahābhārata in the eleventh century. A striking omission is that of chapter 342-353 of the Śānti Parva. This suggests that these chapters were interpolated after the eleventh century A.D. It has been edited in the Kāvyamālā series NO. 28. The Araṇyaparva of the work has also been edited by Mr. BHANDARE.

3. *Bṛhatkathāmañjarī.* This is a summary of Guṇāḍya's Bṛhatkathā. Kṣemendra says that he had a copy of the latter while writing this summary. This can help us in determining the correct form of Guṇāḍhya's Bṛhatkathā. As the Rāmāyaṇa mañjarī and the Bhāratamañjarī are to the Rāmāyaṇa and the Mahābhārata, so the Bṛhatkathāmañjarī must have been to the Bṛhatkathā of Guṇāḍhya. Since the latter is lost, one can form an idea of its volume, subject-matter and form from the Bṛhatkathāmañjarī.

The work is divided into eighteen *lambakas,* nineteenth being added in the end to serve as a finale. The term 'lambaka' is most probably applied to the victory of a hero. Kathāpīṭha introduces the legend of Guṇāḍhya. In the second lambaka, Udayana is glorified while in the third he wins Padmāvati. Naravāhanadatta, the future emperor of the Vidyādharas is born in the fourth lambaka, while in the fifth, Śaktivega comes to him and relates how he went to the city of the Vidyādharas and won four maidens. In the sixth, the legend of Sūryaprabhā is cotinued. In the seventh Kaliṅgadatta, father of Kaliṅgasena, wants Udayana to marry her; he agrees, and when his minister Yaugandharāyaṇa objects, he promises to marry Kaliṅgasena's daughter to Naravāhanadatta. The eight lambaka describes the episodical legend of Velā and her hsuband and ends with the statement that Madanamaṅucukā has been abducted by Mānasavega. The ninth lambaka contains the prince's espousal of Lalitalocanā and her disappearance, the tenth the legends of Vikramāditya, and the eleventh the recovery of Lalitalocanā. In the twelth lambaka, Gomukha tells the tale of Muktāphalaketu, and in the thirteenth the prince finds Madanamaṅcukā with the help of five Vidyādhara maidens, but again losing her, marries the four girls. In the fourteenth lambka the prince married the four girls. In the fourteenth Alaṅkāravatī in the sixteenth Śakti-Yaśas, and in the seventeenth he obtains seven jewels from sage Vāmadeva and kills Mandaradeva. In the eighteenth lambaka, Gopāla and Pālaka resign their tenure of the kingship of Ujjain. Avantivarman weds the heroine and the two are protected against a jealous Vidyādhara by the emperor. The nineteenth lambaka forms the finale.

Kṣemendra is faithful to the copy of Guṇādhya's Bṛhatkaṭhā till the fifth lambaka. He then breaks away from the tradition, and diverges widely. The summary is poetically wortheless. It is dry though sober, and compression of matter often results in obscurity. Kṣemendra tries -to relive his work of the barreness by adding elegant descriptions, but it is a process without any striking results. The work was finished in 1037 A.D. It has been edited in the Kāvyamālā Series No. 69.

4. *Daśāvatāracarita.* It is a poetical abstract of the stories of Viṣṇu's incarnation. The work cannot be considered an independent composition. The subject-matter of the first nine incarnations is taken from the Purānas. The seventh chapter which represents Viṣṇu's incarnation as Rāma, shows novelty of conception. Here the whole of the Rāmāyaṇa is narrated with Rāvaṇa as the central figure. The result is quite happy and the vividness of description as it contains the earliest known reference to the Buddha being considered as an incarnation of Viṣṇu. The narration of the Buddha's life is an abridgement of the story as told in Buddhistic works. The style shows maturity of conception, and is easy and flowing. The work was finished in the Laukika era 41 i.e. 1066 A.D. on the Tripureśa mountain.

5. *Bauddhāvadānakalpalatā.* This work is a collection of Jātaka stories. Kṣemendra composed 107 'pallavas', but his son Somendra added one more to make the number 108 which is considered auspicious. In the introduction, Somendra says that Sajjanānanda requested Kṣemendra to write the Buddhistic birthstories. His dear friend 'Nakka' also requested to the same effect. Kṣemendra undertook the task but left it after writing three Avadānas, was the work seemed too lengthy. But in a dream the

Buddha instructed him to complete the work, while he himself helped him. The teacher Vīryabhadra, an authority on Buddhistic texts also came to assist Kṣemendra. Sūryaśrī was the scribe. The work was finished in the 27th year i.e. 1052 A.D. at the rise of Vaiśākha.

Śākya-Śrī, a Paṇḍita of Kashmir, presented the Avadānakalpalatā to Kun-dgah Rgyal Mtshan, the Lāma of Tibet, in 1202 A.D. It was translated into Tibetan seventy years later by Śoṅ-ton Lochāva. The translation as found by Śarat Candra Das is extremely literal and is considered as the master-piece of Tibetan poetry.

The first forty chapters of the book were lost in India. One manuscript says *"pūrvārdhaṁ kutracit na prāptam"*. These however, can be restored verbatim from the Tibetan version.

The Avadānakalpalatā illustrates six perfections of the Bodhisatava. These are "charity, moral character, patience, dilligence, contemplation and wisdom." It has been edited in the Bibliotheca Indica by Mr. DAS.

6. *Kalāvilāsa.* Critics are unanimous is considering this as Kṣemendra's best work. The book is divided into ten cantos. In canto I, the character of Mūladeva, the famous cheat, is introduced. The rest of the work consists of discourses to Candragupta, his pupil. In the first canto, arrogance is said to be three-fold i.e., crane-like, tortoise-like and cat-like—the last-mentioned being the very height of it, which pervades all men, animals and even the vegetable kingdom. Next, the origin of greed is narrated, and it is said to reside in the trades. The third canto describes the pitiable condition of those in love, and gives an interesting story relevant to the subject of hand. In the next canto the deceitful character of courtesans is exposed. They have sixty-four arts, of which the art of a bawd deserves to be ranked first. Canto V is a satire on the Kāyasthas, the employees of a king. The unscrupulousness of their character is here exposed. Like the incarnations of Viṣṇu, they have sixteen *kalās,* but all contribute to the accumulation of wealth. A humours story is related to show the mean character of a Kāyastha. Canto

VI denounces *'mada'* or arrogance. "Restraint (='dama') in the Kṛta age has become arrogance (='made) in the Kali age." He then divides arrogance into fourteen rather ill-marked divisions. The description of drunkard is really grand. "he cannot differentiate between good and bad, gold and silver, thus though an ascetic, the drunkard goes to hell" (VI 17). He does not feel his self-respect injured when he sees his wife kissing another and he himself is of no strong character. While telling a story of the mythological origin of arrogance, the poet gives an interesting list of places where it resides. Very interesting and pointed is the satire in canto VII, where the bards and the singers are the victims. They deprive people of their wealth by uttering just a few tunes and even then say, "What the devil has he given us?" Though they earn a lot in the morning, they are paupers by noon. Then follows a legendary origin of music. Canto VIII is a satire on goldsmiths. They possess sixty four arts—six of hissing, twelve of movemnts, eleven of thinking new ways of deception, five of weight and so on. Narrating a story the poet says that the mice that undermined the Meru mountain were cursed by gods to be born in the world as goldsmiths. The next two cantos serve as advice to young men, and indicate the means by which one can avoid falling into evil ways. It has been edited in the Kāvyamālā Series No. 1.

7. *Samayamātṛkā.* In this work the poet lays bare the snares of courtesans with great skill. In this work, the hetaira-to-be Kalāvatī is introduced by a barber to an old courtesan, who though owl-faced, crow-necked, and cat-eyed proves an able instructress. The book is divided into 'samayas'. The barber Kaṅka meets the heroine Kalāvatī in the first 'samaya.' In the second 'samaya' the barber gives an amusing and humorous account of the bawd's wanderings in Kashmir. This part of the work is particularly valuable as it mentions several places which can be identified even today. The third 'samaya' contains an elegant description of incidents that take place in the 'prostituere' in the evening. The bawd meets Kalāvatī in the fourth 'samaya' of the work and gives her elaborate instructions, while she divides lovers in eighty classes in the fifth 'samaya', and mentions twenty-three ways in which a lover, having

no money, can be got rid of. The sixth 'samaya' is a fine description of all that happens in the morning in the 'prostituere'. In the last two 'samayas' the heroine is able to take in a young fool and his parents. In the Samayamātṛkā we find the earliest reference to Pāñcāladhārāmaṭṭha and Kṛtyāśramavihāra. The description also mentions ancient salt-trade which still follows the same route. Like the Kalāvilāsa the work is didactic in character and is one of Kṣemendra's finest compositions. It has been edited in the Kāvyamālā Series No. 10.

8. *Cārucaryāśataka.* This is a short poem of one hundred verses in *anuṣṭubh.* The main object of the work is to teach law and polity. Generally the first line of a verse is a moral aphorism, and the second an illustration of the truth embodied in the first. The illustrations are mainly drawn from the epics and the purāṇas. It is of special importance, because it has influenced the Nītimañjarī of Dyā Dviveda (1494 A.D.) and Mugdhopadeśa of Jalhaṇa. The work has been edited in the Kāvyamālā Series No. 2.

9. *Sevyasevakopadeśa.* This is another short poem of sixty-one ślokas. It lays down the duties of the master and the servant, and seeks to better their relations. The last stanza runs thus. "Even ready to honour the learned, and full of the flavours of contentment and sevice, (the author) Kṣemendra by name has composed this Sevāvasara for the eternal bliss of the wise." An auto-biographical touch here is perhaps irresistible. Mr. BHANDARE points out that it is a "vindication of the dignity of service rendered to a worthy master". The work has been edited in the Kāvyamālā Series No. 2.

10. *Darpadalana.* It is quite a long poem consisting of seven chapters called 'vicāras.' In the first chapter Kṣemendra asserts seven causes of pride—high birth, wealth, learning, beauty, valour, munificence and austeirties. He then deals with each of these separately in seven chapters. Each chapter begins with a few generalizations appropriate in form to the cause of pride in hand; he then illustrates them by means of an interesting story in which the pride of the hero has a fall. The poem is didactic and abounds in general maxims and observations in the form of proverbs. It has been edited in the Kāvyamālā Series No. 6.

11. *Deśopadeśa.* In this work Kṣemendra describes in detail his own observations on the customs and notorious characters of the day. The book is divided into eight upadeśas. The first upadeśa ridicules the wicked man. The second criticises the misers; a lenghty caricature of the miser's habits and life in general. "Without rhyme or reason, he falls out with wife and contrives thereby to get rid of his relative of guest. He often foregoes dinner in this intentional fury." In the third upadeśa, Kṣemendra calls a courtesan "a restless dancing mechanical puppet, fitted with strings." In the fourth upadeśa bawds are riduculed while the fifth criticises the 'Viṭa'. The sixth is a satire on the Gauḍa student in a Kashmir University for his high-handed behaviour and arrogance. Old man's marriage is laughed at in the seventh upadeśa, but, alas the description is throughly vulgar. The eighth criticises different types of people—the poet, the quack, the grammarian and so on. It has been edited by Mr. Madhusūdan KAUL, and published by the Kashmir Research Department. The work seems to be one of Kṣemendra's earliest attempts on an original theme. It is in fact the first step to his Kalāvilāsa.

12. *Narmamālā.* This work is akin to the Deśopadeśa in theme. It is divided into three 'parihāsas' or jokes. The main object of ridicule is the villainous Kāyastha. The whole official machinery has in a way been subjected to ridicule while king Ananta is extolled for re-establishing order. It begins with a story giving the origin of the Kāyastha who is "the incarnation of the home-accouontant of the Daityas." He has also been called Divira. The Kāyastha's sole ambition is to become a state-official. He is pointed to be an unmitigated hypocrite without any redeeming feature, and finds pleasure in ruining temples and making the Brāhmaṇas go on hunger strike. The wholly unbearable behaviour of the Kāyastha as an official is vividly described. After his appointment, the Kāyastha and family change clothes, suggesting thereby the evil practice of bribery. The Kāyastha as Gañja Divira and Niyogī is painted in still blacker colours. An elaborate description of the Kāyastha's camp-luggage follows, and a repulsive account of his private life is given. It shows nothing but viciousness. The author

next criticises physicians, astrologers, 'oyāgas' and the 'guru'. The work concludes with the tragic end of the Kāyastha. Who is arrested and put into prison. He is released through the atrocities of his sister-courtesan, but his misfourtunes multiply. All his riches and property and confiscated, and he dies a very sad death. The work has been edited by Mr. Madhusūdan KAUL and published by the Kashmir Research Department.

13. *Caturvargasaṅgraha.* The work seeks to describe the four ends of human life—morality (dharma), practical life (artha), love (kāma) and release (mokṣa). The description is most perfect in the case of love. It has been edited in the Kāyvamālā Series No. 5.

14. *Kavikaṇṭhābharaṇa.* This is a short treatise on the making of a poet. The work is divided into five chpaters or 'sandhis'. The first deals with the effort required for becoming a poet. Such an effort is two-fold—divine and human. The second deals with the training of the poet. It lays down one hundred pieces of advice for the student. These seek to train him both psychically and physically. The third chapter discusses how a poet can compose striking and brilliant poems. Here, the 'camatkāra' is divided into ten classes. The fourth treats of the merits and demerits of poetry. The fifth enumerates the different sciences in which the poet should be well versed in order to write good poetry.

The work is important both for its form and matter. It supplies us with valuable information as regards the lower date of the authors quoted profusely in the examples. The work has been edited in the Haridās Sanskrit Series No. 24. It has also been edited in the Kāvyamālā Series No. 4.

15. *Aucityavicārcarcā.* This is a treatise on literary criticism. It declared *Aucitya* or Propriety as the soul of poetry, which is sustained by means of Rasa or Flavour. Thus the author makes Flavour subordinate to Propriety. The work seeks to show that propriety should be observed in twenty-eight places. Each place is defined by a kārikā which is followed by a discussion. Usually two examples are given, one illustrated Propriety and the other Impropriety. The discussion clearly points out why the verse is

proper or improper. The heading "Kāvyāṅgeṣū" has been left untouched as its scope is unlimited. It has been published in the Haridāsa Sanskrit Series No. 25 and the Kāvyamālā Series No. 1.

16. *Suvṛttatilaka.* This is a work on metrics divided into three chapters or *'vinyāsas'*. The first chapter is called the *'Vṛttāvacaya'* or the 'Selection of Metres'. Twenty-four metres are defined giving examples of each. The second chapter called *'guṇadoṣavarṇanam'* is devoted to a concise exhibition of the merits and demerits as regards metres. The third chapter discusses the use of metres. The last two chapters of this work are particularly valuable. These not only contain the names of many Sanskrit poets, but also attempts the unique task of assigning particular metres to describe particular situations or emotions. Such critical acumen is hardly seen in other writers on prosody. The work has been edited in the Haridāsa Sanskrit Series No. 26 and the Kāvyamālā Series No. 2.

17. *Lokaprakāśa-Kośa.* It is dictionary not differing much in form from the ordinary Sanskrit kośas. WEBER does not consider it to be the work of Kṣemendra. Mr. KAUL also thinks it to be a work of some later author. But as BÜHLER points out, the work is genuinely from the pen of Kṣemendra Vyāsadāsa. BÜHLER writes : "This work gives a great amount of information on the daily life of the Hindus which elsewhere we seek in vain. He gives forms of huṇḍis or letters of exchange bonds, and the like, the titles of most of the Kashmirian officials, in some cases with explanations, a list of the 'paraganās' into which Kashmir was divided. The importance of such an information cannot be over-rated, as all the Kośakāras live too high in the clouds of the Śāstras and poetry to care about such trivial matters as the geography, administration, commerce of the country, etc. etc." The work has not been published as both the manuscripts available—one found by WEBER and the other by BÜHLER—are fragmentary and in very bad condition.

18. *Nītikalpataru.* It is a commentary on a treatise on polity by Vyāsa.

19. *Vyāsāṣṭaka.* It consists of eight verses written to eulogize

the great poet Vyāsa, the author of the Mahābhārata.The work appears as an appendix to Kṣemendra's Bhāratmañjarī. It has been edited in the Kāvyamālā Series No. 28.

Besides the works given above, many others are known by name only. Such works fall distinclty under four heads—those mentioned in (i) the Kavikaṇṭhābharaṇa (ii) the Aucityavicāracarcā (iii) the Suvṛttatilaka and (iv) Miscellaneous.

Works mentioned in the Kavikaṇṭhabharaṇa are Śaśivaṁśamahākāvya, Padyakādaṁbarī, Citrabhāratanāṭaka, Lāvaṇyavatī, Kanakajānakī, Muktāvalī and Amṛtataraṅga-mahākāvya.

Those mentioned in the Aucityavicāracarcā are Vinayavallī, Munimatamīmāṁsā, NItilatā, Avasarasāra, Lalitaratnamālā, and the Kavikarṇikā (if it was a separate work).

The Suvṛttatilaka mentions one Pavanapañcāsika.

The Rājataraṅgiṇī ascribes another work *Nṛpāvali* or *Rājāvali* to Kṣemendra. The work is not available. Evidently it was a chronicle of kings—most probably of Kashmir kings—and was written, as Kalhaṇa says, in verse. The Rājataraṅgiṇī censures the author for carelessness in this work.

Pandit Śiva DATTA ascribed *Hastiprakāśa* to Kṣemendra, but as he himself admits, the ascription is doubtful.[1]

BÜHLER's Kashmir Report gives two works the *Spandanirṇaya* (No. 511) and *Spandasandoha* (No. 517) of Kṣemendra. These can hardly be the works of Kṣemendra Vyāsadāsa, and BÜHLER himself admits this fact. The author as suggested by BÜHLER may be taken to be identical with Kṣemarāja, another pupil of Abhinavagupta, and a commentator on philosophic works.

Mr. Madhusūdana KAUL, has attempted to arrange the works of Kṣemendra in a chronological order. His classification is as follows :

1. In the Kāvyamālā.

(a) Bṛhatkathāmañjarī, Bhāratamañjarī, Ramāyaṇamañjarī.

(b) Pavanapañcāśika, Suvṛttatilaka.

(c) Vinayavatī, Lāvaṇyavatī, Munimatamīmāṁsā, Nītilatā, Avadānakalpalatā, Avasarasāra, Lalitaratnamālā, Muktāvali, Vātsyāyanasūtrasāra, Aucityavicāracarcā.

(d) Padyakādambarī,Śaśivaṁśamahākāvya, Deśopadeśa, Narmamālā, Citrabhāratanāṭaka, Kanakajānakī, Amṛtataraṇgamahākāvya, Caturvargasaṅgraha, Kavikaṇṭhābharaṇa.

(e) Darpadalana, Kalāvilāsa, Samayamātṛkā, Sevyasevakopadeśa, Dasāvatāracarita, Cārucaryāśataka.

Obiviously, the arrangement of works in lists (c) and (d) is open to question. The Aucityavicāracarcā, which Mr. KAUL puts in period (c) quotes two works—the Citrabhāratanāṭaka and the Caturvargasaṅgraha—from (d). Again, the Samayamātṛkā was written in 1050 A.D. and the Avadānakalpalatā in 1052 A.D. Mr. KAUL places the composition of the Avadānakalpalatā long befor that of the Samayamātṛkā. He places the Suvṛttatilaka just after the three summaries, but it cannot be so early as it was obviously written with mature experience. Moreover Mr. KAUL distinguishes the Padyakādambarī and the Vātsyāyanasūtrasāra from the other three summaries without giving any adequate reasons.

Any attempt to construct the chronology of Kṣemendra's works must be based on his three treatises the Aucityavicārcarcā, the Kavikaṇṭhābharaṇa and the Suvṛttatilaka, because the se works are anthological in character. Let us try to arrange these three works in chronological order.

The Aucityavicāracarcā was written in order to teach Ratnasiṁha's son, Udayasiṁha. The Kavikaṇṭhābharaṇa mentions Udayasiṁha, a pupil of Kṣemendra as Mahāśrī and also names his two works the 'lalita' and the 'Bhakti-bhāva'. Evidently the two Udayasiṁhas are identical. Now Udayasiṁha could not have been a 'Mahāśrī' and the author of the two poems before completing his dues, which were obviously completed at least after he had studied the Aucityavicācarcā.Thus the Kavikaṇṭhābharaṇa was composed after Kṣemendra, had finished his Aucityavicāracarcā.

As regards the position of the Suvṛttatilaka, one cannot be sure. Its language, style and the treatment of subject in hand would indicate that it was written before the Aucityavicāracarcā.

Now to a reconstruction of the chronology of Kṣemendra's works.

The first period will naturally consist of the summaries i.e. Rāmāyaṇamañjarī, Bhāratamañjari, Vyāsāṣṭaka, Bṛhatkathāmañjarī, Vātsyāyanasūtrasāra, and Padyakādambarī. Of the first three works, the Rāmāyaṇamañjarī is clearly the earliest, as it does not mention the title 'Vyāsadāsa', which, as we have seen, Kṣemendra accquired only when he had written the Bhāratmañjarī. Moreover it is written in rather an immature style. The Bhāratamañjarī and the Vyāsāṣṭaka, which is merely an apendix to the former, come next. The Bṛhatkathāmañjarī was finished in 1037 A.D. and is definitely later than the other two Mañjarīs. The position of the Vātysāyansūtrasāra and the Padyakādambarī cannot be fixed.

Coming to the other original works, we may be certain that the Deśopadeśa and the Narmamālā were Kṣemendra earliest attempts. After this we lost the thread. We shall have to put the Pavanapañcāśikā, Suvṛttatilaka, Nītikalpataru, Lāvaṇyavatī, Munimatamīmāṁsā, Nītilatā, Avasarasāra, Lalitaratnamālā, Muktāvali, Kalāvilāsa, Samayamātṛkā (1050 A.D.) and Avadānakalpalatā (1052 A.D.) earlier than the Aucityavicāracarcā, because excepting the first three, and the Samayamātṛkā, all others are quoted in this treatise. Then come the Śaśivaṁśamahākāvya, Citrabhāratanāṭaka, Kanakajānakīharaṇa, Amṛtataraṇgakāvya and Caturvargasaṅgraha, all of which are quoted in the Kavikaṇṭhābharaṇa. Kṣemendra, then may have undertaken the composition of scientific works like the Lokaprakāśa, in which the Darpadalana, Sevyasevakopadeśa, Cārucaryāśataka, and Daśāvatāracarita (1066 A.D.) were written.

The above discussion does not divide the various periods in a water-tight mannr. Far from it. While writing summaries, Kṣemendra may have also been trying his hand at original composition, and Deśopadeśa and Narmamālā may have been the products of that period. Similarly works quoted in the Kavikaṇṭhābharaṇa may have been written even before the Aucityavicāracarcā.

Of all the thirty-four works so far attributed do Kṣemendra as many as ninetten have been published[1] while the rest are awaiting publication.

1. For list of the published works with place and dates etc. of publication see the Bibliography.

Chapter II

Kṣemendra's Poetic Art

It is not easy to assess Kṣemendra's literary style in general terms. He has written on widely different subjects and has adapted his style to the subject-matter in a manner that seems to change with every topic. Simple in the Deśopadeśa, Narmamālā and similar works, the style is rather terse in the three treatises on criticism, i.e., the Kavikaṇṭhābharaṇa, Aucityavicāracarcā and Suvṛttatilaka.

There is, however, a great diffrence between the style which Kṣemendra generally adopots and the one which he considers as ideal.

Kṣemendra gives an account of the style he considers ideal in his Kavikaṇṭhābharaṇa and Aucityavicāracarcā. In the Kavikaṇṭhābharaṇa, he writes that a style which is full of faulty words (*śabda-kāluṣya*) and tautology is a blemish in poetry. He quotes examples from Bhaṭṭa Śrī Śivasvāmin who is guilty of both the defects. In his Aucityavicāracarcā he writes that style, above all, should be marked by propriety. A writer should avoid superfluous prefixes—and conjunctions— a fault common to all Sanskrit writers. An author should never think that two synonyms have exactly the same sense and are always interchangeable. Dharmakīrti is censured for using the word 'tanvī' simply for the sake of alliteration, whreas he ought to have used the term 'sundarī'. Śrī Cakra's verse is also faulty, because he has used the conjuct 'ca' superfluously; Kumāradāsa has erred in using a meaningless prefix in his verse.

Kṣemendra then enjoins that a writer should use cases, verbs genders, adjectives and suffixed properly. He gives examples and counter-examples, and finds fault in the verse of well-known writers like Kālidāsa, Bāṇa and Rājaśekhara. He criticises his own verses. This shows that Kṣemendra's own style fall short of the ideal.

Kṣemendra generally imitates the topic style. He had summariese and two epics in the Bhāratamañjarī and the Rāmāyaṇamaṇjarī while he was still a youth. The study of th epiec left an indelible impression on him, and influence his style also. Kṣemendra's style has the same freshness and vigour as Vyāsa's or Vālmīki's has.

In terms of Sanskrit Poetics, Kṣemendra's style appears to follow the Vaidrabhī Rīti. According to Daṇḍin the Vaidarbhī style is characterised by :—

श्लेषः प्रसादः समता माधुर्यं सुकुमारता।
अर्थव्यक्तिरुदारत्वमोजःकान्तिसमाधयः ॥

–काव्यादर्श I. 41.

The above-mentioned are the ten excellences or the *guṇas* of the Vaidarbhī style. Kṣemendra's style is replete with them. He uses puns often and lucidity is the most prominent feature of his style. Equanimity, sweetness and delicacy are also found in his verses. Clearness of expression, force, charm, *samādhi* and *udāratva* are also found in abundance in his works.

Kṣemendra's writings show that his vocabulary was rich. He could use the right word at the right moment. That is why he at his best when describing things. His description of Gautama seeing the dead body burn in the Bauddhāvadānakalpalatā is a masterpiece of narration. The pictures of various places which the heroine of the Samayamātṛkā visits, are vivid and realistic. According to KEITH there is a curious modernity in Kṣemendra's works. His pictures of itinerant singers, prodigal and wearing long hair, of quacks selling fake medicine, and of astrologers, who know nothing, come up to the modern taste.

Kṣemendra shows a very high taste in the use of wit and humour. He is perhaps more inclined towards the lighter than towards the serious side of life; he, for instance, would not provoke the deeper feelings like Bhavabhūti. Kṣemendra finds use for his art in the lampoons and caricatures, and ridiucules the class which they represent. The easiest victims are the Kāyastha, the female mendicant, and the singers. Sometimes his with takes For his wit takes the form of a pithy saying complte in itself. For example "*ekatra dṛṣṭadoṣāṇāṁ sarvatrāśaṅkate manaḥ*" is an excellent translation of "a burnt child dreads fire". He imitates Bhavabhūti when writing.

स तस्य ललितो लोके या यस्य दयितो जनः।

Kālidāsa's *Saubhāgyaphalā hi cārutā* may be compared with this.

Of high taste and originality is Kṣemendra's humour. Sanskrit writers generally employ gluttony to evoke laughter. Bhāsa, the famous dramatist, widened the scope of humour, but few of his successors had the genius to follow his lead. Kṣemendra's humour spirngs out of satire, in which art he is past-master. His humour is full of *camatkāra* and is, indeed of his satire, the Kāyastha, the courtesan, the quack doctor, the astrologer being his special target. The Kāyastha is most frequently the butt-end of his riducule, as he is unscrupulous and incorrigible, a veritable pest of soceity.

Kṣemendra's object seems to be moral reform. He wants to disencumber the society from its evils. To achieve his aim hs uses the same device which Addison used, *i.e. satire* or sarcasitc riducule of men and manners. Kṣemendra has a sharp eye for the loopholes of society. His satire consists in bringing the weak points into prominence, and riduculing them. Like Addison he is reay to strike, but unwilling to wound; Kṣemendra is far from being a misanth rope; he, in fact, is a benefactor of human society. His satire is, therefore, constructive. He does not believe in just condemning a class; on the other hand, he suggests means of reform. This is clear from the tenth canto of the Kalāvilāsa.

One important feature of Sanskrit literary style is the use of the figures of speech (alaṅkāras). Kṣemendra calls them external embellishments only. From this it is clear that he is not very keen on introducing them in his poetry. The figures of speech that he uses are not very complex; they are similes, occasion, and are drawn from the sphere of daily life.They are not gorgeious and are not invaluable like Kālidāsa similes or Subandhu's puns. They lack lustre and do not look prominent. But Kṣemendra does not huddle them together as Bāṇa does; he uses them sparingly.

The metres that Kṣemendra uses are numerous. In his Suvṛttatilaka, he says that one ought to compose verses in many metres and not be content with gaining proficiency in just one or two. He also says that one ought to specialise in a certain metre just as Vidyādhara, Pāṇini, Bhāravi, Ratnākara, Bhavabhūti, Rājaśekhara, and others have done. Following this dictum, and remembering that one cannot become a Mahākavi without composing verses in various metres, Kṣemendra has composed un numerous metres. He has kept apart the use of each metre, which he discusses at length in the third chapter of his Suvṛttatilaka.

Kṣemendra himself has written the bulk of his poetry in Ślokas. The different varieties of his ślokas or anuṣṭups are as numerous as those in the epics. Next come śārdūlavikrīḍita. Kṣemendra has composed a large number of verses in other metres also varrying from the hexa-syllabic tanumadhyā to the twenty-one-syllable sragdharā.

The separate treatment of the literary treatises, viz. the Kavikaṇṭhābharaṇa, Aucityavicāracarcā and Suvṛttatilaka, illustrates in detail the literary standards cultivated by kṣemendra.

Chapter III

Kṣemendra Contribution of Sanskrit Literature

Kṣemendra holds a unique position in the history of Sanskrit litearture. He appears as poet, dramatist, rhetorician, lexicongrapher and historican. He has written numrous works which form important landmarks in several fields of Sanskrit litearture. His works include treatises on poetics, prosody, kāvyas, mahākāvyas, a drama, many didactic poetic compositions, poetical epitiomes of the epics and of Guṇādhyā's Bṛhatkathā, a chronicle of Kashmir kings, and a dictionary. Almost every important branch of Sanskrit literature has been enriched by the facile pen of this versatile genius. Indeed, in the whole range of Sanskrit literature, only Bhoja and Hemacandra have tried their hand on such a variety of sujects, but Kṣemendra displays a depth and originaligy peculiarly his own.

It may not be out of place to consider his works in some detail. Taking his poems first, they can be conveniently divided into three classes—poetical epitomes, didacitc manuals and mahākāvyas.

The epitomes of the epics and of the Bṛhatkathā are works of his early carrer. One may not except much poetic excellence in them, but they are undoubtedly valuable, as they put in a nutshell the nation's treasure before an eager people, who must have enjoyed them. Kṣemendra, the peot-interpreter, was evidently quite popular.

Among the didactic compositions, the Caturvargasaṅgraha, Cārucaryā, and Sevyasevakopadeśa provide a good deal of moral teaching. They are somewhat drab in character, because the moral maxims are a mere catalogue of short utterances, pieces of adivce strung together in verse. Numerous such works have been written by other authors. One can easily judge what little effect they have on the man in the street. Advice seldom reforms an ordinary man, and may sometimes have been the contrary effect. These works may be good collections of advice, but they certainly cannot bring about a reform by themselves Kṣemendra, however, intends them as ancillary to his satirical works. They constitute the constructive part of his criticism.

Kṣemendra's real contribution to didactic literature is found in his works of satire—the Deśopadeśa, Narmamālā, Darpadalana, Samayamātṛkā and Kalāvilāsa. In the Deśopadeśa and the Narmamālā the chief targest of attack are rogues, misers, courtesans, bawds, 'viṭas', students, kāyasthas, and old husbands of young wives. In his Darpadalana he ascertains the causes of pride and shows how proud people are humiliated. In the Samayamātṛkā he lays bare the snares of courtesans. In the Kalāvilāsa he criticises ascetics, doctors, astrologers, singers, goldsmiths, merchants, actors and indeed the whole society.

Kṣemendra's great success lies in his ability to make satirical remarks. The aim of Sanskrit writing has been *Satyam, Śivam* and *Sundaram,* i.e. truth, auspiciousness and beauty. Genearlly in Sanskrit works, we find the three elements, but Sanskrit writers have mostly considered Śivam to mean the story of some great benefactor—Rāma, Kṛṣṇa and others. They speak of the exploits of these heroes in eloquent terms, and seek to reform the world. Such compositions can effect only those persons who have a bitting conscience. They exert littel influence over ordinary men. But as everyday experience shows, men in the street are eaisly susceptible to satire. They are easily affected by it, and if properly employed, satire can become a very effective method of reforming people. It was left to Kṣemendra to harness this power.

Kṣemendra's object was, of course, moral reform. He wanted to rid society of the evils that vitiated it. He saw the prodigality of rich young men. He noticed the junior officers receiving bribes and indulging in other vices. He was aware of the flirtations and the cheatfulness of courtesans, barbers and bawds. He wanted to discourage the illegal and harmful practices of quacks as also of astrologers, who knew nothing. He wanted to eradicate social evils, such as old men marrying young women or students being corrupted and turning truants, or singers lulling people into inaction, or ascetics posing as accomplished persons, while they did not know even the elementary rules of *sandhyā* and so on.

In order to achieve his object, Kṣemendra thought of employing a weapon in the use of which he showed great skill. He had a very sharp eye for weaknesses in human character. He could read the very minds of his victims; and it seems that he had seen all sorts of men in every kind of society—from the pedantic grammarian right up to the cat-eyed and owl-faced bawd. Kṣemendra's method of criticising human character is simple. He finds loopholes in the character of a class, makes them prominent by means of his satire; and then alughs freely at them. He employs the same means of moral reform which Addison and Steele and Swift and Lamb employed in England, but his method is different from theirs. Addition's satire is very mild; he is "ready to strike but unwilling to wound". He only makes the defects in the society prominent, and things that he has done his duty. Swift, often called a misanthrope, mercilessly criticises every poinit—good or bad—in human character and laughs at it in bitterness and hatred. Kṣemendra's criticism is totally different from that. Charles Lamb, the great humorist, also indulges in satire, but his satire is always a handmaid to humour, which pervades every word he writes. Moreover, the scope of the work of these authors is not so wide as Kṣemendra's. Indian society is more complex than any other. There are two reasons for this : first, its peculiarly religious outlook; second, its rigid caste system.

Kṣemendra's criticism is not wholly destructive. It is constructive also, for he does not believe in mrely criticising people for their defects, leaving them ignorant of the means of improvement. In this respect Kṣemendra differs from Swift, whose satire is mainly destructive. Whereas Swift is dubbed as a misanthrope, Kṣemendra appears to be a philanthrope. He suggests means of reform. This is clear from the tenth canto of the Kalāvilāsa, and his works like Cārucaryāśataka, Caturvarga saṅgraha and Sevyasevakopadeśa.

The lead, which Kṣemendra gives in his Kalāvilāsa and Samayamātṛkā, has been taken up by Dyādviveda and Jalhaṇa in their Nītimañjarī and Mughdopadeśa respectively. Other major writers were too much bound by tradition to adopt Kṣemendra's novel methods. The reuslt was that they again reverted to religious or semi-religious poetry, and with one or two exceptions, didactic poetry in Sanskrit, in a way, saw its end with Kṣemendra's witings.

Of great importance are Kṣemendra's Bauddhāvadāna-kalpalatā and Daśāvatāracarita. The Buddhists owe a great debt to Kṣemendra. He has gathered together all the famous 'Jātakas' and narrated them in the Bauddhāvadānakalpalatā. It was a very arduous task and only a man of Kṣemendra's untiring industry could attempt it. In Tibet, the work is regarded as the best both from poetic and religious points of view.

In the Daśavatāracarita, Kṣemendra appears as a religious benefactor. He attempts a task, similar to that which Kabīr and Nānak attempted seven centuries later. He tries to show that Buddhism is just a part of Hinduism, and that Buddhism had developed so much that is superseded even Brāhmanism. There must have been quarrels between the monks and the Brāhmins. In order to put an end of these quarrels, Kṣemendra tries to reconcile the two parties. While enumerating the incarnation of Viṣṇu, he calls the Buddha also an incarnation. This shows his religious tolerance; and in fact, he advises writers not to indulge in bigotry.

Having said this much about Kṣemendra's contribution as a poet, it is meet to consider his contribution as a critic. He has written four treatises on criticism—the Kavikaṇṭhābharaṇa, the Kavikarṇikā, the Aucityavicārcarcā, and the Suvṛttatilaka. The Kavikarṇikā, unfortunately, is not available; the following observations are based on the remaining three works.

In the *Kavikaṇṭhābharaṇa,* Kṣemendra lays down a course

of training for buddhing poets. So far as the general plan of treatise like that goes, he hardly follows the traditional rules. For example, he does not define poetry, nor does he discuss it in detail. This he reserves for the Aucityavicārcarcā. The main intrest of this work lies in his divisions of poetry and the poet's training.

No other author has attempted a division of *'charm'* or realised its important position in poetics; but Kṣemendra by means of his great critical intuition has done even this. He says that a composition without 'charm' cannot be called poetry nor can an author call himself a Poet, if he does not make his verses charming. He then divides into ten classes. The divison is clear, well-marked and comprehensive.

Kṣemendra's course of training a poet is also unique. It is extremely practical in character, and a distinct improvement on Rājaśekhara's Kāvyamīmāṁsā.

If the apprentice is a genuine poet—i.e. if he has poetic faculties in him—such courses can be of great utility. They can help the apprentice in clothing his ideas in an elegant and befitting garb. Moreover they were introduced, most probably, with the aim of attracting people to write verses in Sanskrit. Sanskrit metre, as we all know, is rigidly fixed but for a few 'chandas' which are measured by means of morae. This renders composition in Sanskrit metres extremely difficult. One has to labour very hard in order to become efficient in metrics. The task of expressing his ideas clearly faces the budding poet next. The result is that a great amount of his energy is wasted on the 'form' of poetry. One cannot be at home in the 'form' of Sanskrit poetry without adequate training and constant practice. The treatise on the training of poets, aim at simplifying this task. Obviously the greatest thing required in such works is practicability, because if full of theories which cannot be put into practice, they are useless. Rājaśekhara's Kāvyamīmāṁsā is of that sort. It does lay down a regular programme for the apprentice, but the programme is not practicable; only those, who have nothing else to do but compose poetry, can avail of instructions given in the Kāvyamīmāṁsā. Kṣemendra's Kavikaṇṭhābharaṇa is characterstically practical and anyone—whether a professional poet, or an amateur—can avail of it.

The great contribution, which Kṣemendra makes, through his Kavikaṇṭhābharaṇa, is the training of the apprentice's mind. He lays down rules according to which one should act, as also the manner in which one should keep healthy. He says that psychological training is as important as the training in versification. This makes his instruction still more valuable for the real poet, because it sets up a relation between the mind, the body and the practice in versifying.

In his *Auciyavicāracarcā,* Kṣemendra expalins his ideas about poetry. His notions are revolutionary and based on deep thinking. He does not follow the sayings of the ancient writers blindly, nor does he try to defend their faulty beliefs; on the other hand, like a true and dispassionate critic, he puts forward his own views, and does not shirk criticisinig poets like Kālidāsa and Bhavabhūti. He finds fault with his own verses, and criticises even Bhaṭṭendurāja, the preceptor of his teacher Abhinavagupta.

In this treatise Kṣemendra propounds his theory of *Aucitya* in a rather laconic yet clear manner. The exposition of the theory is characterised by definiteness and common sense. He defines Aucitya, distinguishes it from other constituents of poetry (e.g. excellences, blemishes, figures of speech, flavour and others), speaks of places where it should be present and calls it the very soul of poetry. *Aucitya* in fact pervades every limb of the body of poetry— the word, the sentence, the purport of the piecce, the merit of excellence (guṇa), the figure of speech, the sentiment, the verb, gender, number and case, the adjective, preposition, particle, the time, place, lineage, vow, truth, substance, opinion, character, collecting the eesential genius or inspiration, enquiry, name and wish—in every one of these limbs of poetry does *Propriety,* as its soul, pervade and permeate.

The theory of Properity revolutionises all satndards of criticism. In this school of thought, 'falvour' or Rasa remains as the basis of poetry, while 'propriety' becomes its soul. This gives us a more objective and practical method of criticism. We cannot measure the amount of sentiment by means of any other theory; all the doctrines call this to be purely subjective, and a matter which only a 'sahṛdaya' can decide. But the Aucitya theory indulges in no such vague notions. It gives a practical standard of judging poetry. we can measure the extent to which 'flavour' is present in a particular verse by assessing the propriety in each part of it. Thus, we can know the extent to which 'flavour' has been developed. The 'Aucitya' theory goes a step further. It lays its finger, as it were, on factors which enhance or lessen the charm of the composition. It is an acid test to see what parts or aspects of the composition are improper, and then, we can call them factors lessening the charm of a composition. If we adopt the 'Rasa' theory as the basis of criticism, we shall not be able to say anything definitely. In that case one can have no standard of judging what the cause of abatement in the relish of poetry is. Again, we shall not be in a position to know whether the 'flavour' has been developed to the pitch in a composition or not.

The Aucitya theory makes the elaborate discussions on merits and demerits also useless. Such discussions form the bulk of works of Mammaṭa, Bhoja and Viśvanātha; at any rate they are very prominent in their works. If we examine the traditional divisions and sub-divisions of excellences and demerits, we find that they are not water-tight. A demerit may become a merti, while an excellence may become a demerit; the deciding point in this case is Propriety; and even Mammaṭa and Viśvanātha have acknowledge this. Indeed, Bhoja says that all demerits can become merits on accoutn of proper use. Thus, there is much confusion in this respect, but the whole thing becomes clear if we look at it from the Aucitya point of view. There is no need for divisions and sub-divisions. Anything which is improper is a demerit.

The Aucitya theory is of importance in the field of dramaturgy. Elaborate rules are laid down for the development of 'flavour', the types of minor plots, the different kinds of heroes, villains, heroines and so on. This has resulted in the stagnancy of the Sanskrit drama, just as the stereotyped character of theme arrested the progress of the French and the Greek dramas. All these rules would be unnecessary if 'Aucitya' is kept in view. *Aucity* in everypart of the drama would make the drama more effective and enjoyable; it will guide the write rini the choice of the hero, the villain, the heroine and other minor characters. Propriety of usage (vṛttyaucitya) would result in making the drama more realistic, and therefore, freer towards progress. This last factor i.e., realism has been tatally neglected by writers on dramaturgy; they have not specified whether action should follow the every-day life or not. In most of the dramas—even those considered as the best—the action is most unconvicing e.g. there is frequent introduction of the supernatural element, and even the dialogues are examples of grandiloquence. Similarly there would be no need of regulations fixing the use of Prakrits; it will be regulated by propriety alone.

It may be imagined how comprehensive and practical the theory of Aucitya is. Sanskrit criticism ought to have been recast in the light of this theory, but we are a conservative race, and do not like sudden changes. So propriety was not considered of supreme consideration in poetry. It was made the basis of the divisions of Guṇa and Doṣa, since such a sound theory could not pass altogether unnoticed.

Suvṛttatilaka is a work on prosody,with important contributions to the science of metrics. Some rare features are brought out and discussed. A few petinent remarks may be ventured here.

Like the two treatises on poetics, Suvṛttatilaka is primarily meant for students or aspirant poets. Kṣemendra does not introduce any new metres, nor does he discuss all those used in his own time. Only twenty-seven metres are discussed as against one hundred and eighty-three in Kedārabhaṭṭa's Vṛtta' ratnākara or two hundred and eighty in the Chando-mañjarī of Gaṅgādāsa. His metres are all sama-vṛttas except for Vasantatilakā and Upajāti, but comprehensive is the treatement of the few metres that are handled. Since the treatise is for amaterus, it is characterised by directness and clarity of expressin on and this makes the points clear even though the style is too laconic.

Kṣemendra's special contribution through this work does not consist in his definitions of metres. As Sanskrit metres had been stereotyped long before him, no originality in defining them can be expected; he has, however, attempted a task which no other poet did. He has tried to fix the usag of each metre and has also attempted to bring out clearly the excellences and blemishes of each 'chandas'.

The way in which Kṣemendra fixes the utility of each metre, is not pedantic, nor is it a mere guess-work, nor just a flight of imagination. His observations are scientific and are based on experience. This is clear from the examples he gives; they show that he was so efficient in pointing out the defects in metre, that he could easily detect verses which were defective. Moreover, he could easily ascertain whether a metre had been used in the right place or not. The result is that his contribution is genuine and remarkable.

The Suvṛttatilakạ is important from another point of view; here the author defines the form of poetry. He calls it a beautiful ornamental setting of chosen words and excellences. This gieves us an idea of Kṣemendra's notions about language and style. To him, form was as important as the sense; metres are ornaments of poetry.

The three works—the Kavikaṇṭhābharaṇa, Aucityavicāra-carcā and Suvṛttatilaka—are important in so far as they quote different authors, nearly sixty in number. We know the date of Kṣemendra and therefore can fix the lower limits for the dates of these authors.

Kṣemendra's *Nṛpāvalī* is a chronicle of Kashmir kings. It is unfortunately not extant. Kalhaṇa, in his Rājataraṅgiṇī censures Kṣemendra for his carelessness in the Nṛpāvali. We would have been in a better position to examine Kalhaṇa's remark, had we possesses a copy of the work. Considering the merits of his available works, it may be uncharitable to accuse Kṣemendra of carelessness.

There is a dictioary by Kṣemendra called *Lokaprakāśa kośa.* Buhler writes : "This work gives a great amount of information of the daily life of the Hindus which elsewhere we seek in vain. In this work Kṣemendra gives us examples of *huṇḍīs* titles of Kashmirian officials, sometimes explaining their duties, and a list of *parganas* into which Kashmir had been divided". While it is customary to gather up words that occur in literature, a dictionary of scientific terms, such as the Lokaprakāśakośa, brings all creidt to kṣemendra, because he pays attention to subject of utility like geography, administration and commerce.

Thus, it is seen that Kṣmenedra' works throw a flood of light on contemporary India in general and on Kashmir in particular.

Kṣemendra's contribution to Sanskrit literature is indeed considerable, varied and important. He widened the scope of nearly every branch of literature. Traditional rules were examined and represented; authors were got out of the rut into which they had fallen. His three treatises on poetics fix the 'terminus ad quem', of nearly sixty poets. It is, indeed, a valuable statment in the Bṛhatkathmañjarī, that Kṣemendra had a copy of Guṇāḍhya's Bṛhatkathā before him. If it can be proved that it is a recast of Guṇāḍhya's work, much light will be thrown on the history of the Paṅcatañtra and other apologues which form part of it.

Chapter IV

Kavikaṇṭhābharaṇa

Ancient Sanskrit scholars had a tendency to regulate every process of life. Their modes of worship, sitting, reading, eating, speaking—all were carefully regulated. It is so wonder therefore, that we find elaborate instructions for the budding poet. Rājaśekhara in his Kāvyamīmāṃsā says that the faculty of criticism is an essential quality for a poet. Nay, every writer on poetics had directly or indirectly contributed to the topic "The Making of a Sanskrit Poet" *(Kavi-śikṣā).* Writers like Ānandavardhana, Mammaṭa, Viśvanātha, Bhoja and Jagannātha come under this category. Their works—especially the chapters on merits and demerits of poetry—may be regarded as indirect instructions for those who aspire to become poets. Authors like Daṇḍin, Rudraṭa, Vāmana, Rājaśekhara, Kṣemendra, Hemacandra, and Vāgbhaṭa have treated the subject directly. They have discussed the training of a poet in such detail as to make a whole treatise on the subject.

"The making of apoet"has incidentally given rise to the treatment of topics like the very basis of poetry, kinds of pupils and poets in general, kinds of poetical compsotions and finally instructions to the aspirants.

Daṇḍin, who lived in the seventh century A.D., is the earliest writer on the topic. His treatment of the subject is meagre, and he finishes all he has to say in just three verses. He says :

नैसर्गिकी च प्रतिभा श्रुतं च बहु निर्मलम्।
अमन्दश्चाभियोगोऽस्था कारणं काव्यसंपदः।।

Kāv. I, 103.

न विद्यते यद्यपि पूर्ववासनागुणानुबन्धि प्रतिभानमद्भुतम्।
श्रुतेन यत्नेन च वागुपासिता ध्रुवं करोत्येव कमप्यनुग्रहम्।।

Kāv. I, 144.

तदस्ततन्द्रैरनिशं सरस्वती श्रमादुपास्या खलु कीर्तिमीप्सुभिः।
कृशे कवित्वेऽपि जनाः कृतश्रमा विदग्धगोष्ठीषु विहर्तुमीशते।।

Kāv. I, 105.

"Inborn genius, vast learning that is free from faults, and intense application : these constitute the cause of poetic glory".

"Even though there be not that extra-ordinary genius which depends upon the specific nature of the earlier latent impressions, yet speech cultivated with study and effort, certainly grants her own rare favour."

"Therefore, verily, it behoves those seeking fame to put away sloth, and persistently cultivate speech. For even though the poetic power be meagre, yet people who have made the effort, are able to hold their own in assemblises of the wise".

Thus, according to Daṇḍin inborn genius (naisargiki pratibhā), wide reading free from error, and constant practice—these three are the essentials of poetic enterprise. Daṇḍin gives two pieces of advice—first, the student should worship the goddess of speech, and secondly he should practise regularly. He emphasies like the classical poets the need for constant study and polishing—never resting by day or night. Daṇḍin has nothign to say on the types of students and poets.

Rudraṭa in his *Kāvyālaṅkāra,* has handled the subject at some length. Three ways of mastering the art of poetry are mentioned. These are faculty, culture and practice (*śakti, vyutpatti, abhyāsa).*

Faculty (śakti) is "the power, whereby there is constantly in the concentrated mind, a flash of ideas in various ways". (I, 15). It is twofold—natural and created.

Culture (vyutpatti) is defined as follows :

छन्दोव्याकरणकलालोकस्थितिपदपदार्थविज्ञानात्।
युक्तायुक्तविवेको व्युत्पत्तिरीयं समासेन।।–काव्यालङ्कार I, 18.

"Discrimination between suitable and unsuitable through knowledge of metre, grmmar, arts, the word and meaning—this briefly is culture".

With innate faculty and culture acquired, the formula is to practice as much as possible.

Vāmana, in his *Kāvyālaṅkārasūtravṛiti,* attempts a more comprehensive survey of the subject. He starts by defining the elements or constitutents of peotry. These, according to him, are three—the world, the science, and the miscellaneous :

लोको विद्या प्रकीर्णं च काव्याङ्गानि।

World is "wroldly usage". The various sciences included under the head "Vidyā" are : grammar of words, lexicon, metre, doctrines of the art and of love, politics and so on. The "Miscellaneous" constitutes : perception of aim, application, attendance upon seniors, trial, fancy and concentration. Fancy *(pratibhāna)* is the "seed of poetry" concentration *(avadhāna)* which is its handmaid is secured by two factors, time *kāla)* and place *(deśa)* The place is solitude, while the time is the fourth watch of the night.

Rājaśekhara, author of *Kāvyamīmāṁsā,* treats the subject exhaustively. The whole work is sort of hand-book for those who want to become poets.

Rājaśekhar sets about to find the cause of peotry first. After rejecting the opinions of Śyāmadeva and Maṅgala, he names 'faculty' as the one cause of poetry. He then defines faculty as "that which manifests to mind the words, meaning, the science of poetics, the way of speech and others of the same sort".

या शब्दग्राममर्थसार्थमलङ्कारतन्त्रमुक्तिमार्गमन्यदपि तथविधमधिहृदयं प्रतिभासयति सा प्रतिभा–(Kāvyamīmāṁsa 4)

Faculty is of two kinds : creative (kārayitrī) and critical (bhāvayitrī). The creative faculty may be inborn, acquired or resulting from instruction. Accrodingly the poets are of three kinds : *sārasvata* (Goddess of learning's favourite poet), *ābhyāsika* (poet by practice) and *aupadesśika* (poet by instruction).

सारस्वतः स्वतन्त्रः स्याद् भवेदाभ्यासिको मितः।
औपदेशककविस्त्वत्र वल्गु फल्गु च जल्पति।।

—Kāvya. 4

'The *śarasvata* poet is free (to compose at his will and pleasure); the *ābhyāsika* is limited (in ability and output) while the *aupadeśika* prattles some sweet nonsense'. The poetry of one *(aupadeśika)* remains within the house only; that of another *(ābhyāsika)* may go upto the houses of friends; while that of the champion *(sārasvata)* traverses the mouths of peasnat and professor everywhere as if eager to pervade the whole universe.[1]

The second types of faculty, the critical one (bhāvayitrī) helps one to discern the effort and import of the poet. Thereby the Tree of Poetry bears fruit; otherwise it would be barren. "What, after all, is the difference between the two, on conceives and the other perceives (poetry)?"—Some ask. They are indeed the same. "No" says Kālidāsa; they are quite different, because—

कश्चिद्वाचं रचयितुमलं श्रोतुमेवापरस्ताम्
कल्याणी ते मतिरुभयथा विस्मयं नस्तनोति।
न ह्येतस्मिन्नतिशयवतां सन्निपातो गुणाना-
मेकः सूते कनकमुपलस्तत्परीक्षाक्षमोऽन्यः।।

"One is capable of composing, another is capable of listening only; both ways your mind is well-equipped which makes us wonder. Not indeed do we see a combination of excellent qualities in on one, for (as is well-known) one (type of) stone yields gold, another is only capable of testing it." (Ibid).

Critics *(bhāvakāhā)* are of two kinds, according to Maṅgala: the disapproving *(arocakinaḥ)* and the all-approving *(satṛṇābhayavahāriṇaḥ).*[2] Poets also are similarly to be classified,

1. एकस्य तिष्ठति कवेर्गृह एव काव्यमन्यस्य गच्छति सुहृद्भवनानि यावत्।
न्यस्याविदग्धवदनेषु पदानि शश्वत्कस्यापि सञ्चरति विश्वकुतूहलीव।। (काव्यमी० अ. ४)

2. Vāmana expalians that these two terms should be taken in their secondary sense : discriminating and the undiscriminating. (poets).
अरोचकिसतृणाभ्यवहारिशब्दौ गौणार्थौ। कोऽसावर्थः? विवेकित्वमविवेकित्वं चेति। (Vāmana Ch. II)

says the Vāmana School. They are of four kinds according to Yāyāvarīya : add the jealous ones *(matsariṇaḥ)* and the truth seekers *(tattvābhiniveśinaḥ)*. Indeed, it is so. The faculty to discriminate is natural to some; to some others it is the outcome of profound knowledge (jñānayoniḥ). To those who are divested of discrimination, all poetry is the same. The jealous ones are silent over the merits of others; no merit strikes on their imagination. A critic who is learned and yet free from jealousy is hard to find. Here is an imaginary conversation[2]—

"Oh, who are thou?"

"I am a poet."

"Any new Poem." Recite it, friend."

"Nay, even the talk of it is now abandoned by me."

"Why?"

"Listen. There is no critic at all in his world who can well distinguish merit and demerit and who is himself a good poet. And luckily if there is one, he is not free from jealousy."

And the truth-seeking *(tattvābhiniveśī)* critic is seldom found, perhaps one is in a thousand.[3] What is the use of a *kāvya* which is but ruminated in the poet's mind, and which is not procliamed in the ten quarters by the learned critic?[4] Some critics assess the words, the language and the style *(vāgbhāvaka)* of a *kāvya,* some go deep

---

1. मत्सरिणस्तु प्रतिभातमपि न प्रतिभातं, परगुणेषु वाचंयमत्वात्।
   स पुनरमत्सरी ज्ञाता व विरलः। (काव्यमी० अ० ४)
2. कस्त्वं भ्रा कविरस्मि काप्यभिनवा सूक्ति= सखे पठ्यताम्।
   त्यक्ता काव्यकथैव सम्प्रति मया कस्मादिदं श्रूयताम्।
   यः सम्यग्विविनक्ति दोषगुणय्र सारं स्वयं सत्कविः।
   सोऽस्मिन् भावक एव नास्त्यथ भवेद्दैवान्नं निर्मत्सरः।। (Ibid).
3. शब्दानां विविनक्ति गुम्फनविधीनामोदते सूक्तिभिः।
   सान्द्रं लेढि रसामृतं विचिनुे तात्पर्यमुद्रां च यः।
   पुण्यैँ सङ्घटते विवेक्तृविरहादन्तर्मुखं ताम्यताम्।
   केषामेव कदाचिदेव सुधियां काव्यश्रमज्ञो ज–न।। (काव्यमी० अ० ४)
4. काव्येन किं कवेस्तस्य तन्मनोमात्रवृत्तिना।
   नीयन्ते भावकैर्यस्य न निबन्धा दिशो दश।। (Ibid)

into the poet's heart *(hṛdayabhāvaka),* while some others study the constitutent of emotions *(sāttvikair āṅgikaiḥ kaścid anubhāvaiś ca bhāvakaḥ).* When the learned poet realises the diffrence between his composition and that of others, then he should be regarded as a finishes artist; the bad poet, on the other hand, is not better than a monkey.[1]

Rājaśekhar then proceeds to describe *vyutpatti,* classify the poets and examine the final appeal of finish (*pāka*) of a poem. Wide knowledge is *vyutpatti* according to the elders; because the poet's words are all-embracing *sarvatodikkāḥ).* Powr to discriminate between the proper and the improper *(ucitānucitavivekaḥ)* is *vyutpatti,* says Yāyāvarīya. Ānanda opines that between *pratibhā* and *vyutpatti* the former is more important But Maṅgala favours the latter. Genius often makes up for deficiency in knowledge, whereas knowledge often-times proves impressive even though short of genius. Indeed one feels that a comination of genius and knowledge is highly desirable, says Yāyāvarīya. In fact beauty *(rūpasampat)* bereft of charm *(lāvaṇya),* or charm without beauty is inconceivable.

Both genius and knowledge are to be fouond in a poet worth the name. Poets are of three kinds : *śāstra-kavi* One who fills the work with a knowledge of the system and sciences), *kāvyakavi* (a poet who is proficient in belles-letters) and *ubhaya-kavi* (one who is good at both). Śyāmadeva argues that the latter in superior to the former. "No" says Yāyāvarīya, because each in great in his own sphere; the royal swan cannot indeed drink the moonlight; nor can the *cakora* take away milk from water. Rājaśekhara further classifies the poets to a minute degree : Śāstrakavi is of three sorts; he who describes the sciences, he who infuses poetry into science and he who infuses science into poetry. *Kāvyakavi* is of eight kinds : *racanākavi, śabdakavi, arthakavi, alaṅkārakavi, uktikavi, rasakavi, mārgakavi* and *śāstrārthakavi.* The designations are self, explanatory but are in no way to be regarded as water-tight.

1. यदान्तरं वेत्ति सुघऊँ स्ववाक्यपरवाक्ययः।
   तदा स सिद्धो मन्तव्यः कुकविः कपिरेव वा।। (Ibid).

Rājaśekhara illustrates each type suitably from his vast knowledge of current and contemporary literature. Of the various types of poets, he who can lay claim to most titles is to be regarded as a *mahākavi.*

Next important aspect of poetry that Rājaśekhara deals with is *kāvya-pāka.* What is this *pāka?* It is the literary 'finish' *(pariṇāma),* says Maṅgala, one that is attained by a proper combination of nouns and verbs. The elders think that *pāka* is an unshakeable placing of words. So long as the mind vascillates words are inserted or taken out; but when once they are firmly placed, oh the Goddess of learning has favoured.

आवापोद्धरणे तावद्यावद्दोलायते मनः।
पदानां स्थापिते स्थैर्ये हन्त सिद्धा सरस्वती।।

–काव्यमी० अ. ५

Pāka consists in being averse to change the composition when once made, say the followers of Vāmana. It is no *pāka* but lack of ability or genius, retorts Avantisundarī; because in the case of works of great poets even variant expressions do provide a fine finish. Hence *pāka* may be defined as a combination of words, meaning and expressions that are suited to the *Rasa* or flavour that is being developed by the poet.[1] Then again is the inevitable analysis of the features of *pāka* and no less than nine varieties are marked : *pākas* named after *picumanda, badara, mṛdvīkā, vārtāka, tintiḍīka, sahakāra, kramuka, trapusa* and *nālikera.* When no 'finish' can be discerned, then it is said to resemble *kapittha.* Here one should avoid the first, fourth and seventh varieties; for better not poetise than poetise badly. Bad poetry is living death.

Rājaśekhara then deals with the study of words and sentences (chapter VI). He defined *pada* (the word) as one whose form is determined by grammar and the meaning or significant by the

---

1. गुगालङ्कारीत्युक्तिशब्दार्थग्रथनक्रमः।
स्वदते सुधियायेन वाक्यपाकॄ स मां प्रति।।
सति वक्तरि सत्यर्थे शब्छे सति ग्से सति।
अस्ति तन्न विना येन परिस्रवति वाङमधु।। (काव्यमी० अ० ५)

Nirukta, Nighaṇṭu etc. Then the five *vṛttis—sup, samāsa, taddhita, kṛt,* and *tiṅ*—are explained and illustrated.

In the opinion of Rājaśekhara, a sentence which abounds in merits *(guṇavat)* and which is well embellisehd *(alṅkṛtaṁ ca)* constitutes Poetry *(kāvya).*[1] Some people say that *kāvya* should not be taught because it gives expression to things which are far from truth. But Yāyāvarīya stoutly refutes this remark. There can be nothing untrue *(asatyārtha)* in poetry; what is found by way of explanation *(arthavāda)* of the theme is there not only in *kāvya* but in the Veda, Śāstra and in the world too.[2]

In chapter eight, Rajaśekhara enumerated the sources of poetry : they are twelve according to elders but Yāyāvarīya adds four; hence sixteen sources on the whole—*śruti, smṛti, itihāsa, purāṇa, pramāṇavidyā, rājasiddhāntatrayī, loka, viracanā* and *prakīrṇaka;* add

उचितसंयोगेन, योक्तृसंयोगेन, उत्पाद्यसंयोगेन, संयोगविकारेण च सह षोडश (इति यायावरीयः)।

Each source is suitably illustrated.

For the training of the poet, one would value very much the practical hints that Rājaśekhara gives in the ninth chapter (*kavicaryā*). After going through a course of education in the various branches of learning, one should try one's hand at poetry. This involves reciting of nouns and verbs, the lexicons, metrics and rhetorics. Fine arts are sixty-four.[3] Eight factors are decribes as *kāvya-mātaraḥ*)'mothers of poetry' : peace of mind, intelligence, practice, devotion, talk of the leanred (or, learned assembly), wide knowledge, strong memory and courage.[4]

1. गुणवदलङ्कृतं च वाक्यमेव काव्यम्।
असत्यार्थाभिधायित्वान्नोपदेष्टव्यवं काव्यमित्येके। (अ० ६)
2. नासत्यं नाम किञ्चन काव्ये यस्तु स्तुत्येष्वर्थवाङ।
स न परं कविकर्मणि श्रुतौ च शास्त्रे च लोके च।। (अ० ६)
3. नामधातुपारायणे, अभिधानकोशः छन्दोविचितिः, अलङ्कारतन्त्रं च काव्यविद्याः। कलास्तु चतुःषष्टिरुपविद्याः। (अ० १०)
4. स्वास्थ्यं प्रतिभाभ्यासो भक्तिर्विद्वत्कथा बहुश्रुतता।
स्मृतिदाढर्यमनिर्वेदश्च मातरोऽष्टौ कवित्वस्य।। (अ० १०)

The poet-aspirant must always be pure. Purity is three fold : pure in word, pure in mind and pure in body. The first two aspects are the outcome of study of *śaṣtras,* while the third means—feet with toe-nails pruned, face with betel chewed, body with unguents smeared, valuable but unoppressive dress, head decked with flowers, clean habits—will attract the goddess of speech as it were. Be first to talk and that with a smile; talk always with sense; gather secrets from all quarters (i.e. the secret of conduct, deportment, pronunciation etc.); be averse to blaming others compositions; be faithful to things said and unsaid. These are practical aids to develop a cultured personality and outlook.

The poet's house must be clean and well-kept; separate accommodation must be provided to suit the different seasons; must have a garden with numerous trees and shelters underneath; an artifical hill; lakes and oblong ponds; rivers, seas and whirlpools; a running brook; abounding in peacocks, deer and *hārīta* birds; *crane, cakravāka* and swan, parrot *cakora, kraunīca* and *sārika;* must be capable of warding off summer heat, provided with showers and bowers and swings. When the poet in strained in mind on account of poetic exercise, there must be a set of servants Who obey implicity and silently or there may be none at all, so that the despair of his mind may be easily diverted.

The servants should be well versed in talking in the Apabhraṁśa, while the maid-servants should prefer the use of the Māgadhī tongue. The maids of the inner appartmnets should have a knowledge of Prakrit, Sanskrit and the local tongue, while the student's friends should know all the languages.

The student-poet's scribe should be at home in all the languages. He should be eloquent and able to use appropriate words. He should know the various signs and grimaces, as also all the different characters. He should be a poet himself and a person knowing logic.

The poet's paraphernalia are "a boards with a piece of chalk, a casket, pen and ink, palm leaves or birch bark, leaves of Palmyra, iron nails, and clean mats". But all these things are mere accessories; real poetry lies in one's faculty *(pratibha).*

"The poet should at first examine himself. He should ascertain the limits of his faculty, the language over which he has command, the taste of the public, the subject in which he is strong, has been trained or is interested".

"The poet should see in what places of the production, he is priased or criticised. Then he should exclude the criticised part, and retain the praised one. He should not get disgusted; with himself (i.e. his poetry) on accouont of criticism, and should try to examine himself because *people cannot be cheked"*. Moreover, a poet, like a prophet, is never honoured in his own land!

The poet should study charming works out of curiosity. In this way, his fame would spread in all directions.

Giving further instructions, the author says that a student should not read an incomplete stanza, nor should he recite his new work before one person only, lest the listener should call the new idea his own. He should not make much of his composition, for a prejudiced person cannot judge the merits and demerits of a composition. He should try to conciliate a pround poet by following his metre, but should not recite his verse before one, who thinks himself an extra-odrinary poet.

The poet's routine is as follows : he divides the day and night into eight 'yāmas'. In the first 'yāma' the studnet should get up, perform sandhyā, recite the "sārasvata" hymn, and study the different parts of petry. In the second he should compose stanzas; in the third he should bathe, take food that suits his nature, and talk about poetry and raise or answer questions. In the fourth 'yāma' he should examine the stanzas written that day. At this time he should have no company. He should omit what is redundant, and fill what is wanting. In the fifth 'yāma', the poet should perform sandhyā, worship the goddess of pecch, and go through the corrected stanzas. In the sixth and the seventh 'yāmas' he should sleep soundly and make and effort to get up in the eight 'yama'.

As is clear from the foregoing summary, Rājaśekhara's treatment of the subject is thoughful and exhaustive. But evidently it is not scientific. The four divisions of poetic faculty are unconvincing, and they are not sharply distinguished. The four-fold division of critics also does not carry conviction. The eight kinds of Kāvyakavis are, as Dr. Krishnamacharya has pointed out in his "history of Classical Sanskrit Literature", illogical. Their order also is not true for all times and persons. One may not pass through all the stages enumerated and might still become a great poet. Rājaśekhara leaves the terms 'mahākavi' and 'kavirāja' undefined. According to Rājaśekhara no student of 'aupadeśika' type can become a mahākavī; but there is a striking exception in Śrī Harṣa, the author of the Naiṣadbhīyacarita; and if tradition is to be believed, even Kālidāsa, the prince among Indian poets, was a poet of the 'aupadeśika' type.

Rājaśekhara's method of training the poet, as he himself admits, is not for ordinary studnets. He wants to train a person who is an intellectual giant. The type of palace in which Rājaśekhara wants the poet-apprentice to live is also quite out of question for a prson of meagre or moderate means. The daily programme applies more to professional poets rather than to amateurs. The introduction of 'king-poets' is interesting, and the instructions for them appear quite practicable.

After Rājaśekhara, comes the Kashmirian polymath—Kṣemendra, who lived in the first three quarters of the eleventh century. His *Kavikaṇṭhābharaṇa* is an excellent guide for those who want to obtain a poet's training. Kṣemendra calls his treatment of the subject 'a birds's eye view'; but as we find, it is essentially detailed. In the main outlines he follows Rājaśekhara to some extent, and the Kāvyamīmāṁsā may have provided the inspiration for his own treatise. His treament is free from the defects which are seen in the Kāvyamīmāṁnsā. Kṣemendra sets an entirely new and radical way of training the budding poet. Five successive stages are merked :

तत्राकवेः कवित्वासिः शिक्षा प्राप्तगिरः कवेः ।
चमत्कृतिश्च शिक्षाप्तौ गुणदोषोद्गतिस्ततः ।।
पश्चात्परिचयप्राप्तिरित्यते पञ्च सन्धयः ।।

(a) acquisition of the art of poetry, (b) learning and practice, (c) aim at poetical charm, (d) discrimination between merits and demerits, and (e) lastly, attainment of ease and familiarity. Each of these stages is dealt with in separate chapters. the following is a brief summary of the scheme :

Poetic effort is two-fold : divine and human. The divine lies in reciting the incantation "Oṁ Aiṁ Klīṁ Sauṁ Oṁ Sarasvatyai namaḥ". A continuous recitation of this gives rise to poetic faculty!

As regards the human effort, it differs according to the eype of the student. He is of three kinds—he who can be trained easily, he who has to work hard, and he who cannot be trained.

The method of initiation into the art of poetry differs with each types.

The first (i.e. who can be trained easily) should for the rise of poetic power, hear (poetry) from one well-versed in the art of literary criticism. He should not make a bare logician or a pure grammarian his preceptor, who mars the growth of good poetry".[1]

"When one is well-verse in the grammatical structure consisting of nouns and verbs, and has learnt (lit. laboured in) the composition of metre, on should, with a cheerful heart, devote one's mind to the poems, pleasant by their sweetness."

"One should listen to the tasteful songs, gāthās, and poems written in one's mother-tongue. One should also show taste for considering new meanings (attached) to compositions containing charm." (Kavi. I. 17).

"When absorbed inall the flavous, captivated by the joy in each merit (of poetry), bursting into maturity with the sprnkling of discriminatory powers, the mind gives rise to poetry like a sprout, being ripe from within". (Kavi. I 18)

The second (who has to work hard) "whould study all the works of Kālidāsa, look through works on history, and should save

---

1. कुर्वीत साहित्यविङ सकाशे श्रुतार्जनं काव्यसमुद्भवाय।
न तार्किकं केवलशाब्दिकं वा कुर्याद् गुरुं सूक्तिविकासविघ्नम्।। —Kavi. I 15

the newly--rising fragrance of poetry from the piquant smell of ligic." (Kavi. I. 19)

"He should be fervently devoted to a mahākavi, whose work he wants to imitate, concentrating upon it. He should show, time an agian, the desire to fill in the gaps of a wrod, or a foot (in a stanza)". (kavi I 20).

"For the sake of practice, he should compose in metre, by putting together words even if they do not mean anything, when read as a sentence. He may also change the words of an existing stanza, keeping on to the same meaning." (Kavi. I. 21).[1]

The rhird one is he, who is a logician or a grammarian, or a person unaware of the compositions of great poets. Such a pupil cannot become a great poet even if he is instructed by hundred of special methods. But he may, luckily, gain poetic faculty by reciting the incantation mentioned above.

The advanced studnet should compose verses containing shadow-borrowing, borrowed phraseology, a certian foot, or the entire body. After that he may depend on the skill of poetry thus acquired. Examples of each kind of borrowing are indeed instructive.

Kṣemendra gives one hundred pieces of advice to the students in the second stage of training, as follows : "He should observe the vow in honour of Sarasvatī, make sacrifices and should first of all worship the vanquisher of obstacles (i.e. Gaṇeśa). He should possess

---

1. विज्ञातशब्दागमनामधातुश्छन्दोविधाने विहितश्रमश्च।
काव्येषु माधुर्यमनोरमेषु कुर्यादखिन्–न श्रवणाभियोगम्।।
गीतेषु गाथास्वथ देशभाषाकाव्येषु दद्यात्सरसेषु कर्णम्।
वाचां चमत्कारविधायिनीनां नवार्थचर्चासु रुचिं विदध्यात्।।
रसे रसे तन्मयतां गतस्य गुणे गुणे हर्षवशीकृतस्य।
विवेकसेकस्वकपाकभिननं म–न प्रसूतेऽङ्कुरवत्कवित्वम्।।
पठेत्समस्तान् किल कालिदासकृतप्रबन्धानितिहासदर्शी।
काव्याधिवासप्रथमोद्गमस्य रक्षेत्पुरस्तार्किकगन्धमुग्रम्।।
महाकव्र काव्यनवक्रियायै तदेकचित्= परिचारक्ः स्यात्।
पदे च पादे च पदावशेषसम्पूरणेच्छां मुहुराददीत।। —Kavi I 16-20

discernment, should be devoted to practice, (be interested in) searching (new things), should be confident and should never get tired of work. He should have (the power) to compltet the metre, be always zealous, study the works of others, should read the auxiliary sicience of poetry, and should be able to complete a stanza which is incomplete. He should keep company with good poets, should relish the meaings of long poems (mahākāvya), possess nobility, make friends with the good, be of cheerful mind and put on elegant dress. he should witness a play being staged and have a mind leaning towards the sentiment of love; he should be charitable in poetic symposia, and saturate himself with music. He should be well-versed in etiquette and should show an interest in romantic tales; he should follow history, study beautiful paintings, observe the wroks of art, and witness verious duels;' he should hear the bewailings in sorrow, and visit the cremation grounds and forest. He should wait upon those observing vows, and see perches and mansions. He should eat sweet and oily things, be equitable and free from worry. He should get up when some part of the night still remains, possess presence of mind, be respectful, should sit in an easy manner, sleep during the day and guard himself against cold and heat. He should read magazines and articles, should be well-verse in talking humourously in parties, should observe the behaviour of animate objects, and examine surrounding of sea and mountains. He should notice the movements of the sun, the moon, the stars and have a knowledge of the cycle of seasons, should join people in assemblies and should be able to use the language of the country. He should possess the talents of choosing, eliminating and scrutiny; should be independent, should frequent sacrificial meetings, and other places of learning. He should not be over-anxious for his own exaltation, and should tolerate another's rise; he should feel shy of listening to his own praise and should join others in praising anohter. He should always explain his poems and should avoid hostility and jealousy; he shoul be anxious to excel others intuition and should (be ready) to become the pupil of any person for the sake of learning. He should know the appropriate time to study, and should abide by the taste of the listeners; he should know the significance of gestures and signs and procure things worth providing. He should be able to talk on salient points of his speech and should not be (attached to) one flavour for a long time; he should send forth his choicest works in all directions and should collect other's works. He should leave off the network of longings, be contented and large-hearted, leraned and clever, should be inclined to remain in solitude with none beside. He should not beg, never grow vulgar even when telling stories, be persistent in the composition of poems and at regular intervals he should take rest. He should try to creat something new, and show equanimity in the praise of all the gods, should be able to hear criticism from others and should be profound and firm. He should not indulge in self-praise nor be too humble; should help others to complete (when poems are left unfinished and the original authors cannot complete them); he should express other's mind and what suits others. He should put together words having clarity of meaning, should convey sense suiting the context, should bring out the flavour uncontended; he should be judicious in the matter of putting words in a compound or using them apart. He should see the poem to its finish, possess eloquence in speech; what is proper for one who has acquired the gift of peotry has been said in these hundred pieces of advice." (Kavi II 2-22).

These instructions which point to five sub-stages may be shown in a tabular form as follows :—

Number of stage	Instructions for mode of life	Instructions for study
1	1-13	1-13
2	14-23	24-31
3	32-43	44-51
4		52-74
5	75-100	75-100

This classification is by no means absolute, but it helps a clear understanding.

In the third stage of training, the aspirant poet must learn to infuse charm *(camatkāra)* into his poetry. charm is of ten kinds[1]: (a) that which strikes spontaneously i.e. without effort or deliberation, (b) that which does after effort of deliberation, (c) that which pervades the whole of the expression, (d) that which resides in a part thereof, (e) which is present in words, (f) present in meaning, (g) that which is abiding in the meaing of a word, (h) abiding in the figures of speech, (i) abiding in the sentiment, and (j) abiding in the story of a famour personage. Examples of each kind follows as usual.

In the fourth satege of training, the stuent should be able to distinguish between the merits and the demerits of poetry. Kṣemendra distinguishes merits and demrits on a new basis. These in his own words are : "... her, perspicuity of vocabulary, meaning and flavour,—thes are the three merits of poetry; while defective vocabulary, faulty meaning and insipid flavour are the defects of poetry. Poetry (may be) meritorious or meritless, defective or defectless, and full of both merits and defects" (Kavi IV).

In the fifth and final stage of training, there is necessity for the student to acquaint himself with different scineces and arts. He enumerates eighteen "points of familiarity" which are "the signs to show sovereignty over the kingdom of poetry" (कविसाम्राज्यव्यञ्जन). The eighteen points are logic , dramaturgy, politics, sexual science, the Mahābhārata, the Rāmāyaṇa, means of emancipation, knowledge of the Self, metallurgy, jewellery, the medicinal science, astronomy, archery knolwege of the marks of elephants, horses and men, gambling, deceit and miscellaneous. The miscellaneous includes painting. geography, knowledge of trees and wild animals, familiarity with magnanimity, the usage of calling inanimate thing animate, intimacy with asceticism, discernment, restraint and the like.

It is clear that Kṣemendra's method of treating this delicate sujbect is all his own. He is prepared to seek inspiration from

1. तत्र दशविधश्चमत्कार:–अविचारितरमणीय:, विचार्यमाणरमणीय:, समस्तसूक्तव्यापी, सूक्तैकदेशदृश्य:, शब्दग=, शब्दार्थग=, अलङ्कारग=, रसग=, प्रख्यातवृत्तिगतश्च। Kavi III.

Rājaśekhara's Kāvyamīmāṁsā, but makes distinct improvement on it. He avoids the pitfalls of complexity of division and vaguness of treatment into which Rājaśekhara has fallen. Kṣemendra's treatment is scientific, and his scheme practical. It does not require the student to have the encyclopaedic knowledge as Rājaśekhara's scheme does. kṣemendra wants wide reading the intelligent thinking on the part of his apprentice. He has made his method more prctical by showing different mthods of initiation into poetry for different classes of students.

As has already been shown, Kṣemendra's hundred pieces of advice can be divided into five parts. Each part suggests progressive method of training the student's mind. He emphasizes the training of the mind more than anything else. In this aspect he has definitely improved on Rājaśekhara who has altogether neglected the psychological training of the studnet. Kṣemendra's ten-fold division of excellence is interesting. The bases of division are—(a) with how much effort the excellence can be enjoyed, (b) in what part of the verse does it lie and (c) in what aspect of the verse does it exist. The division seems to be vague at first sight but the examples make the view-points clear.

A further advance that Kṣemendra has made on Rājaśekhara is in the exmaples. Only a few examples are given in the Kāvyamīṃaṁsā, and they ar too inadequate to bring home the point in question. Kṣemendra, however, is a master-hand in providing illustrations. His examples are to the point, and settle the doubts rising in the mind of the reader. Though in the general scheme of training a poet, Kāvyamīmāṁsā was the more popular of the two with the later poets, yet so far as examples are concerned, Kavikaṇṭhābharaṇa carries the palm.

Hemacandra, in his *Kāvyānuśāsana,* has attempted the training of a poet only briefly. According to him "faculty" is the cause of poetry and is two-fold—natural and acquired. Regarding the training of a poet. Hemacandra says, "non-mention of even the actual and mention of even the not-actual, restrictions, dependence like a shadow and so on are the trainings."[1] 'Actual' is of "genius substance, quality, action". and so on; and so is non-actual. He then defines restriction and divides shadow-dependence into four classes. Example follow of course.

Hemacandra's treatment, as will be clear from the above, is extremely concise. In the commentaries Alaṅkāracūḍāmaṇi and Viveka, his point of view has been discussed at length; but the commentaries either quote whole verses from the Kāvyamīmāṁsā or from the Kavikaṇṭhabharaṇa. There is hardly any original thinking.

Vāgbhaṭa, the author of *Vāgbhaṭālaṅkāra* call *fancy* the cause of poetry, *culture* its ornamentation, and *practice* the means of obtaining eloqence in it. The method of training is that at first, the student should put together charming words which may not convey any sense when taken as a whole. Then he should avoid the dropping of the visarga. After that he should try to speak in verses and indulge in verse filling. Tranquillity, fancy, early hours, practice, and an intimate knowledge of the śāstras, these are enumerated as the sources of inspiration. Then the advantages of sitting in the company of poets are mentioned.

Clearly in his instruction to student-poets, Vāgbhaṭa has been strongly influenced by Kṣemendra's Kavikaṇṭhābharaṇa. All that he has done is to take a few points from Kṣemendra's hundred pieces of instrcutions, and put them together.

Arisiṁha's *Kāvyakalpalatā*[1] with Amaracandra's (13th century) Vṛtti is another work on Kaviśikṣā or training of a poet. The work is divided into four 'pratānas', each of which is again divided into 'stabakas'.

---

1. प्रतिभास्य हेतुः। सावरणक्षयोपशममात्रात् सहजा।
मन्त्रादेरौपाधिकी। व्युत्पत्येभ्यासाभ्यां संस्कार्या।
लोकशास्त्रकाव्येषु निपुणता व्युत्पत्ति।
काव्यविचिछक्षया पु–न पु–न प्रवत्तिरभ्यासः।
सतोऽप्यनिबन्धोऽसतोऽपि निबन्धो नियमश्छायाद्युपजीवनादयश्च शिक्षाः।

—Kāvyānusśāsana I 4-10.

(Published by Sri Mahāvīra Jain Vidyālaya, Bombay in 2 vols).

In the first 'pratāna', the first 'stabaka' discusses the various divisions of the book, defines technical terms like ma,bha, etc., and enumerated different kinds of anuṣṭup metre. The second 'stabaka' gives a list of popular metres; it also lays down three schemes for practising these metres. The first way is to complete the metres with verbs or their various grammatical forms—participles, gerunds etc. The six tongues should be used one should also practise 'citrālaṅkāra'. Numerous examples are given. The second way of mastering the use of metres is to describe in verse one's own daily programme, general behaviour, a descriptive passage from an epic or the town in which the student lives. The third way of practising is to borrow another's idea and express it in different words in a different or the same metre. This scheme seems to have been borrowed from Kṣemendra's Kavikaṇṭhābharaṇa. The third 'stabaka' gives a list of useful expletive particles and words for filling up the verse. The fourth 'stabaka' contains a list of words suitable for allteration and pointed sayings, while the fifth enumerates a number of obejcts most suitable for description. It also gives the qualities which are to be described in each of the objects of description.

The first 'stabaka' of the second 'pratāna' gives definitions and examples of conventional, etymological and combined words. The second 'stabaka' describes the use of etymological words while the third gives a list of words suitable for alliteration. The fourth 'stabaka' describes the three powers of speech and in this the author follows Mammaṭa.

The third 'pratāna' opens with divisions of 'śleṣa' and a list of words suitable for puns. The second 'stabaka' lays down the method of describing something in a pun; the third shows how to describe two different objects in a manner that they appear to be the same and the fourth also deals with the same theme. The fifth defines and divides into four kinds the 'Citra-Kāvya'.

The fourth 'pratāna' deals with simile and metaphor is the first stabaka, with the use of figures of speech in the second and the ornamentation of word, form, and letters in the third, fourth and fifth 'stabakas'. The sixth shows how to support one's statement by means of numerals while the seventh gives elaborate instructions as regards verse-filling.

Repetition is the most prominent characteristic of the treatment in this work. The author indulges in too much of "spoon fedding" for the student. This obviously results in making the student's composition stereo typed. As a list of words suitable for puns is given, there is good reason to believe that the student-poet working on the lines suggested by Arisiṁha and Amaracandra will always work out puns only on the words given in the work. Again a list of objects fit for description and a sketch of the items which ought to be mentioned in different descriptions would make these descriptions look similar and hence lifeless. Thus the work, elaborate and comprehensive as it is, is not of much use to the student-poet both because it narrows the field of his activity and because it lays too much stress on figures of speech.

Keśava's *Alaṅkāraśekhara,* and the *Kavikalpalatā* of Deveśvara are also works on 'kaviśikṣā, but they need not be mentioned separately, as they borrow all their thoughts from the Kavikalpalatāvṛtti of Arisiṁha and Amaracandra. Halāyudha's *'Kavi-rahasya'* contains only a list of verbs showing their meaning.

We have surveyed the contributions of all the important Sanskrit writers on Poetics who have touched the subject of training a poet. Rājaśekhara and Kṣemendra easily stand out as the most prominent. Only these two have done original thinking, and have provided inspiration for later writers. they have treated the subject with much throughness,; but as we have already remarked, Rājaśekhara's method of training, his definitions, divisions and sub-divisions are confused, while his examples are hazy. Kṣemendra's method of training, his difinitions, divisions and examples are apt, clear-cut and lucid. Thus the Kavikaṇṭhābharaṇa is a better guide for the apprentice than the Kāvyamīmāṁsā.

We have now to answere one more question—what is the

utility of these courses of training; can there be any such training at all?

Before answering this question we must form a definite idea about a poet. A poet is not a mere versifier or an ordinary bard. He is something higher than these. Rājaśekhara defines as poet *'pratibhāvyutpatimāṁś ca kaviḥ'* i.e. one who possesses faculty and culture is a poet. Different writers have defined faculty in different ways, but all are unanimous in calling it inborn (A poet is born not made). Culture is best defined in Rudraṭa's verse *chandovyākaraṇa* etc. (quoted above). We know from our definition of a poet that faculty and culture are the two elements of poetry. All writers on poetics agree in placing faculty higher than culture. Ānandavardhana, in his Dhanyāloka says, the faculty may hide a defect in culture, but culture cannot conceal lack of faculty. Though culture is treated as of secondary importance, it is considered essential for composing good poetry.

It was to make the poet cultured that courses for the training of poets were suggested. Clearly such courses are of great importance if they are able to put forth a practicable scheme. Other literatures possess no such manuals for poets, but still they have produced writers of great charm. Even in Sanskrit literature, great poets like Vālmīki, Vyāsa, Bhāsa, Kālidāsa, Daṇḍin, Bāṇa, Bhāravi, Bhaṭṭi and Māgha were born long before these manuals were written. The obvious question that faces is "Can there be any such training?" Much may be said on both sides. The results of such handbooks may be desirable and at the same time undesirable. These manuals may make a real poet cultured and thus enable him to express his feelings in a refined manner. These guides may, on the other hand, give rise to mere versifiers with no poetic genius. This has been true for Sanskrit literature also. The manuals have brought forth poets of real charm like Rājaśekhara and Kṣemendra, while they have also produced mere versifiers and poetasters to be seen in large numbers from works written after the twelfth century. In fact, these handbooks show that no real poetic genius entered the field of Sanskrit poetry because progress was barred by the complexity of metres and lack of vocabulary. It is for removing these two obstacles in the way of rising poem that such guides were written. This is clear from the instruction which Kṣemendra gives to an apprentice, namely— he should try to fill in a metre even though the words do not convey any sense when read as a sentence.

Chapter V

Aucityavicāracarcā

The history of Sanskrit peotics shows that at different times different views were current as regards the nature and soul of poetry. Daṇḍin, Bhāmaha, and Ruyyaka gave currency to the view that figures of speech *(alaṅkāras)* are the soul of poetry. Vāmana thought 'Rīti' or style to be the only important thing in poetry (cf. rītir ātmā kāvyasya). Ānandavardhana, Rājaśekhara, Mammaṭa, and Viśvanātha assert that 'Rasa' sentiment is of primary importance in every composition. Kuntaka advocated the view that 'Vakrokti' is the life of poetry. A new era was ushered in the history of Sanskrit poetics by the introduction of 'propriety' *(Aucitya)* in the theory of criticism. The idea of 'propriety' was introduced by Ānandavardhana, but it was Kṣemendra who popularized the view so much that even Mammaṭa, Viśvanātha, and Bhoja, all of whom were staunch beliexers in the 'Rasa' theory, were obliged to give a prominent place to 'propriety' or what Ānandavardhana called "Aucitya". Thus, the credit of propounding the propriety theory goes to Kṣemendra.

The earliest mention of "Aucitya" is found in Daṇḍin. Daṇḍin does not use the term "Aucitya", but his remarks show that it was propriety that he was aiming at. The following verse in the Kāvyādarśa may be cited :

न लिङ्गवचने भिन्ने न हीनाधिकतापि वा।
उपमादूषणायालं यत्रोद्वेगो न धीमताम्।। **II. 51**

Discussing the defects of a simile, Daṇḍin says, "Neither difference in gender and number nor inferiority or superiority, at which the learned people are not pained, is enough to constitute a blemish in a simile."

The idea is that it is only the mind of the wise (later on called 'sahṛdaya') that can finally judge the merit or demerit of a simile. Clearly the verse means that if the wise consider a particular simile to be appropriate, then, even if it does not conform to the traditional rules, it is appropriate.

Another reference to 'Propriety' may be traced in Daṇḍin in the following verse :

न विद्यते यद्यपि पूर्ववासनागुणानुबन्धि प्रतिभानमद्भुतम्।
श्रुतेन यत्नेन च वागुपासिता ध्रुवं करोत्येव कमप्यनुग्रहम्।।

काव्यादर्श, I. 104

"Even though there be not that extra-ordinary genius which depends upon the specific nature of the earlier latent impressions,yet speech cultivated with study and effort certainly grants her own rare favour".

The commentary says, "Here the word 'guṇa' may stand for propriety in composition". (cf. *atratyaṁ guṇapadaṁ kāvyagataucityaparam).*

We can see that Daṇḍin's reference is only indirect, and it is only by a stretch of imagination that we can find any reference to 'propriety' in the Kāvyādarśa. Writers like Bhāmaha, Vāmana and Ruyyaka also do not say anything in regard to 'Propriety'.

Ānandavardhana, who has introduced the idea of 'Propriety', and to whom later writers are indebted for the term 'Aucitya', deals with the topic more seriously and in a detailed manner in his dhvanyāloka.

We shall quote Ānandavardhana to make the point clear. He writes :

द्विविधो हि दोष:–कवेरव्युत्पत्तिकृतोऽशक्तिकृतश्च। तत्राव्युत्पत्तिकृतो दोष: शक्तितिरस्कृतत्वात्कदाचिन्न लक्ष्यते। यस्त्वशक्तिकृतो दोष: स झटिति प्रतीयते।... तथाहि महाकवीनामप्युत्तमदेवताविषयप्रसिद्धसंभोगशृङ्गारनिबन्धनाद्यदनौचित्यं

शक्तितिरस्कृतत्वाद्ग्राम्यत्वेन प्रतिभासते।... एवमादौ च विषये यथौचित्यात्यागस्तथा दर्शितमेवाग्रे। ध्वन्यालोक III. 5

"Demerits are two-fold; either due to lack cf poetic culture or on account of lack of poetic faculty in the poet. There, sometimes the demerit, due to lack of poetic culture, cannot be noticed, because it may be covered by poetic faculty; but the demerit, arising out of the lack of poetci faculty, shows itself at once.... Thus the impropriety contained in describing the ordinary amorous play of high divinities, as composed by great poets, does not look unrefined because its evil effect is dispelled by poetic faculty..... In this and similar instances, the manner in which propriety is not forsaken is shown in the following pages. "

He then goes on :

तस्मादुणाव्यतिरिक्तत्वे गुणस्वरूपत्वे च संघटनाया अन्यः कश्चिन्नियमहेतुर्वक्तव्य इत्युच्यते। तन्नियमे हेतुरौचित्यं वक्तृवाच्ययोः। ध्वन्यालोक III. 5

"Thus we should fix some other standsard of cheking the style whether devoid of merits or full of them. So we say : 'the propriety of the subject and the predicate is the cause (i.e. means) of scrutinizing that".

Explaining the term 'vaktṛ' he says that it includes "the poet or poetic composition". The poetical composition may again be two-fold : first of the hero in the story, secondly of the villain. The hero may be of steadfast and charitable (cf. *dhīrodātta)* or of any other type. Similarly the helper of the hero may be of various types.

'Vācya' ius of many kinds. It may be with reference to the sentiment in Dhvani or to obscurity of sentiment. It may be contained in a mening worthy of being staged or otherwise. It may be dependent on the best style or an inferior one.

Ānandavardhana distinguishes another kind of 'propriety'. He says :

विषयाश्रयमप्यन्यदौचित्यं तां नियच्छति।
काव्यप्रभेदाश्रयतः स्थिता भेदवती हि सा।।

ध्वन्यालोक III. 7

"Still another kind of propriety residing in the substance restrains (i.e., governs) it. (The style) is of various kinds through its employment in different kinds of composition".

He then, distinguishes three kinds of style: (a) where style and merit hold equal position (*saṅghaṭanaikarūpaguṇa),* (b) where style is dependent on the merits *(guṇādhīnasaṅghaṭanā),* and (c) where merits are subordinate to style *(saṅghaṭanāsśrayaguṇā).* In all the three cases propriety is the means of restraint (*niyāmaka)* i.e., it is by propriety that we can test whether a certain kind of style suits a particular sentiment or not. Discussion the phrase "different kinds of composition", Ānandavardhana divides poetry into four classes : 'muktaka', 'paryāyabandha', 'sargabhandha' and abhineyārtha'.

He, then, says :

तत्र मुक्तकेषु रसबन्धाभिनिवेशिनः कवेस्तदाश्रयमौचित्यम्
.... अन्यत्र वा कामचारः। ध्वन्यालोक III. 7

"In the Muktakas, for a poet who wants to bring in sentiment, propriety lies in that (i.e., *Rasa*).... In other places he is free".

He then gives examples of propriety in each of the four divisions of peotry. Here he has metnioned another kind of propriety—propriety in behaviour *(vṛttyaucityas).* The author of the Locana defines propriety in behaviour as "Propriety as regards the conduct of cruel, civilised, and uncultured people"; cf. Paruṣopanāgarikagrāmyāṇām vṛttīnām aucityam).

Summarising the discussion given above he says :

एतद्यथोक्तमौचित्यमेव तस्था नियामकम्।
सर्वत्र गद्यबन्धेऽपि छन्दोनियमवर्जिते।।
रसबन्धोक्तमौचित्यं भाति सर्वत्र संश्रिता।
रचनाविषयापेक्षं तत्तु किञ्चिद्विभेदवत्।।

ध्वन्यालोक III. 8-9

"This propriety, as has been described, controls it (the style) everywhere—even in prose, where there is no rule for metre".

"Style *(racanā)* depending on propriety which is in a composition containing sentiment *(rasabandhokta)* and suits the subject-matter always shines. (But) that (propriety) is of different kinds".

Speaking of the parts of poetry in which propriety should be prominent, he says :

विभावभावानुभावसञ्चार्थौचित्यचारुणः ।
विधिः कथाशरीरस्य वृत्तस्योत्प्रेक्षितस्य वा।।

ध्वन्यालोक III. 10

He then gives examples of each. Propriety of excitants is of three kinds—of mortals only *(kevalamānuṣa),* of divinities only *(kevaladivya),* and of mortals and divinities combined *(divyamānusā).* This distinction, he says, holds good even in the art of love (*rati*).

Speaking of the propriety of grimaces, he says :

अनौचित्यादृते नान्यद्रसभङ्गस्थ कारणम्।
प्रसिद्धौचित्यबन्धस्तु रसस्योपनिषत्परा।।

ध्वन्यालोक III. 10

"Except impropriety, there is no other cause for the abatement in the relish of poetry. A composition containing the well-known propriety is the very secret of *flavour*".

Speaking of propriety in Rasa, he says :

अविरोधी विरोधी वा रसाङ्गिनि रसान्तरे।
परिपोषं न नेतव्यस्तथा स्यादविरोधता।।

ध्वन्यालोक III. 24

"In one prevailing sentiment, another, whether opposite to that or not, should not be developed, or (it should be workd out) in a manner that it does not rival (the main sentiment)". Then Ānandavardhana instructs as to how one should develop a subsidary sentiment. His instructions are not relevant to our topic. So we pass over them, and come to what he has to say about the position of propriety in general. He writes :

वाच्यानां वाचकानां च यदौचित्येन योजनम्।
रसादिविषयेणैतत्कर्म मुख्यं महाकवेः।।

ध्वन्यालोक III. 32

"It is the main business of a mahākavi to bring in line with propriety the subject-matter and the words that express it via media 'rasa' et cetera".

It is clear from the above discussion that Ānandavardhana is all the time considering Aucitya as subordinate to Rasa. He wants to restrict the poetic license by means of Aucitya, so that the poet may not write whatever he likes. Propriety, here, takes the form of some binding rules which regulate the style, accessories, excitants, grimaces, and the subordinate sentiments. The object of this regulation is that all the parts of poetry mentioned above should be in harmony and contribute to the development of the main flavour. Any violation of this regulation would result in the abatement in the relish of poetry *(rasabhaṅga)* and, therefore, must be discredited by all means. Ānandavardhana has missed one important point; he has not defined "Aucitya".

Coming to Kuntala, who in all probability lived after Abhinavagupta, we find that he also has soemthing to say on the subject. Kuntala mentions Aucitya only as a guṇa or merit, which is common to all the three mārgas or styles. He says :

आञ्जसेन स्वभावस्य महत्वं येन पोष्यते।
प्रकारेण तदौचित्यमुचिताख्यानजीवितम्।।

वक्रोक्तिजीवित I. 37

"That is Aucitya whose final object is to convey proper sense,where the excellence of the object is brought out in a direct manner (i.e. through '*abhidhā*' or denotation)."

Another definition of Aucitya found in the Vakroktijīvita is as follows :

यत्र वक्तुः प्रमातुर्वा वाच्यं शोभातिशायिना।
आच्छाद्यते स्वभावेन तदप्यौचित्यमुच्यते।। I. 38

"Where the object of description is covered by the charming nature of the speaker and the hearer—that also is Aucitya".

Thus, according to Kuntala, there are two kinds of Aucitya. It may mean the "striking expression in which the excellence of an object is rightly depicted"; or it may be considered as synonymous with imparting such peculiarities to the object of description as appear to be in harmony with the character of the speaker or the hearer.

He further says :

औचित्यान्तरतम्येन समयो रमणीयताम्।
याति यत्र भवत्येषा कालवैचित्र्यवक्रता।।

वक्रोक्तिजीवित II. 26

"Where there is Vakratā, charm of tense, the tense becomes lovely by the inclusion of propriety".

This means that Kuntala realised that charm of tense at least is based on propriety. Vakrokti may be translated as 'Ingenious speech' implying cleverness and charm as is conveyed by its Hindi rendering of 'बाँकापन', pleasant poignancy.

Kuntala's treatment, obvioulsy, is very meagre, and of no importance in the history of the development of the Aucitya School. He considers propriety as just one of the merits of style. In this respect he seems to have been influenced by Ānandavardhana, who calls propriety, "saṅghaṭanā-niyāmaka". Kuntala contradicts himself when he says that charm of tense is based on propriety.

We now take up, Mahima Bhaṭṭa's *Vyaktiviveka.* Mahima Bhaṭṭa claims that *'dhvani'* can always be reduced to inference, and he severely criticises the Dhavnikāra for not giving any comprehensive definition of poetry. His Vyaktiviveka is just a criticism of the Dhvanyāloka. There is hardly any original thinking in it, but a great deal of pedantry.

Mahima Bhaṭṭa divides propriety into two—that of meaning and that of words. Propriety of meaning he does not discuss because Ānandavardhana has already discussed it. He takes up the discussion of "outward propriety" or "propriety of words". He divides it into various kinds mentioning five—'failure to co-ordinate the parts of a preposition". *(vidheyavimarśa)* 'break in the regular order' *(prakramabheda),* violation of 'syntax' *(kramabheda).* 'tautology '*(Paunaruktya)*' and 'Pleonasm' (vācyavācanam). The first is of two kinds—'paryudāsa' and 'prasajya-pratiṣedha'. Break in regular order may happen in fourteen places. Other improprieties are also divided into various groups.

The summary given above, shows that Mahima Bhaṭṭa's treatment of propriety is incomplete. He gives no definition of Aucitya and considers impropriety as synonymous with demerits *(cf. ime doṣā ity apy ucyante).* Though he divides propreity into two he discusses only one kind of it. The mere fact that Ānandavardhana has dealt with the other kind does not relieve him from the necessity of discussing it. Moreover, he is all the time discussing impropriety rather than propriety with the result that his treatment is a mere nomenclature of negations.

After Mahima Bhaṭṭa, we come to Kṣemendra. Kṣemendra has written a whole treatise, the "Aucitya-vicārācarcā" on the subject. In his work, he has dealt with "propriety" in an exhaustive manner.

Kṣemendra, as he mentions at the end of his "Aucityavicāra-carcā, wrote the work for the training of his pupils. So it has become an invaluable treatise on criticism, and as will be clear from the following summary, the treatment is extremely practical in character.

Having made the preliminary salutations, Kṣemendra writes :

कृत्वापि काव्यालङ्कारां क्षेमेन्द्रः कविकर्णिकाम्।
तत्कलङ्कं विवेकं च विधाय विबुधप्रियम्।।
औचित्यस्य चमत्कारकारिणश्चारुचर्वणे।
रसजीवितभूतस्य विचारं कुरुतेऽधुना।।
काव्यस्यालमलङ्कारैः किं मिथ्यागणितैर्गुणैः।
यस्य जीवितमौचित्यं विचिन्त्यापि न दृश्यते।।

अलङ्कारास्त्वलङ्कारा गुणा एव गुणाः सदा।
औचित्यं रससिद्धस्थ स्थिरं काव्यस्य जीवितम्।।

औचित्य० 2-5.

"Kṣemendra, having composed the 'Kavikarṇikā' a compendium on figures of speech in poetry, and having also discussed its blemishes and subtleties now has undertaken the pleasant task of ruminating on "propriety in poetry" which is the very life of flavour, and an agency for producing effect.

"For a composition in which the soul, namely, propriety is indiscernible, of what use are the ornaments, and merits counted in vain?

"Figures of speech are but ornaments, while merits to speech are mere excellences; but propriety is the abiding life of poetry, full of flavour".

It is clear from the foregoing that Kṣemendra considers propriety to be something distinct from merits and figures of speech. Elucidating his point of view he says :

औचित्यं त्वग्रे वक्ष्यमाणलक्षणं स्थिरमविनश्वरं जीवितं काव्यस्य। तेन विनाऽस्य गुणालङ्कारयुक्तस्यापि निर्जीवितत्वात्।। औचित्य०

"Propriety, whose definition will be given later on, is the abiding and imperishable life of poetry, since without it, poetry is lifeless, though united to elegances and figures of speech".

In order to emphasize this point, he further says :

उचितस्थानविन्यासादलङ्कृतिलङ्कृतिः ।
औचित्यादच्युता नित्यं भवन्त्येव गुणा गुणाः।।

औचित्य० 6

अलङ्कृतिरुचितस्थानविन्यासादलङ्कर्तुं क्षमा भवति। अन्यथा त्वलङ्कृतिव्यपदेशमेव न लभते। तद्वदौचित्यादपरिच्युता गुणा गुणतामासादयन्ति, अन्यथा पुनरगुणा एव।।

"An embellishment is a (real) embellishment, if applied at the proper place; merits are true merits, when they are concomitant with propriety.

"Put at the proper place, ornaments can beautify or else they cannot even pass for decorations. Similarly merits, if they do not fall short of the standard of propriey are merits, otherwise they are blemishes".

Having shown the importance of propriety, and having distinguished it from merits and figures of speech, the author defines propriety as follows :

उचितं प्राहुराचार्याः सदृशं किल यस्य यत्।
उचितस्य च यो भावस्तदौचित्यं प्रचक्षते।।

औचित्य 7

"The great masters have called that to be proper which is verily suited to a certain thing. The abstract idea of being proper, goes by the name of propriety".

Kṣemendra is quoting the "ācāryas" in this defnition. No such definition in Āandavardhana's Dhavanyāloka or Abhinavagupta's Locana is found; and these two were the only personages whom he could address as "Ācāryas". It must therefore be said that the credit of defining Aucitya belongs to Kṣemendra and by the term "ācāryas" he simply means "authentic writers".

After this Kṣemendra sets about to determine the scope of "propriety". He mentions twenty-eight places in which propriety should be present. These, in his own words, are as follows :

पदे वाक्ये प्रबन्धार्थे गुणेऽलङ्करणे रसे।
क्रियायां कारके लिङ्गे वचने च विशेषणे।।
उपसर्गे निपाते च काले देशे कुले व्रते।
तत्त्वे सत्त्वेऽप्यभिप्राये स्वभावे सारसंग्रहे।।
प्रतिभायामवस्थायां विचारे नाम्न्यथाशिषि।
काव्यस्याङ्गेषु च प्राहुरौचित्यं व्यापि जीवितम्।।

औचित्य० 8-10

"They say that propriety, which is the very life of poetry, should necessarily exist in the word, sentence, meaning of the composition, merits, figures of speech, flavour, verb, syntax, gender, number, adjective, prefix, particle, tense, context, family, surrounding, essence, force, nature, winding up of essences, intuition, stage, thought, nomenclature, benediction, and other limbs of poetry".

The expression "kāvyāṅgeṣu ca" is there. This means that besides the places enumerated above, propreity should pervade all limbs of poetry.

Having enumerated all the places of propriety, and having defined its nature, Kṣemendra gives illustrations of propriety and impropriety in each place. By means of his great critical power, he mentions the rason for which he considers the use of a certain noun, adjective or verb improper and suggests improvements. This shows the practical character of his work.

Kṣemendra's discussion of propreity in sentiment is very detailed. In the first place, he illustrates the propriety of each sentiment, giving as many as twenty examples in all. Having finished with the sentiments one by one, he takes up the question of propriety in combining the various sentiments. He writes :

यथा मधुरतिक्ताद्या रसाः कुशलयोजिताः।
विचित्रास्वादतां यान्ति शृङ्गाराद्यास्तथा मिथः।।
तेषां परस्पराश्लेषाकुर्थादौचित्यरक्षणम्।
अनौचित्येन संस्पृष्टः कस्येष्टो रससंकरः।।

औचित्य० 17-18

"Just as the sweet, bitter and other falvours, when mixed cleverly, taste wonderful, similarly the erotic and other sentiments, when put together in a clever way give indescribable enjoyment. One should maintain propriety when putting together the sentiments. To whom is the counterfeit mixture of sentiments, touched by impropriety, welcome?"

Here Kṣemendra has obviously been influenced by Ānandavardhana. He, infact, quotes the verse 'virodhī vā' etc. But Kṣemendra elucidates his point of view by means of cleverly chosen examples. He makes the whole thing clear and shows how it can be put into practice, while Ānandavardhana indulges in mere theory.

This gives Kṣemendra's treatment of "propriety in sentiment" a touch of originality.

He then quotes different authors showing where propriety or impropriety in combining the various sentiments lies. In the discussion on the propriety of cases, Kṣemendra discusses all the seven cases one by one, giving, as usual, examples and counter-examples.

Kṣemendra does not explain what he means by the expression "limbs of poetry". He does not show how to find propriety or impropriety in it. He asks the reader to excuse him for this, the reason being that these limbs of poetry are innumerable and examples would never end. He asks the student to find out propriety in such places himself.

Clearly Kṣemendra's "Aucityavicāracarcā" shows great improvement on Ānandavardhana's and Kuntala's treatment of "Propriety". Kṣemendra has propounded a school of thought which might be called the *Propriety School.* It considers propriety as the soul of poetry and as important as Rasa.

Kṣemendra is the propounder of this school. His treatments of "Propriety" is complete in itself. He defined the term, lays down practical rules according to which the theory can be applied in criticism, and distinguishes it from merits, sentiments and figures of speech.

Coming to the later writers on poetics, we find that Mammaṭa's treatment of propriety is meagre. He discusses it in the chapter on demerits alone. He writes : "Through propriety of the speaker and of attribution, a defect becomes a merit, or becomes neither a merit nor a demerit". Cf. :—

वक्त्राधानौचित्यवशाद्दोषोऽपि गुणः क्वचित्ववचिन्नोभौः ।। काव्यप्र० सू० ८

Mammaṭa mentions fifteen such cases.

It is clear that propriety has been given only a secondary place in the Kāvyaprakāśa. It is trated only as a standard of judging merits and demerits and has nothing to do with Rasa.

King Bhoja, in his voluminious treatise the

Sarasvatīkaṇṭhābharaṇa has treated Aucitya very meagrely. He, a follower of the Rasa school, made 'propriety' subordinate to style and language, and confused it with merits and demerits.

Bhoja mentions under the head 'Demerits in the meaning of a sentence' *(vākyārthadoṣa)* one demerit as *Aucityaviruddha,* 'not conforming to propriety'. He cites an example coming merits, he gives an example of the above-mentioned demerit also. In his example he does not point out what impropreity has become propreity. and for what reasons.

Bhoja, in his chapter on Alaṅkāras treats 'Propriety'as subordinate to style and language. He divides it into six classes; they are as follows :

(a) *Viṣayaucitya* which makes a figure of speech a real ornament of poetry.

(b) *Vācyaucitya* consists in using the proper language—Sanskrit, Prakrit or Apabhraṁśa—on different occasions.

(c) *Deśaucitya* means propriety in using the language with reference to the country. For example, the Gurjaras like Apabhraṁśa.

(d) *Samayaucitya* consists in propriety as regards the language spoken at the time.

(e) *Vaktṛviṣayaucitya* means propriety in using the language according to the status of the speaker.

(f) *Arthaucitya* means propriety in the use of form of language (verse or prose) according to the subject.

From the above account, it is clear that Bhoja quite changed the status of Propriety. It was considered as of secondary importance, and was treated as if it had nothing to do with the soul of poetry.

In his *Kāvyānuśāsana,* Hemacandra lays down rules for a student of poetry to follow. One of these rules is :

सतोऽप्यनिबन्धोऽसतोऽपि निबन्धो नियमश्छायाद्युपजीवनादयश्च शिक्षाः ।

काव्यानुशासन I.10

"Non-mention of even the actual and mention of even the non-actual restrictions, dependence in the form of shadow, and so on are the trainings". The Vṛtti on the Kārikā says :

आदिशब्दात्पदपदादीनां च काव्यान्तराद्यथौचित्यमुपजीवनम्।

"The expression 'and so on' indicates that borrowing of the feet or expression from another poem should be proper".

Explaining this the anonymous commentary says :

पुंसः कालातिपातेन चौर्थमन्यद्विशीर्यते।
अपि पुत्रेषु पौत्रेषु वाक्चौर्यं न विशीर्यते।।
इत्याशङ्कयाह–यथौचित्यमिति ।

"A person's other thefts are forgotten in course of time, but plagiarism is not forgotten even generations after generations. Apprehending this, he says, 'according to propriety".

Propriety, then; is mentioned in the chapter on demerits of poetry. Hemacandra says :

विसन्धिन्यूनाधिकोक्तास्थानस्थपदपतत्प्रकर्षसमाप्तपुनरात्ताविसर्गहत-वृत्तसंकीर्णगीर्मतभग्नप्रक्रमानन्वितानि वाक्यस्य।

"Absence of *sandhi,* either more or less syallbles than required, gradual decay, repetition, wrong placing of visargas, faulty metre, confusion of ideas, break in the sequence in the case of mode of address".

The *'visandhi'* demerit, due to obscurity disapperas in case there is propreity of speaker; then through his speech, harshness does not remain a demrit. Cf. :—

वक्त्राद्यौचित्ये चेति वक्ष्यमाणत्वाद् दुर्वचकादौ न दोषः।

Hemacandra calls 'improper meaning of a word' *(anucitārthatvaṁ padasya)* a demerit. In this part of the chapter the word 'improper' *(anucita)* occurs again and again.

He then goes on to enumerate cases where through the propriety of the speaker a demerit becomes an excellence or does not remain a demerit. In the chapter on merits, he says :

यद्यपि गुणेषु नियता वर्णादयस्तथापि वक्तृवाच्यप्रबन्धौचित्या-द्वर्णादीनामन्यथात्वमपि। तत्र वाच्यप्रबोधनापेक्षया वक्त्रौचित्यादेव वर्णादयः।

"Though the classification of the merits of poetry is rigid, yet through the propriety of the speaker, or the subject matter, or the composition, the classification may even be altered. There, neglecting the consideration of subject matter, the calssification and others are (fixed by) the propriety of the speaker alone".

Thus, according to Hemacandra, the propriety of the speaker is of greater importance than that of the subject-matter or composition.

Concluding his remarks on merits of poetry, he says, "similarly propriety in other places should be followed" *evam anyad apy aucityam anusartavyam*). He further says that the effect of a sentiment may be marred by impropriety *(anaucityāc ca)*.

Hemacandra's treatment of propriety is quite detailed. But he also has treated propriety as only of secondary importance. He has associated it mainly with 'merits and demerits'. In this he follows Mammaṭa who, as we have seen, assigns a similar position to propriety.

Hemacandra has not defined 'propriety' and he has made no rigid classification. The parts of poetry in which propreity should be found are, according to him, the speaker, the subjectmatter and the composition. This view is very vague. He gives us no definite examples to show how we should know whether a certain stanza contains propriety or not.

Viśvanātha, in his *Sāhityadarpaṇa,* has treated propriety very briefly. He writes :

अन्येषामपि दोषाणामित्यौचित्यान्मनीषिभिः।
अदोषता च गुणता ज्ञेया चानुभयात्मता।।

साहित्यदर्पण VII. 32

"Similarly the wise should watch other demerits giving up their defective character or becoming merits or neither of the two through propriety'.

According to Viśvanātha, therefore, propriety lies at the very basis of the classification of merits and demerits in poetry. He mentions twenty cases in which demerits become merits through the propriety of use. Besides these, the poetic conventions, though untrue, are not demerits; on the other hand, they are merits.

After Viśvanātha, the great luminary among literary critics of Sanskrit was Jagannātha Paṇḍita. In his famous *Rasagaṅgādhara* he does not develop the theme of Aucitya to the extent to which Kṣemendra has done. However, he brings in *Aucitī* as an attribute of good poetry in his treatment of the force of word. At the same time he is of opinion that faculty *(Pratibhā)* alone is the source of poetry.

From the short sketch of the history of Sanskrit poetics, given above, it is clear that the concetpt of *propreity* has had many a rise and fall. Bharata spekas of Aucitya implicitly when he treats of ornaments and decorations in the make up of characters. Daṇḍin, in his Kāvyādarśa, makes only indirect mention of the conception and does not use the term 'Aucitya'. Ānandavardhana, or more correctly Dhvanikāra, first introduced the idea in his Dhvanyāloka. Kuntaka, in his Vakroktijīvita, recognizes, its existence, but considers it only as of secondáry importance. Mahima Bhaṭṭa, a casuistic and pedantic critic of the Dhvani doctrine, accords 'Aucitya' a half hearted recognition. In Kṣemendra the theory of propriety found a real champion, and he is so much impressed by it that he ventures to propound that as a school of thought. But Ksemendra did not find any followers. Those of the Rasa school-Mammata, Bhoja, Hema-candra and Visvanatha-though recognizing the importance of ' Aucitya ' confuse it with merits and demerits.

After this discussion , we may still ask : what is the distinction between 'propriety' and 'merit'?

Kṣemendra has already answered this question in his *Aucityavicāracarcā.* He says that merits are only excellence of poetry, while propriety is its life and soul. To understand this point fully, we have to revert to Rājaśekhara's conceptions of point fully, we have to revert to Rājaśekhara's conception of Kāvyapuruṣa.[1] Of the 'Poetry-incarnate' the figures of speech are the ornaments—the necklace, the arme, and so on. The mertise are the virtues, just as man has several virtues—charity, purity, truthfulness, sincerity and so on; similarly poetry also has excellences—'mādhurya' (sweetness), 'ojas' (force) and the like. These excellences possess the same status which virtues have in a man. Lack of ornament does not bring discredit to one. Lack of virtues brings about some lowness of opinion about him, but he is considered a man all the same. Simlarly a poetic composition cannot be condemend outright if it does not abound in figures of speech. Lack of excellence may lower its value, but it might still claim to be good poetry.

Coming to the question of 'Rasa' or flavour in poetry, we find that the most influential school of thought—the Rasa School—believes that Rasa or flavour is the very life of poetry (cf. *vākyaṁ rasātmakaṁ kāvyam).* According to this school, poetry cannot exist without flavour. Kṣemendra, however, does not seem to hold that view. We shall be able to elucidate this point if we revert to our metaphor of Kāvyapuruṣa.

There are two things which are necessary for the existence of man—body and soul. The body is made up of the five elements and is susatined by the vital essence. This essence includes the seven fluids and is an elementary ingredient. Soul, on the other hand, is absolutely necessary for sustenance of life in human body. Both the vital essence and soul are of more or less the same importance for life. Now, Kṣemendra says that 'Aucitya' or 'propriety is like the soul in the body of poetry, while Rasa or flavour is like the vital essence. Thus, in a way Kṣemendra places Aucitya higher than even Rasa.

---

1. शब्दार्थौ शरीरं, संस्कृतं, मुखं, प्राकृतं बाहुः।
जघनमपभ्रंशः पैशाचं पादौ, उरो मिश्रम्।
समः प्रसन्नो मधुर उदार ओजस्वी चासि।
उक्तिचणं ते वचो, रस आत्मा, रोमाणि छन्दांसि।
प्रश्नोत्तरप्रवह्लिकादिकं च वाक्केलिः, अनुप्रासोपमादयश्च त्वामलङ्कुर्वन्ति।

It must have been clear by now that 'Aucitya' or 'Propriety' is fundamentally different from poetic excellences. The difference lies in the importance of the two for poetry.

Similarly the distinction between impropriety and demerits is also very sharp. The difference lies in the extent to which each of the two lowers the value of poetry. According to Kṣemendra, who, as we have seen, considers propriety to be the soul of poetry, impropriety would lower the value of the composition very much. It may efface all charm and may even produce the contrary effect. A common 'doṣa', would not abate the relish of poetry to such an extent.

Having made clear the difference between propriety, impropriety, merits, demerits and flavour, we may, before closing the chapter, study the importance of the 'Propriety Theory'.

The introduction of this doctrine, revolutionizes all standards of criticism. It is extremely practical in character. The critic can definitely point out the defective parts by just seeing where the impropriety lies. In this respect it is more useful than even the 'rasa' theory which is purely subjective. The Propriety theory renders useless the lengthy, intricate, and often confused classification of guṇa and doṣa. The only standard of judging the two, according to this doctrine, is *propriety*.

Chapter VI

Suvṛttatilaka

The Indian system of prosody exhibits an artifice which is peculiar and ingenious. Sanskrit metres are measure either by quantity or number of syllables, both with and without rhyme : sometimes they are most rigidly restricted, while at times they give ample latitude. Thus, in variation of metres, Sanskrit prosody is the richest of all.

Broadly speaking a Sanskrit stanza has four verses. We do come across stanzas having three, five or even six verses, but they are merely exceptions to the genral rule. The Prakrit prosody exhibits a greater variety in the length of the stanzas; we find stanzas having even sixteen verses.

Sanskrit metres can roughly be classified into two : those measure by number of syllables *(varṇa)*, and those measured by syllabic instants *(mātrā)*. The former are the most numerous and the most popular. Among the Sanskrit metres which are measured by *mātrā* like the hexametre of Greek and Latin, the Āryā and the Vaitālīya are the most popular.

Coming to Varṇachandas, or metres regulated by number of syllalbes we find that these occur in stanzas having four verses each. The metres can be divided into three classes according as all the four verses are similar, the alternate are similar, or all dissimilar. In the case of these metres, the number of syllables in each verse varies from one to twenty-six. There are metres having as many as one less than one thousand syllables; but they form a class by themselves. Considering the three sub-divisions given above and the rigidity of scheme, the variety of possible metres becomes almost infinte. Bhāskara's Līlāvatī givees a method of calculating the number of possible metres.

On account of the great number of subdivisions, the *śloka,* which is the most commonly used stanza in Sanskrit verse and which is denominated from the Anuṣṭubh variety, forms a distinct class. The most simple kinds of the *śloka* are those consisting of iambic and trochaic feet exclusively. The rest are calld 'Vitāna'.

The above, in brief, is the outline of Sanskrit Prosody. The science of Prosody held an important place in Sanskrit literature—even as early as the Brāhmaṇas. The Śāṅkhyāyana Śrautasūtra, the Nidānasūtra, the Ṛkprātiśākhya, Kātyāyana's Anukramaṇis to the Ṛgveda and the Yajurveda—all contains chapters on Prosody Later on, Prosody was included among the six Vedāṅgas, and was designeated as the 'foot of the Veda' *(chandaḥ pādau tu vedasya).* The work which is regarded as a Vedāṅga, is Piṅgala's Chandassūtra. Later on, Bharata, in his Nāṭyassāstra, writes, "There is no word without metre; nor is there any metre without words" *(chandohīno na śabdosti na cchandaś śabdavarjitam).* Writing about the importance of prosody in dramaturgy, he writes "one should apply oneself to speech; it is regarded as the body of dramaturgy". This shows how important the Sanskrit writers considered prosody.

As is the case with all other scientific branches of Sanskrit litearture, the earliest extant work on prosody—the Chandassūtra of Piṅgala—is a work complete in itself. Piṅgala ranks as an ancient sage, and is sometimes identified with Patañjali. His work seems to be old and discusses metres which are not used in Kāvya literature. It is probable that the treatise was written in a period during which writers on lyrics were experimenting in metrical effect. Though the work is regarded as a Vedāṅga, it discusses mostly secular prosody. The names of the metres look like "epihtets of beloveds". We cannot account for this phenomenon clearly. Piṅgala uses the algebraic symbols employing 'la' for a short and 'ga' for a long syllalbe; 'ma' denotes 'molossus' and so on.

Next we come to the Nāṭyaśāstra by Bharata. It is a treatise on dramaturgy and deals with metres only because they are an important part of drama. We cannot determine Bharata's date exactly. The lower limit may, as P.V. KANE suggest, be accepted as third century A.D. In chapter XIV of the work are defined the algebraic symbols; metres having Vedic names are also discussed here. Bharata finishes his treatment of Prosody in chapter XV after defining sixty-eight metres and five kinds of Āryā. He does not use the algebraic notation in defining metres; he, however, states which syllable should be long and which short.

Varāhamihira's Bṛhatsaṁhitā, though a treatise on astronomy, deals with metres in chapter 104. As Dr. KEITH has suggested, arāhamihira lived somehwere in the sixty century A.D. In this work, he defines sixty-three classical metres simultaneosly with planetary movements. A metres is defined in the verse having the same syllabus. The reference is not at all important from the point of view of the history of Prosody.

Chapter 328-335 of the Agnipurāṇa deal with Prosody. P.V. KANE suggests that the last date for the Agnipurāṇa may be the seventh century A.D. The author of these chapters follows closely Piṅgala's Chandassutra both inform and matter. Chapter 328 contains definitions of the algebraic symbols like 'la', 'ga', 'ma' and so on. In the next three chapters Gāyatrī, Jagatī, and Utkṛti are defined. In chapter 332, seventeen metres, regulated by number and position of syllalbes, are dealt with. The next chapter contains a discussion of ten 'Ardha-sama' metres. Seventy-two metres with caesura are defined in chapter 334; these metres are divided on the genus of Vedic metres. The division of meteres that he gives is traditonal i.e., 'sama', 'ardhasama' and 'viṣama'. The same division is found in Piṅgala's Chandassūtra and Bharata's Nāṭyasśāstra. Chapter 335 of the Agnipurāṇa contains miscellaneous metres like Gāthā, and deals with 'prastāra' etc.

The Śruta-bodha, another treatise on Prosody, is ascribed to Kālidāsa, though there is no justifiable ground for this ascription. The author writes as if he is speaking to his beloved or his wife. It begins in the usual manner with the definitions of the algebraic symbols, and the tratditional division of metres into three classes. The author, then, defines thiry-nine metres all of which are classical. He does not use the algebraic system, but only indicates the numbers of the long and short syllables. The verse in which the author defines a metre is also composed, as in the Bṛhatsaṁhitā, in the same syllabus. The author is careful enough to mention the caesura in nearly every case; this he does in terms of technical words like 'giri', 'aśva', 'sūrya', and others, all of which denote certain numbers.

All the works mentioned above, follow the same scheme in their treatment of metres. They show hardly any originality, and very only in the number of metres discussed. The form of discussion is stereotyped in every case. The treatment is only superficial and no critical faculty whatsoever is exhibited. The authors merely define the syllabus of the metres and think that they have done their duty.

We now come to an author whose work shows great originaligy in the treatment of metres; and that is Kṣemendra's *Suvṛttatilaka.* The work, by no means comprehensive, is very important as it forms a land-makr in the history of Sanskrit Prosody. Kṣemendra treats the subject in a manner which is all his own; the work is primarily meant for students. The author writes :

"Kṣemendra composes for his intelligent pupils; the Suvṛttatilaka of charming letters ....."

"Having examined the metres, and considering their (respective) charm, this collection is made (of metre) loved by eminent poets;—metres which are chiefly used in the making of poetry". Suv. I, 4-5.

Thus, Kṣemendra does not pretend to be comprehensive in his short treatise. In the first chapter he defines the algebraic symbols and the 'gaṇas'; then he selects twenty-seven most popular metres and defines them giving one exmaple each. Excepting one—which is a quotation from Vyāsa—Kṣemendra illustrates the definitions of all the metres by his own verses. He follows the algebraic system in his definitions, which are composed in Śloka form. The metres chosen vary from the hexa-syllabic Tanumadhyā to Sragdharā which has twenty-one syllable. The most numerous are those that contain eleven syllables; these number seven.

The second chapter of the Suvṛttatilaka discusses the excellences and blemishes of metres in genral, and also with speicla reference to the metres defined in Chapter I. This is a unique task. No other extant work of Sasnskrit Prosody—not even any posterior to the Suvṛttatilaka—contains such information. This shows how great a critic Kṣemendra was. Speaking in a general manner Kṣemendra says that there is no caesura in metres cotaining six or seven syllables. He further writes :

"Lovely metres, if short, look charming with compounds, and if long, with lack of compounds; or as the context suits them". Suv. II, 3.

After these general observations, Kṣemnedra takes up one by one the metres defined in Chapter I. A brief summary of this is as follows :

Anuṣṭup. The fifth syllable should be short and the sixth long; but as exceptions to this rule are found in the compositions of great poets, so *appeal to the ear* is of the greatest importance.

Upajāti. Though the scheme of this metre is fixed, yet one should make the first sylallbe of the first foot short. If this is note done, the verse does not please the ears.

Dodhaka. It ought to have a break after every three syllables, otherwise it loses rhythm and its pause.

Śalinin. The joints of this metre are loosely knit; one should try to strengthen them; great effort is needed in bringing force in this metre. Śālinī, according to Kṣemendra, becomes forceful if one introduces harsh-sounding present participles and 'visargas' at the end.

Rathoddhatā. It shoul have 'visargas' at the end of its fee, othrwise it will lack lustre.

Svāgatā. All its feet should begin with the letter 'sa' and end with 'visargs'.

Toṭaka. It should have flowing rhybhm, and quick movement. The feet of the verse in this metre should contain harsh letters.

Vaṁśastha. It should not contain long compounds. The feet should have 'visargas' at the end and should be free from sandhi.

Drutavilambita. Its feet should begin with quick movement but end in a slow one. There should be no sandhis.

Praharṣiṇī. Three of the syllables in each foot should have the vowel 'a', and the rest should possess quick time.

Vasantatilakā. The verse in this metre should either begin with the vowel 'a' or its first syllable should contain that sound. The verse should be forceful and free from knots of conjunct consonants.

Mālinī. It should have 'visargas' at the end of its feet and compounds in the latter half. The writer should avoid a jarring note.

Narkuṭa. The verse in this metre looks charming with the pause after two syllables in the beginning, after three and four next, and after five in the end.

Pṛthvī. The words should be places separately and not knit down in compounds. If, however, the letters are vigorous, and the vowel 'a' occurs frequently, compounds may be used.

Hariṇī. The pauses should be liquid and quick; in no case should they be slow. They should exist only in the first three feet, while the last foot should have quick rhythm.

Śikhariṇī. The metre is forceful by nature. Its force is increased if the 'visargas' at the end are dropped. There should be no pauses in this case.

Mandākrāntā. The first four syllables should have slow rhythm, while the six in the middle should be put together in as extremely cleve manner.

Śārdūlavikrīḍita. The vowel 'a' should begin the syllable and 'visargas' should end a foot, otherwise the vers in this metre losses all its charm. The words should be put separately in the first half, but should be knit into compounds in the second half. The metre is harsh and should not be used in a delicate flavour.

Sragdharā. The feet should begin with a syllable having the vowel 'a'; that failing, it must be long. The feet should end with 'visargas' and the pauses should not be mixed up.

Having discussed some of the merits and defects of metres. Kṣemendra lays down their special usages. He divides poetry into four—science, poetry, a work on poetry admitting scinece, and a work on science admitting poetry. Science he defines as marked with all the requisties of poetry; poetry is the beautiful ornamental setting of chosen words and meanings, poetry admiting science is found in all the four objects of human existence. and gives instruction to every one. The works of Bhaṭṭi and Bhaumaka are cases of science admitting poetry. The division is clearly founded on both the matter and the form of composition. Kṣemendra enjoins that one should use the proper metre at the proper place. In works on poetry admitting science, extremely long metres should not be used, while in cases of science admitting poetry, the length of the metre varies according to the flavour.

After the general remarks given above, Kṣemendra takes up a few metres and shows their usages. These are as follows :

Anuṣṭup. It shoul be used in writing works on science because it makes the meaning clear. It may also be used in works which imitate the Purāṇas in style and matter, which are didactic or which aim at clear exposition. Other occasions of using the metre are the firs chapter of an epic poem written in 'sargas', or where the long theme is summarised or where both instruction and story have an equal status.

Upajāti. It may be used in describing the beauty of a noble heroine or of spring.

Rathoddhatā. It is best employed in the description of excitants like the moon-rise etc.

Vaṁśastha. It should be used in explaining the six-fold policy.

Vasantatilakā. It should be employed in a description where the dreadful and the heroic sentiments are contained.

Mālinī. It should be used at the end of a 'sarga' if it has quick movement.

Śikhariṇī. It is of special use on the occasion of discrimination.

Hariṇī. It should be used in riduculing people, or in speech made in anger.

Pṛthvī. It should be used in riduculing people, or in speech made in anger.

Mandākrāntā. It finds its best use in describing separation in the autumnal season.

Śārdūlavikrīḍita. This metre should be used in praising kings.

Sragdharā. It may be employed in describing hurricanes etc.

Dodhaka, Toṭaka, and Narkuṭa should be put in the form of a Muktaka stanza. They have no regulations as regards flavour.

Kṣemendra concludes his remarks by demanding variety of metres from poets. He says that one, who can compose in only one ro two metres, is never honoured. he, however, admits that great poets like Vidyādhara, Bhāravi, Ratnākara, Bhavabhūti, Kālidāsa, Rājaśekhara and others have shown preference for one metre. Thus Kālidāsa specializes in the Mandākrāntā, Bhavabhūti in the Śikhariṇī, Rājaśekhara in the Śārdūlavikrīḍita, and so on. Kṣemendra's view, therefore, is that while one should specialize in one metre, one shuld be able to compose verses in other metres as well.

Evidently, Kṣemendra's Suvṛttatilaka stands promeinent among all the works mentioned hitherto. In this work the author is not satisfied with simply defining the syllabus of the metres. He points out their merits and defects and also suggests places where these metres should be used. This last part of his task in extremely difficult. It needs great critical faculty, wide reading and much expeirience. So difficult in this task that even though Kṣemendra had given the lead, none of the sucessros had the ability to take it up. The result is that Ksemendra's Suvṛttatilaka remains the only treatise that analyses the metres critically. Another strong point of this treatise is the illustrations. In the first chapter of the work, these are mostly the author's own, in the second chapter they are mostly taken from other authors. As a ruel, the examples are apt, and make clear the author's point of view. In the third chapter the examples have been chosen carefully and they illstrate the point well.

We now come to the *Chandonuśāsana* by Hemacandra. We know Hemacandra's date for certain; he lived during 1088-1172 A.D. The work follows the traditional scheme and contains only the definitions of metres. It is divided into eight chapters Chapter I contains the exposition of algebraic symbols. Chapter II consists of definitions of 401 'sama' metres. The definition are all given in algebraic notation. Ardhasama and Viṣama metres are defiend in chapter III, while metres measured by morae—Āryā, Galita, Khañjaka and others—are defined in Chpater IV. Chapter V contains Utsāha and other metres Chapter VI shows verses having six lines, and Chapter VII, those having two lines. Prastāra i.e., enumeration of all sorts of combinations of syllables and other metres are found in Chapter VIII.

Hemacandra' style is laconic; he tries to compress the sense in the briefest space possible. The Chandonuśāsana is full of definitions of metres in the algebraic symbols, and the author does not give even a single example by way of illustration.

We shall now take up Kedārabhaṭṭa's *Vrttaratnākara.* The work has been very popular with later writers and is quite comprehensive. We cannot be sure about teh date of Kedārabhaṭṭa, but it is certainly not later than the fifteenth century A.D. The work is divided into six chapters and explains 136 metres.

The first chapter contains the explanation of algebraic symbols like 'la', ga', 'ma' etc. Metres are divided into the traditional division of two—those measures by morae and those by syllables. In Chapter II, Āryā, Vaitālī and similar metres measure by morae are mentioned. Chapter III contains definitions of 'Sama' metres; Chapter IV of 'Ardhasama', and Chapter V of 'Viṣama' Chapter VI describes the six 'pratyāyas', 'prastāra' etc.

Kedārabhaṭṭa's method is the same as Hemacandra's. He also defines metres by means of algebraic notations and gives to examples. Numerous commentaries, however, have been written on the work and they supply suitable examples. Most prominent of these is the one written by Nārāyaṇa in 1545 A.D. The metres are carefully chosen thought no critical insight is shown in their treatment. The whole treatise is a mere compilation of definitions. The work became popular with later writers probably because it contained the most widely used metres defined in a style which makes it easy for the student to learn the definitions by rote.

The *Chandomañjarī* of Gaṅgādāsa comes next. The date of Gaṅgādāsa is disputed and may well be put in the sixteenth century A.D. The work is divided into six 'stabakas' and follows the traditional ruels. Stabaka I defines 'laghu', and cites the cases where a short syllable becomes a long one. Stabaka II defines 'Sama' metres, Stabaka III six 'Ardhasama' metres, and Stabaka IV seven 'Viṣama' metres. Āryā, Vaitāla and other metres measured by morae are defined in Stabaka V. In the sixth Stabaka, prose style is divided into three—Vṛttaka, Utakalikāprāya, and Vṛttagandhi. These three dividsion of prose style correspond to the three *rītis*.

Though Gaṅgādāsa touches all the aspects of the metres, he fails to analyse them critically, show their good and bad points and indicate their special usages.

Dāmodra's *Vāṇībhūṣaṇa* is the last work on Prosody in Sanskrit, worthy of mention. Dāmodara's date is not certain. He cannot be identified with Dāmodara, son of Lakṣmīdhara and author of Saṅgītadarpaṇa. The author of the Vāṇībhūṣaṇa is of Dīrghaghoṣa family; he, therefore, cannot be the same Dāmodara gupta who wrote the Kuṭṭanīmata in the last quarter of the eighth century A.D. The Vāṇībhūṣanā is a short treatise consisting of just two chapters. Chapter I contains the exposition of symbols like 'ma', 'ja', 'na' and so on, mentions the deities of gaṇas, the rules of short and long vowels, and the traditional two-fold divisionof metres. Chapter II defines nearly one hundred metres both 'Sama' and 'Viṣama'. The metres are arranged according to the number of syllables in them.

Form the foregoing summary it must have been clear that the science of Prosody was regarded as of great importance in the study of literature. The works mentioned above are only a part of the great volume of literature on the subject. so popular was versification that even dry subjects like grammar, and logic were explained inverses. From the above it will be clear that all the writers on Prosody have simply defined and classifeid the metres. They have not looked into the special characteristics of each metre. It was left to Kṣemendra to attempt this most arduous task. As has been said above, his tratment is characterised by clarity of exposition and great critical acumen. He lays down the usage of each metre. This practice is both advantageous and dertimental to Prosody; if it results in dogmatic rules it must be discouraged, because say thought can be embodied in any metre. It is the context that decided whether a metre suits the thought or not. On the other hand, if it serves as a mere guide to a novice in poetics, it can go a long way in helping him to use the right metre.

[illegible] and Hemacandra have developed this subject in their treatises, but Kṣemendra appears to be quite original in his treatment.

A study of Kṣemendra's works reveals that they were written in accordance with the doctrines propounded in his Kavikaṇṭhābharaṇa. For instance, his didactic poems, the Samayamātṛkā, the Kalāvilāsa, the Darpadalana, the Sevyasevakopadeśa, and the Cārucaryāśataka illustrate his [illegible] (Kavi II 6) i.e., "familiarity with the ways of the world", and [illegible] (Kavi II 10) i.e., "special didactic skill". His epitomes of the Epics and the Nṛpāvalī bear testimony to the fact that he was pursuing the principle of [illegible] (Kavi II [illegible]) i.e., "acquaintance with history". In his Daśāvatāracarita he illustrates his [illegible] (Kavi II 19) i.e., "[illegible] in the praise of all deities"; in the Padyakādambarī his [illegible] (Kavi II [illegible]) i.e., "sparkling interest in romances"; in the Citrabhāratanāṭaka his *nāṭakābhinayaprekṣā* (Kavi II 15) i.e., "fondness for dramatic performances", and in his works on poetics *kāvyāṅgavidyādhigama* (Kavi II 3) i.e., "a knowlege of ancillary disciplines". Since all his works are complete, one might say that he follows faithfully *prārabdhakāvyanirvāha* (Kavi II 22) i.e., "seeing a poem to its finish". In fact all the one hundred instructions to the poet are amply illustrated in his works; and it may be concluded that the Kavikaṇṭhābharaṇa was a product of his mature genius.

In his Aucityavicāracarcā Kṣemendra has developed the theme of PROPRIETY as essential to poetry. He has illustrated under twenty-eight headings how propriety can either be displayed or violated. His forceful arguments and discussions and his clear enunciation of principles in defence of what he believes to be poetry, point to his remarkable conception of poetic art and its practice. His Aucityavicāracarcā, like his Kavikaṇṭhābharaṇa, is a mine of quotations from his contemporaries as well as predecessors and fully illustrates his contention *vyutpattyai sarvaśiṣyatā* (Kavi II 14) i.e., "readiness to become other's disciple for poetic culture", *paronmeṣaślāghā* (Kavi II 14) i.e., "eagerness to emulate or excel

Translation of

Kṣemendra's Kavikaṇṭhābharaṇa, Aucityavicāracarcā and Suvṛttatilaka

महाकविश्रीक्षेमेन्द्रविरचितं

कविकण्ठाभरणम्

Kavikaṇṭhābharaṇa or A Necklace for Poets

प्रथमः सन्धिः

First Link

जयति जितसुधाम्भः सम्भवद्वाग्भवश्री-
रथ सरससमुद्यत्कामतत्त्वानुभावा।
तदनु परमधामध्यानसंलब्धमोक्षा
रविशशिशिखिरूपा त्रैपुरी मन्त्रशक्तिः[1] ।। १ ।।

1. Victorious is the Mystical Energy known as Traipurī (i.e., belonging to *tripura*[2])—the Mystical Energy, which possesses the lustre of the Vāgbhava Bīja (i.e. ऐं) emanating from teh ambrosial waters, which has the potency of the evolving Kāma-tattva Bīja (i.e. क्लीं). full of charm, and which grants salvation, when contemplated as the Supreme Splendour (i.e. सौं), and which, thus exists in the form of the Sun, the Moon and the Fire.[3]

---

1. ऐं क्लीं सौः इति त्रिपुराख्यमन्त्रमहिमेत्यर्थः।
2. A spell or charm so called. It also, no doubt, reminds one of the greatest exploits of Śiva, who had to summon all power at his command in order to quell the formidable enemies, the demons of the *three cities.* The Mystic Energy (*mantrasśakti*) which enabled Śiva to destroy the Tripuras is what is contemplated here.
3. In the Tantrik language the Sun, the Moon and the Fir are technical terms which denote the creative trinity. They are represented by the syllables ऐं, क्लीं and सौ restpectively in the mystical formula which, when effective, grants wisdom, glory and powr. See Tantrik Texts Vol. I and Tantrābhidhāna by Tārānātha Vidyāratna. The 'Bīja' is the germ and forms the essential part of the Mantra or the incantation.

शिष्याणामुपदेशाय विशेषाय[1] विपश्चिताम्।
अयं सरस्वतीसारः क्षेमेन्द्रेण प्रदर्श्यते।।२।।

2. By Kṣemendra is brought into being this Epictome of Eloquence—(Substance of Speech). for the instruction of pupils and for the specialization (in learning) of the larned.

तत्राकवेः कवित्वाप्तिः शिक्षा प्राप्तगिरः कवेः।
चमत्कृतिश्च शिक्षाप्तौ गुणदोषोद्गतिस्ततः।।३।।
पश्चात्परिचयप्राप्तिरित्येते पञ्च सन्धयः।
समुद्दिष्टाः क्रमेणाषां लक्ष्यलक्षणमुच्यते।।४।।

3-4. Acquisition of the art of peotry by one who is not a poet, instruction for one who has obatined mastery over speech, (infusing) charm (in poetry) when one has received training, then differentiation between merits and demerits, and last of all, complete mastery (over the art of poetry)—these are the five[2] chapters (lit. links or joints) which are prosposed. Their definitions and illustrations will be given in due course.

[3]सुविभक्तिसमन्वितं बुधैर्गुणसंयुक्तममुक्तसौष्ठवैः।
रचितं पदकैः सुवर्णवत्कविकण्ठाभरणं विचार्यताम्।।५।।

5. Let the wise bestow thought upon this Kavikaṇṭhābharaṇa,[4] which is endowed with well-meaning caseforms *(suvibhaktisamanvitam),* which is graces by qualities *(guṇasaṁyuktam),* which is wreathed from words not dispossessed of elegance *(amuktasauṣṭhavaiḥ padahai racitam),* which contains melodious syllalbes (*suvarṇavat);* and which, thus, resembles an (actual) golden necklace for poets *(suvarṇavat Kavikaṇṭhābharaṇam),* having well-marekd sections

---

1. विशेषज्ञानार्थमित्यर्थः।
2. CF. पञ्चसन्धयः as in a Sanskrit drama, viz., मुख, प्रतिमुख, गर्भ विमर्श and निर्वहण.
3. सुप्तिङादिविभक्तिभिख्यत्र शोभनमानादिविभागेन च युक्तं, शब्द–सौन्दयंसमेतैः पदैर्युतं, अन्यत्र सन्दरैरलंकारपदकैर्युक्तं च, कविकण्ठाभरणं विद्वद्भिर्विचारणीयमिति भावाः।
4. Mark the double entendre of *Kavikaṇṭhābharaṇa* to well brought out by the oet.

(suvibhaktisamanvitam,), with a thread passing through it *(guṇavat)* and with its beautiful pendants well set *(amuhtasauṣṭhavaiḥ padakai racitam).*

And now, he who is not a poet (akavi) in instucted to acquire poetic ability. First of all there is divine effort, then human.

ॐ स्वस्त्यङ्कं स्तुमः सिद्धमन्ताद्य[1] मितीप्सितम्।
उद्यदूर्जप्रदं देव्या ऋॠलृलॄनिगूहनम् ॥६॥

6. We parise the symbol of success,[2] which is accomplished, and dear to heart, because it is the primaeval one; it bestows (on one) ever-increasing strength and hides with intiself the syllables ऋ, ॠ, लृ, लॄ, symbolic of the goddess of speech.

एकमैश्वर्यसंयुक्तमोजोवर्धनमौषधम् ।
अन्तरान्तः कलाखण्डगलद्धनसुधाङ्कितम्॥७॥

7. It is unique, fullof prospeirty, a medicine to add to one's (poetic) vigour; it is extremely secret and is marked with the auspicious nectar exuding from the digit (or the moon).

चन्द्रोच्छलज्जलं प्रोज्झदज्ञानं टठसंयुतम्।
डम्बरप्रौढकिरणं तथतां दधदुन्नतम्॥८॥

8. It gets overflowing elixir from the moon; it dispels ignorance, and contains ट and ठ, has a multitude of luxuriant rays of light; it is exalted andbears the form of त and थ.

परं फलप्रदं बद्धमूलोद्भवमयं वपुः।
रम्यं लघुवरं शर्म वर्षत्सर्वसहाक्षरम्॥९॥

9. Taking form from a well-rooted source (the *bījamantra*), it bestows the highest rewards. It is lovely and eminently brief or light. It rains bliss. It is all endruing and imperishable.

---

1. अन्तर्मनसि सिद्धम्, आद्यं प्रथममित्यतो हेतोरीप्सितमभीष्टम्।
2. *Svastyaṅkam* may be taken to denote Swastika, a kind of mystical cross made to denote good luck. It is a mark of auspiciousness. *Svasti* is also soemtimes personified as a goddess. Sometimes it is related to the worship of Gaṇesśa.

एतां नमः सरस्वत्यै यः क्रियामातृकां जपेत्[1]।
क्षेममैन्द्रं स लभते भव्योऽभिनववाग्भवम्।। १०।।

10. Bow to such Sarasvatī. He is the blesed one who recites the Kriyāmātṛkā[2] and obtains the supreme security[3] arising from the root-formula.

श्वेतां सरस्वतीं मूर्ध्नि चन्द्रमण्डलमध्यगाम्।
अक्षराभरणां ध्यायेद्वाङ्मयामृतवर्षिणीम्।। ११।।

11. One should contemplate in one's mind Sarasvatī, who is white in form residing in the middle of the lunar circle, who has the ltetters for the ornaments (or whose ornaments never perish) and who showers nectar in the form of learning.

त्रिकोणयुगमध्ये तु तडित्तुल्यां प्रमोदिनीम्।
स्वर्गमार्गोद्गतां ध्यायेत्परामममृतवाहिनीम्।। १२।।

12. One should contemplate, in the centre of the two traingels, Sarasvatī, Supreme goddess, who rejoices being triumphant, who, like lighting, flashes through the heavenly regions, and who is the very river of ambrosia.

निर्विकारां निराकारां शक्तिं ध्यायेत्परात्पराम्।
एषा बीजत्रयी[4] वाच्या त्रयी वाक्काममुक्तिसूः।। १३।।

13. One should contemplate upon the unchaning and formless mystic power which is higher than the highest. It is expressed through the three-fold seed (the *bījamantara*). It is that Vedic Speech *(trayī-vāh)* which grants desire and emancipation.

---

1. 'अन्तः' इतिपदमारभ्य 'सहाक्षरम्' इत्यन्तेन पदकदम्बकेन अकारादि क्षकारान्तमातृका-वर्णस्वरूपां वाग्देवतां 'सरस्वत्यै नम' इति मन्त्रेण जपेदित्यर्थः

2. The stanzas 6 to 9 contains the Skt. *varṇamālā* which our author designates as *Kriyāmātṛkā*. This *varṇamālā* shmbolises the form of speech.

3. Mark the use of *kṣemam aindram* which has a side reference to the author's own name.

4. बीजत्रयं पूर्वोक्तमेव ग्राह्यम्।

काव्यक्रियेच्छाङ्कुरमूलभूमिमन्विष्य विश्रान्तिलवेन मोक्षः।
न्यावधाने मदनस्य मोक्षस्तृतीयबीजे सकलेऽस्ति मोक्षः।। १४।।

14. Delivernance follows when one seeks, with little rest, the regions where sprouts the desire to creat poetry. Love's freedom follows with concentration on the second one (viz., Kāmatattva of the first stanza). And emancipation is there in the third basic formula, (conceived) in its entirety.

Now, human effort.

Pupils, who are to be initiated inot the art of poetry, are of three kinds—those who can accomplish (the work) with little effort, those who can be trained with difficulty and those who are incapable (of any training).

तत्र प्रथम

कुर्वीत साहित्यविदः सकाशे श्रुतार्जनं काव्यसमुद्भवाय।
न तार्किकं केवलशाब्दिकं वा कुर्यादगुरुं सूक्तिविकासविघ्नम्[1] ।। १५।।

The first one—

15. For the sake of poetic inspiration, the pupil should gain knowledge rather at the feet of a man of literature. He should not make a logician or a mere grammarian his preceptor, because they hinder the flowering of good poetry.

विज्ञातशब्दागम[2] नामधातुश्छन्दोविधाने विहितश्रमश्च।
काव्येषु माधुर्यमनोरमेषु कुर्यादखिन्नः श्रवणाभियोगम्।। १६।।

16. When one has studies with effort the grammatical structure consisting of nouns and verbs, and has worked out methods of versification, one should with a cheerful heart, devote one's mind to listening to poems, pleasant by their sweetness.

गीतेषु गाथास्वय देशभाषाकाव्येषु दद्यात्सरसेषु कर्णम्।
वाचां चमत्कारविधायिनीनां नवार्थचर्चासु रुचिं विदध्यात्।। १७।।

17. One should listen to the tasteful songs, gāthās (folklore)

---

1. सुकाव्याविभू 'तिप्रतिबन्धकम्।
2. व्याकारणशास्त्रम्।

and poems written in one's local tongue. One should also cultivate a taste for discussing novel interpretations arising from delightful compositions.

रसे रसे तन्मयतां गतस्य गुणे गुणे हर्षवशीकृतस्य।
विवेकसेकस्वकपाकभिन्नं मनः प्रसूतेऽङ्कुरवत्कवित्वम्।। १८।।

18. When absorbed in the various flavours, captivated by the joy in each poetic quality, bursing into maturity with the sprinkling of discriminatory talents, the mind gives rise to peotry like a sprout, being ripe from within.

अथ द्वितीय:-

पठेत्समस्तान्किल कालिदासकृतप्रबन्धानितिहासदर्शी।
काव्याधिवासप्रथमोद्गमस्य रक्षेत्पुरस्तार्तिकगन्धमुग्रम्।। १९।।

Then the second one—

19. with an eye on history, the second one should study all the works of Kālidāsa, and should save the newly rising fragrance of poetry from the pungent smell of logic.

महाकवेः काव्यनवक्रियायै तदेकचित्तः परिचारकः स्यात्।
पदे च पादे च पदावशेषसम्पूरणेच्छां मुहुराददीत।। २०।।

20. He should remain fervently devoted to the great poet (mahākavi), whose work he sets as his ideal, always concentrating upon it for the production of new poetry. He should have, time and again, the desire to fill in the gaps in a word or in a foot (in a stanza), or in the part of a foot.

अभ्यासहेतोः पदसन्निवेशैर्वाक्यार्थशून्यैर्विदधीत वृत्तम्।
श्लोकं परावृत्तिपदैः पुराणं यथास्थितार्थं परिपूरयेच्च।। २१।।

21. For the sake of practice, he should compose in a metre, by putting together words even if they do not mean anything, when read as a sentence. He may also change the words of an already composed stanza keeping on to the same meaning.

The one having no meaning is as follows : (it being merely an attempts at simple versification without caring for sense).

आनन्दसन्दोहपदारविन्दकुन्देन्दुकन्दोदितबिन्दुवृन्दम् ।
इन्दिन्दिरान्दोलितमन्दमन्दनिष्यन्दनन्दन्मकरन्दवन्द्यम् ।।

(It may be translated as follows, but it is meaningless :) Heap of joy, lotus-like feet, *kunda,* the moon, drops arising from roots, shaken, rage, swinging, oozing slowly, gladdening, honey worshipful.

An example of sustaining the old sense by a change in the words of the verse is as follows :

वागर्थाविव सम्पृक्तौ वागर्थप्रतिपत्तये।
जगतः पितरौ वन्दे पार्वतीपरमेश्वरौ।।

वाण्यर्थाविव संयुक्तौ वाण्यर्थप्रतिपत्तये।
जगतो जनकौ वन्दे शर्वाणीशशिशेखरौ।।

In order to comprehend the word and its meaning, I bow to Pārvatī and Parameśvara, the parents of the world, who are united like word and its meaning.

अथ तृतीयः

यस्तु प्रकृत्याश्मसमान एव कष्टेन वा व्याकरणेन नष्टः।
तर्केण दग्धोऽनलधूमिना वाऽप्यविद्धकर्णः सुकविप्रबन्धैः।। २२।।
न तस्य वक्तृत्वसमुद्भवः स्याच्छिक्षाविशेषैरपि सुप्रयुक्तैः।
न गर्दभो गायति शिक्षितोऽपि संदर्शिते पश्यति नार्कमन्धः।। २३।।

Then the third—

22-23. On him, who, by his nature, is like a stone, or has been depirived of initiative (lit. spoiled) by tedious grammar, or has been consumed by the smouldering fire of logic, or whose ears have never been perforated by listeining to the compositions of eminent poets, eloquence cannot down even by special instructions well-employed. An ass cannot sing though trained; a blind person cannot see the sun though shown.

इति ततसुकृतानां प्राक्तनानां विपाके
भवति शुभमतीनां मन्त्रसिद्धं कवित्वम्।
तदनु पुरुषयत्नैर्धर्मितामभ्युदेति
स्फुरति जडधियां श्रीशारदा साधनेन।। २४।।

24. As a reward for the extensive good deeds done in previous births, glorious Śāradā (poetry) becomes manifest to intelligent persons (accomplished) through mystical incantations. She reveals herself to sensible ones through effort, and dawns upon the full through as expedient.

इति श्रीव्यासदासापराख्यक्षेमेन्द्रकृते कविकण्ठाभरणे

कवित्वप्राप्तिः प्रथमः सन्धिः।

Here ends the first link 'Acquisition of the Art of Poetry' in the NECKLACE FOR POETS composed by Kṣemendra alias Vyāsadāsa.

द्वितीयः सन्धिः

Second Link

छयोपजीवी पदकोपजीवी पादोपजीवी सकलोपजीवी।
भवेदथ प्राप्तकवित्वजीवी स्वोन्मेषतो वा भुवनोपजीव्यः।। १।।

छायोपजीवी यथा भट्टभल्लटस्य–

नन्वाश्रयस्थितिरियं तव कालकूट!
केनोत्तरोत्तरविशिष्टपदोपदिष्टा।
प्रागर्णवस्य हृदये वृषलक्ष्मणो[1]ऽथ
कण्ठेऽधुना वससि वाचि पुनः खलानाम्।।

यथा च श्रीमदुत्पलराजदेवस्य–

मात्सर्यतीव्रतिमिरावृतदृष्टयो ये
ते कस्य नाम न खला व्यथयन्ति चेतः।
मन्ये विमुच्य गलकन्दलमिन्दुमौले-
र्येषां सदा वचसि वल्गति कालकूटः।।

पदकोपजीवी यथा मुक्ताकणस्य–

यथा रन्ध्रं व्योम्नश्चलजलदधूमः स्थगयति
स्फुलिङ्गानां रूपं दधति च यथा कीटमणयः।
यथा विद्युज्ज्वालोल्लसनपरिपिङ्गाश्च ककुभ-
स्तथा मन्ये लग्नः पथिकतरुखण्डे स्मरदवः[2]।।

---

1. नीलकण्ठस्य।
2. कामाग्निः।

यथा चैतद्भ्रातुश्चक्रपालस्य–

सरस्यामेतस्यामुदरवलिवीचीविलुलितं
यथा लावण्याम्भो जघनपुलिनोल्लङ्घनकरम्।
यथा लक्ष्यश्चायं चलनयनमीनव्यतिकर-
स्तथा मन्ये मग्नः प्रकटकुचकुम्भः स्मरगजः।

पादोपजीवी यथामरकस्य–

गन्तव्यं यदि नाम निश्चितमहो गन्तासि केयं त्वरा
द्वित्राण्येव दिनानि तिष्ठतु भवान्पश्यामि यावन्मुखम्।
संसारे घटिकाप्रणाल[1] विगलद्वारा समे जीविते
को जानाति पुनस्त्वया सह मम स्याद्वा न वा सङ्गमः।।

यथा मम–

हंहो स्निग्धसखे! विवेकबहुभिः प्राप्तोऽसि पुण्यैर्मया
गन्तव्यं कतिचिद्दिनानि भवता नास्मत्सकाशात्क्वचित्।
त्वत्सङ्गेन करोमि जन्ममरणोच्छेदं गृहीतत्वरः
को जानाति पुनस्त्वया सह मम स्याद्वा न वा सङ्गमः।।

सकलोपजीवी यथार्यभट्टस्य–

शब्दैर्निसर्गकटुभिर्मलिनस्वभावाः श्रोत्रं खला निगडवत्परितस्तुदन्ति।
श्रव्यैरलुप्तमदबन्धतयाऽतिमञ्जुमञ्जीरवत्तु सुजना जनयन्ति मोदम्।।

यथा च भट्टबाणस्य–

कटु कणन्तो मलदायकाः खलास्तुदन्त्यलं बन्धनशृङ्खला इव।
मनस्तु साधुध्वनिभिः पदे पदे हरन्ति सन्तो मणिनूपुरा इव।।

भुवनोपजीव्यो यथा भगवान्व्यासः। तथा चोक्तम्–

इदं कविवरैः सर्वैराख्यानमुपजीव्यते।
उदयं प्रेप्सुभिर्भृत्यैरभिजात इवेश्वरः।।

1. (A poet) while composing may thrive in the shadow of another poet, or on his words *(pada),* or on his feet (pāda=metricla line) or on his entire composition. Or, he may thrive on his own faculty acquried by effort. Or he may, through his own genius, become a feeder to the poet-world.

---

1. जलनिर्गमस्थानम्। वारा-जलेन।

(i) Now, "thriving in another's shadow"—Example, Bhaṭṭa Bhallaṭa—

'O fatal poison, who advised you to seek these resorts, excelling one another in succession? First, you dwelt in the heart of the ocean,then in Śiva's throat and now you live in the speech of the wicked'!

(ii) Again Utpalarājadeva—

'Whose mind do not the wicked afflict—the wicked whose eyes are obscured by darkenss aggravated by malice, and in whose speech, methinks, the fatal poison reveals, forsaking even the tender neck of the moon-crested god?'

(iii) 'Thriving on borrowed words"—Example, Muktākaṇa's verse—

'As the smoky clouds, when moving, cover the cavity of the sky, as the glow-worms assume the form of sparks of fire, and as the quarters get tawny by flashes of bright lightning, I am led to believe that travellers must have been caught in a woodland-conflagration of love'.

(iv) Compare his brother Cakrapāla's (verse)—

'As in this lake of loveliness the water of grace rolling in ripples in the form of folds on her belly is transgressing the banks of (her) thighs, and as the multitude of fish moving about is visible in the form of (her0 tremulous eyes, I think the elephant of love, with its temples displayed in the form of her prominent breasts, had dived".

(v) "Thriving on borrowed feet"—Example, Amaraka's verse—

'Well, if you must go, you will certainly go, where is the hurry? Stay for just two or three days[1] so that I may keep looking at your face. Who knows whether, again, there would be a union at all between you and me in this world, where life is (passing away) like the trickling of water from a water-pot used in measuring time?'

Compare (with the above verse) mine—

1. *V.L. padāni (Subhāṣitāvalī* 1059).

'Well, dear friend, Viveka (Discretion), I have got you after many good deeds. You are not to go away from me anywhere for some days. In your company, I wish to make haste and put an end (once for all) to birth and death; for who knows whether, again, three would be a union at all between you and me?"

(vi) 'Thriving on wholesale borrowal", as in Ārya Bhaṭṭa's verse—

'The ill-natured wicked poeple pain the ears in every way (lit. from all sides) by words naturally harsh, like the sound of chains; and the virtuous ones captivate (the mind) by words compact and wothty of hearing and sounding sweet like anklets'.

Compare (with the above) Bāṇa's verse—

'The wicked, like fetters, echo harshly, leave a mark, and wound deeply, while the good, like jewelled anklets, ever charm the mind with sweet sounds'.

(vii) "A feeder for the whole world—as the venerable Vyāsa. Verily, it is said—

'This epic (mahābhārata) provides meterial for composition to all the great poets, like a noble master twho provides sustenance to all dependents who desire to prosper".

(The author) now speaks of the injunctions to one who has acquried the gift of poetry.

व्रतं सारस्वतो यागः पूर्वं विघ्नेशपूजनम्।
विवेकशक्तिरभ्यासः सन्धानं प्रौढिरश्रमः।। २।।

2. He should observe the vow in honour of Sarasvatī (the goddess of leaning), make sacrifices and should first of all worship the vanquisher of obstacles (i.e. Gaṇeśa). He should possess discernment, should be devoted to practice, (be interested in) searching (new things), should be confident and should never get tired of work.

वृत्तपूरणमुद्योगः पाठः परकृतस्य च।
काव्याङ्गविद्या[1] धिगमः समस्यापरिपूरणम्।। ३।।

१. महाकविकाव्यछन्दोनुशासनादि।

3. He should have (the skill) to complete metres, be always zealous, study the works of otehrs, should read the auxiliary sciences of poetry and should be able to complete a stanza which is incomplete.

सहवासः कविवरैर्महाकाव्यार्थचर्वणम्।
आर्यत्वं सुजनेमैत्री सौमनस्यं सुवेषता।।४।।

4. He should keep company with good poets, should relish the meanings of epic poems (mahākāvyas). Possess nobility, make friends with the good, be of cheerful mind, and put on elegant dress.

नाटकाभिनयप्रेक्षा श्रृङ्गारालिङ्गिता मतिः।
कवीनां सम्भवे दानं गीतेनात्माधिवासनम्।।५।।

5. He should witness a play being staged, and have a mind leaning towards the sentiment of love, should be charitable in poetic symposia and saturate himself with music.

लोकाचारपरिज्ञानं विविक्ताख्यायिकारसः।
इतिहासानुसरणं चारुचित्रनिरीक्षणम्।।६।।
शिल्पिनां कौशलप्रेक्षा वीरयुद्धावलोकनम्।
शोकप्रलापश्रवणं श्मशानारण्यदर्शनम्।।७।।

6-7. He should be weel-versed in etiquette and should show an intrest in romantic tales (ākhyāyikās). He should learn history, study beautiful paintings, observe the skill of artists and witness various duesl; he should hear th bewailing in sorrw and witness the cremation grounds and forests.

व्रतिनां पर्युपासा च नीडायतनसेवनम्[1]।
मधुरविमशनं धातुसाम्यमशोकता।।८।।

8. He should wait upon those observing vows and observe roosting places of birds and mansions for human beings. He should eat sweet and oily things, should have harmony of humours and be free from worry.

---

1. कपोतादिनिवासस्थानसेवनम्

निशाशेषे प्रबोधश्च प्रतिभा स्मृतिरादरः।
सुखासनं दिवा शय्या शिशिरोष्णप्रतिक्रिया।। ९।।

9. He should get up when some part of night still remains, possess presence of mind, be respectful; should sit in an easy manner, should enjoy a nap during the day and guard himself against cold and heat.

आलोकः पत्रलेख्यादौ गोष्ठीप्रहसनज्ञता।
प्रेक्षा प्राणिस्वभावानां समुद्राद्रिस्थितक्षिणम्।। १०।।

10. He should observe paintings and leaf-cutting, should be clever in talking humorously in parties, should observe the behaviour of animate objects and examine the pnysical surroundings of seas and mountains.

रवीन्दुताराकलनं सर्वर्तुपरिभावनम्।
जनसङ्घाभिगमनं देशभाषोपजीवनम्।। ११।।

11. He should notice the movements of the sun, the moon and the stars and should have a knowledge of the cycle of seasons, should join people's assemblies, and should be able to use the languages of the country.

[1]आघानोद्धरणप्रज्ञा कृतसंशोधनं मुहुः।
अपराधीनता यज्ञसभाविद्यागृहस्थितिः।। १२।।

12. He should possess the talents of selecting and rejecting, and should have the ability to scrutinize, should be independent, should frequent the secrificial meetings and places of learning.

अतृष्णाता निजोत्कर्षे परोत्कर्षविमर्शनम्।
आत्मश्लाघाश्रुतौ लज्जा परश्लाघानुभाषणम्।। १३।।

13. He should not be over-anxious for his own exaltation and should tolerate another's rise; he should feel shy of listening to this own praise, and should join in the praise of others.

---

1. स्थापननिष्कानज्ञानम्

सदा स्वकाव्यव्याख्यानं वैरमत्सरवर्जनम्।
परोन्मेषजिगीषा च व्युत्पत्त्यै सर्वशिष्यता।। १४।।

14. He should be always ready to explain his poems and should avoid hostility and jealousy. He should be anxious to excel others in enlightenment and should (be ready) to act as pupil to any person for the sake of learning.

पाठस्यावसरज्ञत्वं श्रोतृचित्तानुवर्तनम्।
इङ्गिताकारवेदित्वमुपादेयनिबन्धनम् ।। १५।।

15. He should know the proper time to study and should abide by the taste of listeners, he should know the significance of gestrues and signs and procure things worth providing.

उपदेशविशेषोक्तिरदीर्घरससङ्गतिः ।
स्वसूक्तप्रेषणं दिक्षु परसूक्तपरिग्रहः।। १६।।

16. He should be able to develop the salient points of his talk and should not be solely (atached to) one flavour for a long time; he should send forth his choicest works in all directions and should collect others's works.

वैदग्ध्यं पटुताभङ्गिर्निःसङ्गैकान्तनिर्वृतिः।
आशापाशपरित्यागः सन्तोषः सत्त्वशीलता।। १७।।

17. He should be learend and clever. He should possess sparkling wit and should love to remain in solitude with none beside. He should get out of snares of longings, be contented and large-hearted.

अयाचकत्वमग्राम्यपदालापः कथास्वपि।
काव्यक्रियासु निर्बन्धो विश्रान्तिश्चान्तरान्तरा।। १८।।

18. He should neither go a-begging nor stoop to vulgarity even in his narratives. He should be persistent in the composition of poems and at regular intervals he should take rest.

नूतनोत्पादने यत्नः साम्यं सर्वसुरस्तुतौ।
पराक्षेपसहिष्णुत्वं गाम्भीर्यं निर्विकारता।। १९।।

19. He should try to create something new, and show equanimity in the praise of all the gods, should be able to suffer criticism at others's hands, and should be profound and firm.

अविकत्थनतादैन्यं[1] परेषां नष्टयोजनम्।
पराभिप्रायकथनं परसादृश्यभाषणम्।। २०।।

20. He should not indulge in self-praise nor feel too humble; should help others to complete (when poems are left unfinished and the original authors cannot complete them);he should expalin others's import and say what suits others.

सप्रसादपदन्यासः ससंवादार्थसङ्गतिः।
निर्विरोधरसव्यक्तिर्युक्तिर्व्याससमासयोः ।। २१।।

21. He should put together words having clarity of meaning, and should convey sense suiting the context.He should bring out the flavour uncontended; he should be judicious in the matter of putting words in compounds or using them apart.

प्रारब्धकाव्यनिर्वाहः प्रवाहश्चतुरो गिराम्।
शिक्षाणां शतमित्युक्तं युक्तं प्राप्तगिरः कवेः।। २२।।

22.He should see the poem to its finish, possess adroit eloquence in speech. What is proper for one, who has acquired the gift of poetry, has been said in these hundred pieces of advice.

इति बहुतरशिक्षालक्षणक्षीणदोषे
प्रभवति गतनिद्रे प्रातिभे सुप्रभाते।
कविरविरविलुप्तव्याप्तिभिः सूक्तपादै-
र्नयति नवनवत्वं भावभावस्वभावम्[2] ।। २३।।

23. Thus when his flaws have been removed by pursuing these tenets of training, a poet is at his best in the morning hours when he has shaken off his sleep and his genius has a free play.

---

1. आत्मप्रशंसादीनत्वयोरभावः।
2. दोषाः वक्ष्यमाणाः शब्दकालुष्यादयोऽन्यत्र दोषा रात्रिः, सूक्तानां पादैः श्लोकचतुर्थांशैरन्यत्र किरणैः, भावानां पदार्थानां ये रत्यादयो भावास्तेषां स्वभावमन्यत्र पदार्थसत्तास्वभावम्; अन्यत्सुगमम्।

At that time he represents the nature of various sentiments and emotions of beings in ever fresh glow in his poetry, which does not lose sight of pervasiveness. The poet in this manner acts the sun, who rises at the time when the end of the night is proclaimed by many a recital and, who, chasing away gloom, brings light into being and displays all objects in their fresh garb by means of his omniscient rays.

इति श्रीव्यासदासापराख्यक्षेमेन्द्रकृते कविकण्ठाभरणे द्वितीय सन्धिः।

Here ends the second link 'Instructions to One who has obtained Mastery over Speech' in the NECKLACE FOR POETS composed by Kṣemendra alias Vyāsadāsa.

—•—

तृतीयः सन्धिः
Third Link

Now, (the author) speaks of (the way in which) a trianed poet can display charm in what he says—

अथ शिक्षितस्य कवेः सूक्तिचमत्कारमाह–

सुकविरतिशयार्थी वाक्चमत्कारलोभा-
दभिसरति मनोज्ञे वस्तुशब्दार्थसार्थे।
भ्रमर इव वसन्ते पुष्पकान्ते वनान्ते
नवकुसुमविशेषामोदमास्वादलोलः।। १।।

1. A good poet, desirous of excellence (in poetry) and out of eagerness for charm in speech, pursues the heart bewitching art of composition containing matter and words full of meaning; just as a bee restless on account of his (love) for flavour, hovers in spring over a garden beautiful with flowers in quest of fresh floral fragrance.

Bereft of charm, a poet is not poet, nor a poem a poem.

नहि चमत्कारविरहितस्य कवेः कवित्वं, काव्यस्य वा काव्यत्वम्

एकेन केनचिदनघर्मणिप्रभेण
काव्यं चमत्कृतिपदेन विना सुवर्णम्।

निर्दोषलेशमपि रोहति कस्य चित्ते
लावण्यहीनमिव यौवनमङ्गनानाम्।। २।।

चमत्कारविरहो यथा मालवरुद्रस्य-

वेल्लत्पल्लव संमिलल्लत लसत्पुष्प स्फुटत्कुड्मल
स्फूर्जद्गुच्छभर क्वणन्मधुकरक्रीडाविनोदाकर।
रक्ताशोक सखे! दयां कुरु हर प्रारब्धमाडम्बरं[1]
प्राणाः कण्ठमुपागताः प्रियतमो दूरे त्वमेवंविधः।।

चमत्कारो यथा कालिदासस्य-

रक्तस्त्वं नवपल्लवैरहमपि श्लाघ्यैः प्रियाया गुणै-
स्त्वामायान्ति शिलीमुखाः स्मरधनुर्मुक्ताः सखे! मामपि।
कान्तापादतलाहतिस्तव मुदे तद्वन्ममाप्यावयोः
सर्वं तुल्यमशोक! केवलमहं धात्रा सशोकः कृतः।।

तत्र दशविधश्चमत्कारः-अविचारितरमणीय[१]: विचार्यमाणरमणीय[२]: समस्तसूक्तव्यापी[३] सूक्तैकदेशदृश्य[४]: शब्दगत[५]: अर्थगत[६]: शब्दार्थगत[७]: अलङ्कारगत[८]: रसगत[९]:, प्रख्यातवृत्तिगतश्च[१०]।

अविचारितरमणीयो यथा मम शशिवंशे-

शूराः सन्ति सहस्रशः सुचरितैः पूर्णं जगत्पण्डितैः
संख्या नास्ति कलावतां बहुतरैः शान्तैर्वनान्ताः श्रिताः।
त्यक्तुं यः किल वित्तमुत्तममतिः शक्नोति जीवाधिकं
सोऽस्मिन्भूमिविभूषणं शुभनिधिर्भव्यो भवे दुर्लभः।।

विचार्यमाणरमणीयो यथा मम पद्यकादम्बर्याम्-

अङ्गेऽनङ्गज्वरहुतवहश्चक्षुषि ध्यानमुद्रा
कण्ठे जीवः करकिसलये दीर्घशायी कपोलः।
अंसे वीणा कुचपरिसरे चन्दनं वाचि मौनं
तस्याः सर्वं स्थितमिति न तु त्वां विना कापि चेतः।।

समस्तसूक्तव्यापी यथा मम शशिवंशे-

माधुर्यानुभवेऽपि ते सुवदने तीक्ष्णा. कटाक्षाः परं
पर्यन्तस्थितताररका अपि नृणां रागानुबन्धोद्यताः।
नैवोज्झन्ति विवेकिनश्चपलतामुत्सेकसंवादिनी-
माश्चर्यं श्रवणौ स्पृशन्ति च पुनमरं च [2]कुर्वन्त्यमी।।

---

1. पल्लवादिस्वसमृद्धिसमुदायम्। 2. कामम्।

सूक्तैकदेशदृश्यो यथा मम पद्यकादम्बर्याम्–

नित्यार्चा हृदयस्थितस्य भवतः पद्मोत्पलैश्चन्दनै–
स्त्वद्भक्तिस्त्वदनुस्मृतिश्च मनसि त्वन्नाममन्त्रे जपः।
सर्वत्रैव घनानुबन्धकलना त्वद्भावना सुभ्रुव–
स्तस्या जीवविमुक्तिरेव दिवसैर्देव! त्वदाराधनात्।।

शब्दगतो यथा मम चित्रभारतनाटके–

इतश्चञ्चच्चूतच्युतमधुचया वान्ति चतुराः
समीराः सन्तोषं दिशि दिशि दिशन्तो मधुलिहाम्।
निशान्ते कान्तानां स्मरसमरकेलिश्रममुषो
विजृम्भन्ते जृम्भाकलित[1]कमलामोदसुहृदः।।

अर्थगतो यथा मम लावण्यवत्याम्–

सदासक्तं शैत्यं विमलजलधारापरिचितं
घनोल्लासः क्ष्माभृत्पृथुकटकपाती वहति यः।
विधत्ते शौर्यश्रीश्रवणनवनीलोत्पलरुचिः
स चित्रं शत्रूणां ज्वलदनलताप भवदसिः।।

शब्दार्थगतो यथा मम पद्यकादम्बर्याम्–

किञ्चित्कुञ्चितकामकार्मुकलतामैत्री विचित्रा भ्रुवो–
नर्मोक्तिः स्मितकान्तिभिः कुसुमिता प्रागल्भ्यगर्भा गिरः।
रागोत्सङ्गनिषङ्गिभिः सरसतासंवादिभिर्विभ्रमै–
रायुष्यं परमं तया रतिपतेः प्राप्तं मृगाक्ष्या वयः।।

अलङ्कारगतो यथा मम लावण्यवत्याम्–

स्तनौ स्तब्धौ तीक्ष्णं नयनयुगलं निम्नमुदरं
भ्रुवोर्वक्राः वृत्तिर्विहितसुनिमारो[2]ऽधरमणिः।
तथासन्ने दैवादियति विषमे दुर्जनगणे
गुणी मध्ये हारः स्पृशति तव दोलातरलताम्।।

रसगतो यथा मम कनकजानक्याम्–

अत्रार्यः खरदूषणत्रिशिरसां नादानुबन्धोद्यमे
रुन्धाने भुवनं त्वया चकितया योद्धा निरुद्धः क्षणम्।
सस्नेहाः सरसाः सहासरभसाः सभ्रूभ्रमाः सस्पृहाः
सोत्साहास्त्वयि तद्बले च निदधे दोलायमाना दृशः।।

---

1. विकसित। 2. यति विनाशकः।

प्रख्यातवृत्तिगतो यथा मम शशिवंशे–

अग्रं गच्छत यच्छत स्वपृतनां[1] व्यूहक्षितिं रक्षत
क्षोणीं पश्यत नश्यत ततरं मा मा स्थितिं मुञ्चत।
यत्नात्तिष्ठत पृष्ठतस्तनुभिदामुग्रा गतिः पत्रिणा-
मित्यासीज्जनभञ्जने रथपथे पार्थस्य पृथ्वी श्रुतिः[2]।।

2. How can a composition, even though containing beautiful and flawless syllables but bereft of words of exquisite sense, even as burnished gold without the priceless gem to illumine, appeal to the heart of any one, like the youth of a woman devoid of the grace of beauty?

(i) Without charm, for instance, Mālavarudra's (verse)—

'O Red Aśoka tree, my friend, with your leaves moving, creeprs inter-twining, flowers looking bright, buds bursting, bunches of flowers glistening, the repository of the joy of (amorous) sport of humming bees, be kind; desist from this external display that you have started. My life is about to end (lit. the breath has come to the very throat to expire), the Dear One is at a distance and you are of such a sort'.

(ii) With charm, for instance, Kālidāsa's (verse)—

'You are red with fresh sprouts, I am also impassioned with the commendable virtues of my beloved; to you come the bees and to me, O friend, the arrows *(śilīmukhāḥ)* discharged from cupid's bow; strokes of woman's foot bring joy to you, so do they to me. O Aśoka, so much is common between you and me, but alas, God made me full of sorrow (sa-śoka) but you free from it (a-śoka)'.

This charm is of ten kinds—charm which one accrues without thoughtful effort or deliberation; charm for which one has to deliberate; charm pervading the whole of the composition; charm residing in a part of the verse; charm found in words; in meaning; both in word and meaning; in figures of speech; in sentiment; and lastly charm residing in the story of a famous personality.

(i) 'Spontaneous charm', as in my Śaśivaṁṣa—

---

1. स्वसेनाम्।
2. एवं रथाध्वनि अर्जुनेन श्रुतमित्यर्थः।

'There are thousands of valiant warriors, the world is full of learned men of solid character, the artists are innumerable, those after peace have in large numbers retired to forests. But rare to find in this world is the blessed one, the ornament of this earth, the repository of auspicious things, the high-minded one, who can give away his wealth, which is more than life'.

(ii) 'Charm which has to be thought out' (is found), for instance, in (a verse) in my Padyakādambarī—

'In her limbs stays the fire of love, in eyes the pose of meditation and in her throat her breath. On the sprout-like hand, the cheek rests for long, on the shoulder the guitar on the expanse of her bosom the sandal-paste, and silence in her speech. Thus everything of hers seems stable, but not her mind which reamins unsteady in your separation'.

(iii) 'Charm residing in the whole of the verse', as in a (verse) in my Śaśivaṁśa—

'O beautiful one, though mixed with sweetness, your side glances are yet extremely sharp; though the pupils of your eyes rest in the corners, yet they are ready to bind others in love; though possessed of discernment yet they do not renounce their tremulousness which becomes a source of pride. How strange![1] They touch the ears and yet generate love (cause death)'.

(iv) 'Charm, seen in one part of the verse', as in a verse in my Padyakādambarī—

'Through daily worship of yours, residing in the heart, with red and blue lotueses and sandla paste, devotion to you, your remembrance, constant muttering of your name—everywhere a display of deep devotion to you, and absorption in you. O lord, that sweet-browed on will in a few days achieve emancipation in this very life'.

(v) 'Charm, residing in words', as in this verse in my Citrabhāratanāṭaka—

'From here blow the charming breezes in all directions possessed

1. 'Touching of ears' indicates abstinence from doionig bad thing. Mark the antithesis.

of honey dripping from the juicy mangoes, comforting the honey-lickers (i.e. bees). They, taking away, at the end of the night, the fatigue of the loving pair, tired of amorous sport in the battle of love, grow strong and shrae the joy (lit. become friends) of full-blown lotuses'.

(vi) 'Charm, residing in the meaning', as a verse in my Lāvaṇyavatī—

'Your sword of bright lustre, smiting the huge armies of monarches possesses always an intense cold (i.e. sharpness of edge) increased by the stream of pure water. But stragne to say that it, beaming with the lusture of ear lotuses of the goddess of heroic valour, causes an affliction (as if) of blazing fire, to your enemies'.

(vii) 'Charm, residing in word and meaning', as is shown in my Padyakādambarī—

'That fawn-eyed lady has obtained an extremely long lease of life for the lord of Rati, since the movements of her eye-brows are wonderful, resembling the creeper-like bow of Kāma, slightly bent; her amorous talk is blooming with smiles and her speech is insipired by boldness and her coquetish behaviour conforms to her feelings of intense love, bordering on passion'.

(viii) 'Charm, residing in the figure of speech', as in a verse of mine in the Lāvaṇyavatī—

'Hard (or cruel) are the breasts while the pair of eyes is sharp (or merciless), the belly low (or mean), the eyebrows crooked (or cunning), the jewel-like lower lip a killer of ascetics even. Through ill luck dwelling among such extremely wicked company, the virtuous (lit. wellstrung) necklace demonstrates (lit. touches) at the middle the dangling movements of the swing'.

(ix) 'Charm, residing in the flavour', as in a verse in my Kanakajānakī—

'Here, while the noise in the act of killing Khara, Dūṣaṇa and Triśiras, was filling the world, the noble and valiant warrior was held back by you for a moment, bewildered as you were, and he did cast on you and that army tremulous glances full of love, full of fondness, bright with smile, mixed with the play of the eyebrows, and full of longings and courage'.

(x) 'Charm, residing in the story of a famous person', in a verse in my Śaśivaṁśa—

'Move forward', 'Control the army', 'Guard the arena' of the battle-array', 'Observe the movements of the army', 'Run away quickly', 'Do not leave your post', 'Hold on with effort', 'The speed of body-piercing arrows is very swift',—these wre the voluminous voices which were heard when the people were routed by Arjuna on the battle-field.'

इत्युक्त एष सविशेषचमत्कृतीनां सारः प्रकारपरभागविभाव्यमानः।
कर्पूरवेम इन वाङ्धुगन्धयुक्तेश्वैत्रासवस्य सहकाररसाधिवासः॥ ३॥

3. Here has been described the essence of all special charms, looking bright through its proper division and logical sequence. It is just like the blending of a little quantity of camphor with the honeyed fragrance of speech or like the mingling of sweet mango juice with the wine of spring time.

इति श्रीव्यासदासापराख्यक्षेमेन्द्रकृते कविकण्ठाभरणे
चमत्कारकथनं तृतीयः सन्धिः।

Here ends the third link, namely 'Exposition of Charms of Poetry' in the NECKLACE FOR POETS of Kṣemendra alias Vyāsadāsa.

—•—

चतुर्थः सन्धिः
Fourth Link

Now to merits and demerits distinguisted—

अथ गुणदोषविभागः-

काव्यैकपात्रविलसद्गुणदोषदुग्ध
पाथःसमूहपृथगुद्धरणे विदग्धाः।
जानन्ति कर्तुमभियुक्ततया विभागं
चन्द्रावदातमतयः कविराजहंसाः॥ १॥

तत्र शब्दवैमल्यमर्थवैमल्यं रसवैमल्यमिति त्रयः काव्यगुणाः। शब्दकालुष्यमर्थकालुष्य रसकालुष्यमिति काव्यदोषाः। सगुणं निर्गुणं सदोषं निर्दोषं सगुणदोषं च काव्यम्।

शब्दवैमल्यं यथा मम पद्यकादम्बर्याम्–

तत्कालोपनते वयस्यनिधने हा पुण्डरीकेति त-
न्मोहव्यञ्जनमशमभञ्जनमलं जीवस्य सन्तर्जनम्।
कुञ्जव्यापि कपिञ्जलेन करुणं निस्पन्दमाक्रन्दितं
येनाद्यापि च तैः स्मृतेन हरिणैः शष्पं परित्यज्यते।।

अर्थवैमल्यं यथा मम शशिवंशे–

स्निग्धश्यामलशाद्वले फलतरुच्छायानिपीतातपे
चञ्चद्वीचिचयोच्छलत्कलकले निःसङ्गगङ्गातटे।
अन्योन्याभिमुखोपविष्टहरिणे स्वस्थैर्यदि स्थीयते
तत्का श्रीः किमकाण्डभङ्गुरसुखैर्मोहस्य दत्तोऽञ्जलिः।।

रसवैमल्यं यथा मम पद्यकादम्बर्याम्–

अथोद्ययौ बालसुहृत्स्मरस्य श्यामाधवः[1] श्यामललक्ष्मभङ्ग्या।
तारावधूलोचनचुम्बनने लीलाविलीनाञ्जनबिन्दुरिन्दुः ।।

शब्दकालुष्यं यथा भट्टश्रीशिवस्वामिनः–

[2]उत्खातप्रखरा सुखासुखसखी खड्गसिता खेलगा
वैशृङ्खल्यखलीकृताखिलखला खे (खा) त्खेटकैः ख्यापिता।
खेटादुत्खनितुं निखर्वमनसां मौर्ख्यं मुखात्खक्खटं
निःसख्यान्यनिखर्वसर्वमणिभूराख्यातु संख्यानि वः।।

अर्थकालुष्यं यथा तस्यैव–

[3]पित्रापि त्रायते या न खलु खलधृताज्ञानमात्रापमात्रा
स्योनस्योनस्थितेर्भूरनुनयविरमद्दामपाशाप्यपाशा ।
वर्षावर्षाम्बुपातात्त्रुटिततृणवसत्यश्रियातां श्रियातां
सौरी सौरीष्टयाग्रे सरदिह जनतां साश्नुवानां श्नुवानाम्।।

रसकालुष्यं यथा भट्टनारायणस्य वेणीसंहारे–

भानुमत्या नकुलप्राणिस्वप्नदर्शने पाण्डवनकुलस्वैरसङ्गमेर्ष्यासद्भावश्च-क्रवर्तिमहिष्याः सामान्यनीचवनितावत्।।

---

1. रजनीपतिश्चन्द्रः।
2. अत्र वक्तुरभिप्रेतस्यार्थस्य सम्भवेपि शब्दानां कुटिलत्वाच्छब्दकालुष्यम्।
3. अत्र सरलशब्दसत्त्वेऽपि वक्त्रभिप्रेतार्थबोधानिष्पत्तेरर्थकालुष्यं बोध्यम्।

सगुणं यथा कालिदासस्य–

श्यामास्वङ्गं चकितहरिणीप्रेक्षणे दृष्टिपातं
गण्डच्छायां शशिनि शिखिनां बर्हभारेषु केशान्।
उत्पश्यामि प्रतनुषु नदीवीचिषु भ्रूविलासा-
न्हन्तैकस्थं क्वचिदपि न ते चण्डि! सादृश्यमस्ति।।

निर्गुणं यथा चन्द्रकस्य–

स्तनौ सुपीनौ कठिनौ ठिनौ ठिनौ कटिर्विशाला रभसा भसा भसा।
मुखं च चन्द्रप्रतिमं तिमं तिमं अहो सुरूपा तरुणी रुणी रुणी[1]।।

सदोषं यथा भट्टश्रीशिवस्वामिनः–

आद्यत्वावधि शिण्ढि शिण्ढ दृढतागूढानि गूढेतरां
प्रौढिं ढौकय पिण्ढि पिण्ढि च रुजं रुढापरूढां तया।
मूढं मूढममूढयस्व हृदयं लीढ्वाथ मूढ्वा तमः
सोऽव्यूढामिति च प्रभापरिवृढाव्यूढा द्रढिम्नेऽस्तु वः।।'

निर्दोषं यथा श्रीभीमसाहेः सान्धिविग्रहिकस्येन्द्रभानोः–

स्नातुं वाञ्छसि किं मुधैव धवलक्षीरोदफेनच्छटा-
छयाहारिणि वारिणि द्युसरितो दिक्पूरविस्तारिणि।
आस्ते ते कलिकालकल्मषमषीप्रक्षालनैकक्षमा
कीर्तिः संनिहितैव सप्तभुवनस्वच्छन्दमन्दाकिनी।।

सगुणदोषं यथा भट्टमयूरस्य–

अस्तव्यस्तत्त्वशून्यो निजरुचिरनिशानश्वरं(रः)कर्तुमीशो
विश्वं वेश्मेव दीपः प्रतिहततिमिरं यः प्रदेशस्थितोऽपि।
दिक्पा(क्र)कापेक्षयाऽसौ त्रिभुवनमटतस्तिग्मभानोर्नवाख्यां
यातः शातक्रतव्यां दिशि दिशतु शिवं शोचिषामुद्गमो वः।।

1. Just as the Swan Royal is capable of separating milk from water mixed in the same pot, so also the great poets, gifted with an intellect clear as the moon, and erudite in the art of distinguishing merits from demerits, manifesting themselves in the same poem, know, by constant application, how to distinguish good from bad poetry.

Here, purity of words, purity of sense and purity of flavour—

---

1. नास्मिन्पद्ये कोप्यनुप्रासेन गुण इति निर्गुणं पद्यमिदन्।

these are the three merits of poetry; while impurity of words, sense and flavour are respectively the defects of poetry. A poem (may be) meritorious or meritless; defective or defectless, or may have both merits and defects.

(i) 'Purity of Words', as in my Padyakādambarī—

'Then at the friends' death, which occurred at that time, Kapiñjalal cried in a pitiful manner, 'O Puṇḍarīka' as he stood motionless; the lament showed his (state of) stupefaction; it was powerful enough to rend rocks and shock lives, as it pervaded the bowers. Recollecting it, the deer, even today, give up their food (grass)'.

(ii) 'Purity of sense', as in my Śaśivaṁśa—

'Of what avail are the riches? Of what avail the joys which termiante suddenly any moment? Farewell[1] to delusive desires, if one can stay in good spirits on the lonely banks of the ganges, resounding with the splashing of the moving ripples, with lovely dark-green meadows, the sun's heat being absorbed by the shade of fruit-trees, and the deer sitting in a group facing one another'.

(iii) 'Purity of flavour', as in my Padyakādambarī—

'Then there did rise the moon, the Lord of the Night and a friend of Cupid from boyhood, The Moon, with a coquetish small black speck inprominence, it being nothing more than a drop of collyrium wiped off in the act of kissing the eyes of his luminary spouse'.

(iv-v) 'Impurity of word and sense' is illustrated in Śivasvāmin's two verses. The defects are apparent at the very reading of the stanzas. They bear no translation.

(vi) Impurity of flavour as in Bhaṭṭanārāyaṇa's veṇīsaṁhāra—

On seeing in a drem, a mongoose (Nakula) the evil longing of Bhānumatī, the queen of a monarch, for a free union with Nakula is in the manner of an ordinary low-born woman.

---

1. *Mohastya datto ṅjaliḥ* : 'folded hands shown to *moha*' literally; folded hands are a sign of hearty farewell.

(vii) 'Full of Merit', for instance, in Kālidāsa's (verse)—

> 'I see your limbs in the night, your glances in the gaze of frightened gazelles, the beauty of your cheeks in the moon, your hair in the plumage of peacocks, and the amorous play of your eye-brows in the tiny ripples of the river. O wrathful woman, the like of you, all in one, can be found nowhere'.

(viii) 'Devoid of merit', as in Candraka's verse—

'The breasts are well-developed and hard. The hips are massive and strong. The face is like the moon. Ah, the damsel is indeed beautiful'.[1]

(ix) 'With defect', as in Bhaṭṭa Śrī Śivasvāmin's verse—

A mere reading of the stanza with expression like śiṇḍhi *śiṇḍhi, piṇḍhi piṇḍhi,* will reveal the defect.

(x) 'Without defect' as in the verse of Śrī Bhīmasāhi Sāndhivigrahika Indrabhānu—

'Why do you, in vain, want to bathe in the water of the celestial Ganges—water which excels the beauty of the foam of the white milky ocean and extends upto the ends of quarters; especially when there is at hand the Ganges of your own fame freely pervading the seven regions and capable of washing off the soot of sins of the Kali age?'

(xi) 'With both merit and defect', as in Bhaṭṭa Mayūra's verse —

> 'May the rising radiance of the fierce-rayed sun command bliss for you—the sun, who roams in the three worlds, who is free from chaos and terminates night by his glow, who even staying in other regions is capable of brightening the whole universe just as a lamp does a house, and who at present has resorted to the eastern direction, known as such only by reference to space and time'.

1. The repetition *ṭhinau*, *bhasā bhasā,* etc. is simply meaningless.

इति गदितगुणार्थी त्यक्तनिर्दिष्टदोषः
[1]कविरुचिरपदस्थश्चक्रवर्तित्वसिद्ध्यै।
किमपि कृतविवेकः साधुमध्याधमानां
नृप इव परिरक्षेत्संकरं वर्णवृत्तेः[2] ।। २ ।।

2. Thus in order to achieve the role of a prince among poets, after having established oneself in the welcome position of a poet, one with a desire for the merits mentioned above, discardign all the defects and differenticating the best, the mediocre, and the worst (composition and then authors), should look to the proper usage of speech, just as a king keeps up the distinction among he different castes and professions inorder to achieve sovereignty, discriminating among the high, the middle, and the low classes'.

इति श्रीव्यासदासापराख्यक्षेमेन्द्रकृते कविकण्ठाभरणे
गुणदोषविभागश्चतुर्थः सन्धिः।

Here ends the fourth link, namely, 'A Classification of Merits and Demerits', in the NECKLACE FOR POETS of Kṣemendra alias Vyāsadāsa.

—•—

पञ्चमः सन्धिः
Fifth Link

Now (the author) speaks of the aesthetics of the cultivation of peotic art—

अथ परिचयचारुत्वमाह–

नहि परिचयहीनः केवले काव्यकष्टे
कुकविरभिनिविष्टः स्पष्टशब्दप्रविष्टः।
विबुधसदसि पृष्टः क्लिष्टधीर्वेत्ति वक्तुं
नव इव नगरान्तर्गह्वरे कोऽप्यघृष्टः ।। १ ।।

---

1. कवे रुचिरमुत्कृष्टं यत्पदं तत्र स्थित इत्यर्थः।
2. शब्दव्यापारसांकर्यमन्यत्र ब्राह्मणादिवर्णवृत्तिसाङ्कर्यम्।

तत्र तर्कव्याकरणभरतचाणक्यवात्स्यायनभारतरामायणमोक्षोपासात्मज्ञानधातुवाद- रत्नपरीक्षा वैद्यकज्यौतिषधनुर्वेदगजतुरगपुरुषलक्षणद्यूतेंद्रजालप्रकीर्णेषु परिचयः कविसाम्राज्यव्यञ्जनः।

तर्कपरिचयो यथा मम पद्यकादम्बर्याम्-

यत्प्राप्यं न मनोरथैर्न वचसा स्वप्नेऽपि दृश्यं न य-
त्तत्रापि स्मरविप्रलब्धमनसां लाभाभिमानग्रहः।
मोहोत्प्रेक्षितशुक्तिकारजतवत्प्रायेण यूनां भ्रमं
दत्ते तैमिरिकद्विचन्द्रसदृशं खे नूनमाशाकृषिः।।

व्याकरणपरिचयो यथा भट्टमुक्तिकलशस्य-

द्विगुरपि सद्वन्द्वोऽहं गृहे च मे सततमव्ययीभावः।
तत्पुरुष कर्म धारय येनाहं स्यां बहुव्रीहिः[1] ।।

भरतपरिचयो यथा भट्टश्रीशिवस्वामिनः-

[2] आतन्वन्सरसां स्वरूपरचनामानन्दिबिन्दूदयं
भावग्राहि शुभप्रवेशकगुणं गम्भीरगर्भस्थिति।
उच्चैर्वृत्ति सपुष्करव्यतिकरं संसारविष्कम्भकं
भिन्द्योद्वो भरतस्य भाषितमिव ध्वान्तं पयो यामुनम्।।

चाणक्यपरिचयो यथा मम पद्यकादम्बर्याम्-

स्वामी प्रमादेन मदेन मन्त्री कोपेन राष्ट्रं व्यसनेन कोपः।
छिद्रेण दुर्गं विषमेण सैन्यं लोभेन मित्रं क्षयमेति राज्ञाम्।।

वात्स्यायनपरिचयो यथा भट्टदामोदरगुप्तस्य-

[3] अधरे बिन्दुः कण्ठे मणिमाला कुचयुगं शशप्लुतकम्।
तव सूचयन्ति सुन्दरि! कुसुमायुधशास्त्रपण्डितं रमणम्।।

भारतपरिचयो यथा मम देशोपदेशे-

भगदत्तप्रभावाढ्या कर्णशल्योत्कटस्वना।
सेनेव कुरुराजस्य कुट्टनी किन्तु निष्कृपा[4] ।।

---

1. वृषद्वयवान् सुखदुःखादिद्वन्द्वसहश्चाहं, मद्गृहे सदा व्ययो न भवति, तस्माद्धे जन तत्कर्मत्वं कुरु येनाहं बहुधान्ययुक्तः स्यामित्यर्थः।
2. सरसां श्रृङ्गारादियुतामन्यत्र सरोवराणाम्, बिन्दवः सन्ध्याख्या अन्यत्र जलबिन्दवस्तेषामुदयो यत्र, भावाना हि रत्यादीनां ग्राहकमन्यत्र प्रतिबिम्बग्राहकम्, पुष्करवाद्यादिसम्बद्धं, सकमलं च, काव्यानन्ददानात्संसारनिवर्तकमन्यत्रपूतत्वात्तथाभूतमन्यत्सुगमम्।
3. अत्र कार्यात्कारणानुमानेन न्यायशास्त्राभिज्ञता कवेर्बोध्या।
4. भगदत्ताख्यराज्ञः प्रतापेन सम्पन्नाऽन्यत्र योनिमाहात्म्ययुता, कर्णशल्याख्ययोरद्वयशब्दोत्कटाऽन्यत्र श्रोत्रे शल्यवदुत्कटशब्दकारिणी, कौरवसेना कृपाचार्ययुता कुट्टनी तु निर्दयेत्यर्थः।

रामायणपरिचयो यथा भट्टवाचस्पतेः–

जनस्थाने भ्रान्तं कनकमृगतृष्णान्धितधिया
वचो वैदेहीति प्रतिपदमुदश्रु प्रलपितम्।
कृतालङ्काभर्तुर्वदनपरिपाटीषु घटना
मयाऽऽप्तं रामत्वं कुशलवसुता न त्वधिगता।।

मोक्षोपायपरिचयो यथा मम मुक्तावल्याम्–

निरासङ्गा प्रीतिर्विषयनियमोऽन्तर्न तु बहिः
स्वभावे भावानां क्षयजुषि विमर्शः प्रतिदिनम्।
अयं संक्षेपेण क्षपिततमसामक्षयपदे
तपोदीक्षाक्षेपक्षपणनिरपेक्षः परिकरः।।

आत्मज्ञानपरिचितिर्यथा मम चित्रभारतनाम्नि नाटके–

पृथुशास्त्रकथाकन्थारोमन्थेन वृथैव किम्।
अन्वेष्टव्यं प्रयत्नेन तत्त्वज्ञैर्ज्योतिरान्तरम्।।

धातुवादपरिचयो यथा राजशेखरस्य–

नखदलितहरिद्राग्रन्थिगौरे शरीरे
स्फुरति विरहजन्मा कोऽप्ययं पाण्डुभावः।
बलवति सति यस्मिन्सार्धमावर्त्य हेम्ना
रजतमिव मृगाक्ष्या कल्पितान्यङ्गकानि।।

रत्नपरीक्षापरिचयो भट्टभल्लटस्य–

द्रविणमापदि भूषणमुत्सवे शरणमात्मभये निशि दीपकः।
बहुविधोर्व्युपकारभरक्षमो भवति कोऽपि भवानिव सन्मणिः।।

वैद्यकपरिचयो यथा मम पद्यकादम्बर्याम्–

अङ्गं चन्दनपङ्कपङ्कजबिसच्छेदावलीनं मुहु
स्तापः शाप इवैष शोषणपटुः कम्पः सखीकम्पनः।
श्वासाः संवृततारहाररुचयः सम्भिन्नचीनांशुका
जातः प्रागतिदाहवेदनमहारम्भः स तस्या ज्वरः।।

ज्योतिःशास्त्रपरिचयो यथा विद्यानन्दस्य–

द्यामालोकयतां कलाः कलयतां छायाः समाचिन्वतां
क्लेशः केवलमङ्गुलीर्गणयतां मौहूर्तिकानामयम्।
धन्या सा रजनी तदेव सुदिनं पुण्यः स एव क्षणो
यत्राज्ञातचरः प्रियानयनयोः सीमानमेति प्रियः।।

धनुर्वेदपरिचयो यथा मम कनकजानक्याम्–

आर्यस्यास्त्रघनौघलाघववती सन्धानसम्बन्धिनी
स्थाणुस्थानक[1] सौष्ठवप्रणयिनी चित्रक्रियालङ्कृतिः।
निष्पन्देन मयाऽतिविस्मयमयी सत्यस्थितप्रत्यया
संहारे खरदूषणत्रिशिरसामेषैव दृष्टा स्थितिः।।

गजलक्षणपरिचयो यथा मम कनकजानक्याम्–

कर्णाभ्यर्णविकीर्णचामरमरुद्विस्तीर्णेनिःश्वासवा–
च्छङ्कच्छत्रविराजिराज्यविभवद्वेषी विलीनेक्षणः।
स्मृत्वा राघव! कुञ्जरः प्रियतमामेकाकिनीं कानने
सन्त्यक्तां चिरमुक्तभोगकवलः क्लेशोष्मणा शुष्यति।।

तुरगलक्षणपरिचयो यथा ममामृततरङ्गनाम्नि काव्ये–

आवर्तशोभी पृथुसत्त्वराशिः फेनावदातः पवनोरुवेगः।
गम्भीरघोषोऽद्रिविमर्दखेदादश्वाकृतिं कर्तुमिवोद्यतोऽब्धिः।।
उच्चैःश्रवाः शक्रमुपाजगाम स विश्वसाम्राज्यजयप्रदोऽश्वः।
जग्राह हेलाघनशङ्खशब्दनिवेदिताशेषशुभं तमिन्द्रः।। (युग्मम्)

पुरुषलक्षएणपरिचयो यथा कालिदासस्य–

व्यूढोरस्को वृषस्कन्धः सालप्रांशुर्महाभुजः।
आत्मकर्मक्षमं देहं क्षात्रो धर्म इवाश्रितः।।

द्यूतपरिचयो यथा चन्द्रकस्य–

यत्रानेके क्वचिदपि गृहे तत्र तिष्ठत्यथैको
यत्राप्येकस्तदनु बहवस्तत्र नैकोऽपि चान्ते।
इत्थं नेयौ रजनिदिवसौ तोलयन्द्वाविवाक्षौ[2]
काल· काल्या सह बहुकलः क्रीडति प्राणिसारैः।।

इन्द्रजालपरिचयो यथा श्रीहर्षस्य–

एष ब्रह्मा सरोजे रजनिकरकलाशेखरः शङ्करोऽयं
दोर्भिर्दैत्यान्तकोऽसौ सधनुरसिगदाचक्रद्विश्चतुर्भिः।
एषोऽप्यैरावणस्थस्त्रिदशपतिरमी ेविदेवास्तथान्ये
नृत्यन्त्यो व्योम्नि चैताश्चलचरणरणन्नूपुरा दिव्यनार्यः।।

---

1. स्थाणुवत्स्थानकं धन्विस्थितिविशेषः।
2. द्यूतपाशकौ।

प्रकीर्णे चित्रपरिचयो यथा भगवतो व्यासस्य–

अतथ्यान्यपि तथ्यानि दर्शयन्ति विचक्षणाः।
समे निम्नोन्नतानीव चित्रकर्मविदो जनाः।।

देशपरिचयो यथा मम शशिवंशे–

भोजैर्भञ्जनभीरुभिर्विलुलितं व्यामीलितं मालवै-
र्मद्रैर्विद्रुतमेव यातमसकृन्मार्गादधे मागधैः।
वङ्गानाभिमन्युकङ्कणरवैर्व्राते पुरः सूचिते
मीनैः सङ्कुचितं परस्परधृतैर्नीरन्ध्रमन्धैः स्थितम्।।

वृक्षपरिचयो यथा मम कनकजानक्याम्–

जम्बूबिम्बकदम्बनिम्बबकुलप्लक्षाक्षभल्लातक-
द्राक्षाकिंशंककर्णिकारकदलीजम्बीरकोदुम्बरैः।
सा सन्तानकबिल्वतिल्वतिलकश्लेष्मातकाऽऽरग्वध-
न्यग्रोधार्जुनशातनासनवनश्यामान्ददर्शाश्रमान्।।

वनेचरपरिचयो यथा मम तत्रैव–

वामस्कन्धनिषण्णशार्ङ्गकुटिलप्रान्तार्पिताधोमुख-
स्यन्दच्छोणितलम्बमानशशकान्पाणिरखलच्चामरान्।
ज्यान्तप्रोतकपोतपोतनिपतद्रक्ताक्ततूणीरका-
न्साऽपश्यत्करिकुम्भभेदजनिताक्रन्दान्पुलिन्दान्पुरः।।

औदार्यपरिचयो यथा मम चतुर्वर्गसहे–

मान्यः कुलनिः कुलजात्कलावान्विद्वान्कलाज्ञाद्विदुषः सुशीलः।
वनी सुशीलाद्धनिनोऽपि दाता दातुर्जिता कीर्तिरयाचकेन।।

अचेतनचेतनाध्यारोपपरिचयो यथा मच्छिष्यमहाश्रीभट्टोदयसिं
हस्य ललिताभिधाने महाका[illegible]े–

इह विकसदशोकास्तोकपुष्पोपहारै-
रयमतिशयरक्तः सक्तसुस्निग्धभावः।
त्रिभुवनजयसज्जः प्राज्यसाम्राज्यभाजः
प्रथयति पृथुमैत्रीं पुष्पचापस्य चैत्रः।।

भक्तिपरिचयो यथाऽस्यैव भक्तिभवनाम्नि महाकाव्ये–

बाल्यादेव निरर्गलप्रणयिनी भक्तिर्भवानीपतौ
जन्मायासविकासवासितमनःसंवाससन्दायिनि।

प्रायः प्राक्तनकर्मनिर्मितमहामोहप्ररोहापहा
भव्यानां भवभीतिभञ्जनसखी सञ्जायते सन्मतिः।।

विवेकपरिचयो यथा मच्छिष्यराजपुत्रलक्ष्मणादित्यस्य–

आशापाशविमुक्तियुक्तममलं सन्तोषमान्यं मनः
सेवायासविवर्जितं विहरणं मायाविहीनं वचः।
चण्डीशार्चनमात्मशुद्धिजननी गङ्गेव सत्सङ्गतिः
सोऽयं सन्तरणे परः परिकरः संसारवारांनिधेः।।

प्रशमपरिचयो यथा मम चतुर्वर्गसहे–

चित्तं वातविकासिपांसुसचिवं रूपं दिनान्तातपं
भोगं दुर्गतगेहबन्धचपलं पुष्पस्मितं यौवनम्।
स्वप्नं बन्धुसमागमं तनुमपि प्रस्थानपुण्यप्रपां
नित्यं चिन्तयता भवन्ति न सतां भूयो भवग्रन्थयः।।

1. A petty poet, unfamiliar with the cultivation of poetry, always busy labouring in the art of versificationa and knowing only the literal sense of words, is at his wits' end when questioned in an assembly of the wise; just as a clown, newly come to town, is stranded in the streets and alleys thereof.

Therefore, familiarity with the following is indicative of soverignty among poets—logic, grammar, dramaturgy, politics, eugenics, the Mahābhārata, the Rāmāyaṇa, means of emancipation, spritiual science, metallurgy, science of jewels medicine astronomy, archery, a knowledge of the auspicious signs of elephants, horses and men, art of gambling, of magic and sorcery and other miscellaneous arts.

(i) 'Familiarity with logic', as in my Padyakādambarī—

'The young with their minds deluded by love, (have) the perverseness to aspire after that which is inaccessible even to desire or speech, and which is invisible even in dreams. Surely, the harvest of hopes creates delusion among the youthful, just as one mistakes a pearl-oyster for silver, or one suffering from an eye-disease sees two moons in the sky'.

(ii) 'Familiarity with grammar', as in Bhaṭṭa Muktikalaśa's verse—

'I have two cows. A conflict of pain and pleasure goes on in my mind. There is nothing to spend in my house. Therefore, O man, think of a profession which brings me abundant enough corn'.[1]

(iii) 'Familiarity with dramaturgy', as in Bhaṭṭa Śrī Śiva Svāmin's verse—

'May the water of the Yamunā dispel your gloom (ignorance) like the work of Bharata—the former displays a liquid formation and the latter also explains the eight sentiments in the construction of a drama; the former composed of delicious drops of waters, and the latter exalted in the interesting development of the *bindu* (a sudden development of a secondary incidence); the former pleasing the heart and the latter delaing with the emotions; the former possessing healthy properties for the bathers and the latter mentioning the characterisitics of an interlude acted by inferior characters; the former possessing a great depth and the latter referring to a grave 'garbha'sandhi, the former rolling and swelling and the latter indicating the superior style; the former containing clusters of lotuses and the latter comprising a description of the art of dancing; the former terminating the course of transmigration and the latter describing interludes'.[2]

(iv) 'Familiartiy with politics *(cāṇakya)*' as in my Padyakādambarī—

'A king perishes through negligence, a minister through pride, an empire through wrath, a treasury through vice, a fortress through a breach, an army through an illplanned strategy, and a friend through greed'.

(v) 'Familiarity with Vātsyāyana' as in Bhaṭṭa Dāmodaragupta's verse—

'O beautiful damsel, a mark of a bite on your lower lip, a series of such markes on your neck, a scratch with a finger nail (śaśa-plutakam i.e. of the form of a hare's leap) on your breats,—

1. Mark the beautiful stringing together of the names of grammatical compounds with an underlying double sense.
2. Mark the marvellous use of double entendre.

these show that (you have been) enjoyed (by one) well-versed in the art of love making'.[1]

(vi) 'Familiarity with the Mahābhārata' as in my Deśopadeśa—

'The baws with invaluable lustre imparted to her by her vulva, and with a shrill voice piercing hte ear like an arrow, is like the army of the Kuru King with (power) imparted by the valour of Bhagadatta, and possessed of the terrible noise of Karṇa and Śalya, but with the difference that the (the bawd) has no mercy while the army is devoid of Kṛpācārya.'

(vii) 'Familiarity with the Rāmāyaṇa', as in Bhaṭṭa Vācaspati's verse—

'With my mind blinded with the mirage of gold, I wandered in the towns with tears streaming (from my eyes) at every step and crying out, 'O give me'. What efforst did I not make to propitiate my master, however ill-natured? But I did not attain wealth which brings wlefare. Thus did I imitate Rāma, who, with his mind blinded by the desire for the golden deer, did roam in the Janasthāna forest, did cry out the name of Vaidehī shedding tears at every step, did assault Rāvaṇa's many faces, but did not, after all, find the mother of Kuśa and Lava (Sītā)'.[2]

(viii) 'Familiarity with the means of emancipation', as in my Muktāvalī—

'Devotion without attachment, discipline of the senses, not only externally but internally, daily deliberatin on the perishing nature of beings—this, in short, is the entourage for those whose ignorance has vanished in order to attain the immortal position—an entourgae, which needs no preoccupation with austeirites and other acts of initiation'.

(ix) 'Familiarity with the spiritual science', as in my drama named Citrabhārata—

'What is the use of ruminating over the (lit. chewing the cud of

1. 'bindu', 'maṇimālā' and 'śaśaplutaka' are technical terms and are explained in the fourth and the fifth chapter of Vātsyāyana's Kāmasūtra.
2. Mark the significant double entendre.

the) rigmarole of manifold scineces? Those who would know the reality ought to seek with effor the innermost Light'.

(x) 'Familiarity with metallurgy', as in Rājaśekhara's verse—

'On her body, yellowish white like a piece of turmeric and scratched with nails, a palish hue, arising from separation, makes its appearance and (the palish hue) becoming more and more prominent makes the limbs of the fawn-eyed one look like silver mixed with gold'.

(xi) 'Familiarity with the art of examining jewellery' as in Bhaṭṭa Bhallaṭa's verse—

'There is seldom seen an excellent gem like your honour, serving as welath in trouble, an ornament in a festival, a refuge in fear, a lamp at night, capable of confering manifold benefits'.

(xii) 'Familiarity with medical science', as in my Padyakādambarī—

'The heat (of love) dries up her limbs like a curse, the body is covered with sandal-paste and lotus-filaments; her tremor shakes her friends, her breath is (irregular) like the (movement of her) long tremulous necklace disturbing her silkne garments. that heat of love in her case has developed into a high fever which starts with a crucial pain and a burning sensation.'

(xiii) 'Familiarity with astronomy', as in Vidyānanda's verse—

'Observing the sky, calculating the altitude, computing the days on fingers—all this is a futile effort on the part of astrologers, Blesses is that night, auspicious is that day and fortunate that moment, when the lover roaming in cognito comes within the range of the sight of the beloved'.

(xiv) 'Familiarity with archery', as in my Kanakajānakī—

'Steadily did I behold even before, a similar and very amazing posture of your honour relating to the drawing of the bow at the time of killing Khara, Dūṣanā and Triśiras—the posture, which possessed the grace of a bowman's stand, known as Sthāṇu-Sthānaka (Śiva's posture) and which was as decorative as in a painting was convincing of firm determination like truth itself'.

(xv) 'Familiairty with the characteristics of elephants', as in my Kanakajānakī—

'O son of Raghu, the elephant, the breeze for whose breath is wafted by the chowries (moving) near his ears, who is indifferent to the princely grandeur though decorated with conchshells and the umbrella, with his eyes sunken and his comforts given up since long, is languishing through the fire of greif while remembering (his) lovely beloved separated from him in the forest'.

(xvi) 'Familiarity with the characteristics of horses', as in my poem called Amṛtataraṅga—

'The horse Uccaiśśravas (by name), the bestower of soverigntyu over the entire world appraoched Indra—the horse, looking bright with its curling mane, a mass of immense courage, white with foam of swift speed like that of wind, of deep sonority imitating the very ocean which was afflicted at the destruction of mountains and was ready to assume as it were the hose's appearance—the ocean, charming with eddies, sheltering huge animals in its recesses, white with foam, of swift speed like wind and roaring deeply. Indra accepted him, whose auspicious character was revealed by the joyful blowing of conches etc."

(xvii) 'Familiarity with the characteristics of man', as in Kālidāsa's verse—

'He was broad-chested, with shoulders like those of a bull, tall like a śāla tree, and with long arms; thus he looked like Heroism incarnate in a body strong enough to discharge its duties'.

(xviii) 'Familiarity with gambling', as in Candraka's verse—

'In the house where there were many, only one remains, where there was only one, many appear and in the end not even one remains. Thus balancing the day and the night as two dice pieces, Kāla, of endless duration, along with Kālī, plays with human beings as with chess-men or dice-pieces'.

(xix) 'Familiarity with the art of magic', as in Śrī Harṣa's verse—

'O Queen, here is Brahmā seated on the lotus; here is Śankara with the digit of the moon on his crest; here is the killer of demons, with four arms marked with bow, sword, mace and the disc; here is the lord of the gods seated on the Airāvata; and here are the other gods, and here are the clestial damsles dancing in the air with jingling anklets on their moving feet'.

(xx) 'Knowlege of the art of painting 'under' miscellaneous arts', as in reverd Vyāsa verse—

'The clever show's unreal as real, just as one knowing the art of painting (shows) high and low on an even level'.

(xxi) 'Familiarity with the country', as in my Śaśivaṁśa—

'On hearing the noise of bracelets of Abhimanyu, the multitude of Vaṅgas ran away before him; the Bhojas, fearing that they would be uprooted, took to their heels; the Malavas disappeared, the Madras fled, the (soldiers) of Magadha left the scene of battel many a time, the Mīnas withdrew and the Āndhras in a body stood apart'.

(xxii) 'Familiarity with trees', as in my Kanakajānakī—

'She saw the mhermitages darkened with the forests of Jambu, Bimba, Kadamba, Nimba, Bakula, Plakṣa, Akṣa, Bhallātaka, Drākṣā, Kiṁśukta, Karṇikāra, Kadalī, Jambīraka, Udumbara, Sanstānaka, Bilva, Tilva, Tilaka, Śleṣmātaka, Aragvadha, Nyagrodha, Arjuna, Śātana and Āsana'.

(xxiii) 'Familiarity with wild life', as in the same work of mine—

'She is front of her saw mountaineers, who were rasing a cry at the piercing of the frontal globes of elephants, from the crooked ends of whose bows resting on their left shoulders were hanging hares with their faces downwards dripping with blood, from whose hands *camarī* deer were slipping away, whose quivers were stained with blood coming out from the young ones of pigeons strung at one end of the bow-string'.

(xxiv) 'Familiarity with magnanimity', as in my Caturvargasaṅgraha—

'A person of high family is of course to be honoured, but even more than him the one who knows some art as well, and more than the artist the learned, more than the learend the man of good character, more than the man of good character the rich, more than the man of riches the one given to charity, and the charitable has his reputation surpassed by one who never supplicates'.

(xxv) 'The art of animating the inanimate' as in the poem, Lalitābhidhāna of my pupil, Śrī Bhaṭṭodayasiṁha—

> 'Here does the spring month showering hepas of blooming aśoka flowers display an intensity of affection for the flower-bowed god who enjoys an exalted sovereignty—the spring month, which is deep red in affection and harbours feelings of love and is out to conquer the three worlds'.

(xxvi) 'Familiairty with the idea of devotion' as in the poem, called Bhaktibhava, by the same author—

> 'To the blessed is born from their very early years that good sense, which brings about an unimpeded and ardent devotion to Śiva, which affords an abiding satisfactions to the mind revolving in the troublesome and repated births, which consumes the off shoots of great delusion resulting from previous deeds, and which is a helper is putting an end to the fear of wordly existence'.

(xxvii) 'Familiarity with principles of discretion', as in the composition of my pupil, Rājaputra Lakṣmaṇādiya—

> 'A pure mind, dignified in contentment and free from noses of yearnings, a behaviour devoid of weary subservience to others, a speech free from fruad, an adoration of Śiva, a company of the good producing self-purification—this indeed is a unique entourgae in crossing the ocean of wordly existence.'

(xxviii) 'Familiarity with the principles of Peace and Rastraint', as in my Caturvargasaṅgraha—

> 'Mind, an associate of dust wafted by wind; beauty passing away like the afternoon sun; pleasures tottering like the joints of a dilapidated house; youth (evanascent) like the bloom of flowers; meeting with kinsmen, as dream; this body, a public place for water-service on the roadside;—even reflecting on thes, the good do not suffer from wrold bondage'.

इत्युक्ता रुचिरोचिता परिचयप्राप्तिर्विभागैर्गिरां
दिङमात्रेण विचित्रवस्तुरचनामैत्रीपवित्रीकृता।
यद्यस्त्यत्र नवोपदेशविषये लेशेऽप्युपादेयता
तत्सद्भिर्गुणकौतुकादवसरः श्रोतुं समाधीयताम्।। २।।

2. Thus has been narrated in an agreeable form the cultivation of speech in different branches (of experience). It is just an indication and it has been sanctified by its association with some fine poetic pieces. If there be anything in it, howsoever small, worthy of acceptance as a piece of advice, then let the good give it a chance of listening to, just by way of curiosity for merit.

कृत्वा निश्चलदैवपौरुषमयोपायं प्रसूत्यै गिरां
क्षेमेन्द्रेण यदर्जितं शुभफलं तेनास्तु काव्यार्थिनाम्।
निर्विघ्नप्रतिभाप्रभावसुभगा वाणी प्रमाणीकृता
सद्भिर्वाग्भवमन्त्रपूतविततश्रोत्रामृतस्यन्दिनी ।। ३।।

3. Having firmly adopted human and divine means for the creation of poetry whatever good was gatherd by Kṣemendra, may that good bring blessings to those who seek poetry. Let their speech be regarded by the good as standard—the speech, which is rendered delightful under the influence of unimpeded poetic vision and which sheds ambrosia for the ears sanctified by the muttering of the Vāgbhava Bījamantra.

इति श्रीव्यासदासापराख्यक्षेमेन्द्रकृते कविकण्ठाभरणे
परिचयप्राप्तिः पञ्चमः सन्धिः।

Thus ends the fifth link "Acquisition of Poetic Culture" in the NECKLACE FOR POETS of Kṣemendra alias Vyāsadāsa.

काश्मीरेषु पृथुप्रतापसवितुः कीर्त्यंशुतारापतेः
प्रौढारातिवनानलस्य धनदस्येन्प्रस्य भूमण्डले।
विश्वाकारवतः पुनः कलियुगे विष्णोरिवोत्साहिनो
राज्ये श्रीमदनन्तराजनृपतेः काव्योदयोऽयं कृतः।।

This poem was written in the reign of the glorious king Ananta

Rāja of Kashmir who was the sun of immense lustre, the moon of beaming fame, the radiant forest fire for the hosts of foes, the very Kubera and Indra on this earth, and adventurous as the very Viṣṇu of Universal Form appearing in the Kali age.

इति कविकण्ठाभरणं समाप्तम्।

Here ends the Necklace for Poets.

महाकविश्रीक्षेमेन्द्रकृता

औचित्यविचारचर्चा

Aucityavicāracarcā or A Critical Discourse on the Theory of Propriety

कृतारिवञ्चने दृष्टिर्येनाञ्जनमलीमसा।
अच्युताय नमस्तस्मै परमौचित्यकारिणे॥ १॥

1. My homage to the Imperishable One (i.e. Viṣṇu[1]), who, the doer of what is extremely proper made his eyes black with collyrium in order to delude his foes.

कृत्वापि काव्यालङ्कारां क्षेमेन्द्रः कविकर्णिकाम्।
तत्कलङ्कं विवेकं च विधाय विबुधप्रियम्॥ २॥
औचित्यस्य चमत्कारकारिणश्चारुचर्वणे।
रसजीवितभूतस्य विचारं कुरुतेऽधुना॥ ३॥ (युग्मम्)

2-3. Kṣemendra, even having written "Kavikarṇikā" (Ear-ornament for Poets[2]), a compendium on figures of speech in poetry, and having also discussed its blemishes and subtleties, now has undertaken the pleasant task of pondering over "Propriety in Poetry". Which is the very life in flavour, and an agency for producing charm.

काव्यस्यालमलङ्कारैः किं मिथ्यागणितैर्गुणैः।
यस्य जीवितमौचित्यं विचिन्त्यापि न दृश्यते॥ ४॥

4. Of what use are the ornaments (i.e. figures of speech) and the useless enumeration of merits for a composition in which its very life, viz. *Propriety,* is not visible even though sought for?

1. Reference is here perhaps to Viṣṇu as Mohinī Incarnation.
2. Another work by Kṣemendra.

अलङ्कारास्त्वलङ्कारा गुणा एव गुणः सदा।
औचित्यं रससिद्धस्य स्थिरं काव्यस्य जीवितम्।। ५।।

परस्परोपकारकरुचिरशब्दार्थरूपस्य काव्यस्योपमोत्प्रेक्षादयो ये प्रचुरालङ्कारास्ते कटककुण्डलकेयूरहारादिवदलङ्कारा एव, बाह्यशोभाहेतुत्वात्। येऽपि काव्यगुणाः केचन तल्लक्षणविचक्षणैः समाम्नातास्तेऽपि श्रुतसत्यशीलादिवद्गुणा एव, आहार्यत्वात्। औचित्यं त्वग्रे वक्ष्यमाणलक्षणं स्थिरमविनश्वरं जीवितं काव्यस्य, तेन विनाऽस्य गुणालङ्कारयुक्तस्यापि निर्जीवत्वात्। रसेन श्रृङ्गारादिना सिद्धस्य प्रसिद्धस्य काव्यस्य धातुवादरससिद्धस्येव तज्जीवितं स्थिरमित्यर्थः।। १-५।।

5. Figures of speech are but ornaments, while merits of speech are mere excellences; but *Propriety* is the abiding life of poetry, full of (lit. accomplished) flavour.

> The numerous figures of speech like smile, metaphor and others belonging to poetry, which is constituted by words and their meaning—both plesant and promoting each other's snese—are just like the golden bracelet, the ear-ring, the armlet, or the necklace, etc., as they bring about only exteriro charm. Also, whatever merits of speech have been enumerated by those well-versed in defining them, are merely good qualities like learning, truth, strong character and the rest, because they are acquired. *Propriety,* whose definition will be given later on, is the abiding and imperishable *soul* of poetry, since without it, poetry is lifeless, though yoked to qualities and figures (of speech). Essence of poetry, sustained and ornated through flavour like erotic and others, is firmly established, like (the life of a man) susatined and made firm by a preparation of quick-silver.

अक्तार्थस्यैव विशेषमाह–

उचितस्थानविन्यासादलङ्कृतिरलङ्कृतिः।
औचित्यादच्युता नित्यं भवन्त्येव गुणा गुणाः।। ६।।

अलङ्कृतिरुचितस्थानविन्यासादलङ्कर्तुं क्षमा भवति, अन्यथात्वलङ्कृतिव्यपदेशमेव न लभते। तद्वदौचित्यादपरिच्युता गुणा गुणतामासादयन्ति, अन्यथा पुनरगुणा एव।

In explanation of what has been said, he says—

6. An embellishment is a (real) embellishment if applied at the proper place; merits are always (real) merits when they are not divested of propriety.

Put at the proper palce, ornaments could beautify, otherwise they do not even deserve to be called adornments. Similarly merits, if they do not fall short of propriety, are merits, otherwise they are blemishes.

यदाह

कण्ठे मेखलया नितम्बफलके तारेण हारेण वा
पाणौ नूपुरबन्धनेन चरणे केयूरपाशेन वा।
शौयण प्रणते रिपौ करुणया नायान्ति के हास्यता-
मौचित्येन विना रुचि प्रतनुते नालङ्कृतिर्नो गुणाः।। ६।।

Wherefore he says—

'Who do not suffer mockery by (putting on) the girdlestring around the neck, the radiant necklace around the waist, the anklets on hands, the bracelets on feet, and (by showing) might against the prostrated and compassion towards foes? Similarly, neither figures of speech nor the merits look charming without propriety'.

किं तदौचित्यमित्याह–

उचितं प्राहुराचार्याः सदृशं किल यस्य यत्।
उचितस्य च यो भावस्तदौचित्यं प्रचक्षते।। ७।।

What then is *Propriety?* (The author) says—

7. What befits a particular thing is what the great masters call proper. The sate of being proper is *Propriety.*

That which is suited to a certain thing is called proper; its abstract notion is called "Propriety".

यत्किल यस्यानुरूपं तदुचितमुच्यते, तस्य भावमौचित्यं कथयन्ति।। ७।।

Now, in order to indicate the principal places, where propriety, the very life of the entire body of peotry, can chiefly be perceived, (the author) says—

अधुना सकलकाव्यशरीरजीवितभूतस्यौचित्यतस्य प्राधान्येनोपलभ्यां स्थितिं दर्शयितुमाह–

पदे वाक्ये प्रबन्धार्थे गुणेऽलङ्करणे रसे।
क्रियायां कारके लिङ्गे वचने च विशेषणे।। ८।।
उपसर्गे निपाते च काले देशे कुले व्रते।
तत्त्वे सत्त्वेऽप्यभिप्राये स्वभावे सारसङ्ग्रहे।। ९।।

प्रतिभायामवस्थायां विचारे नाम्न्यथाशिषि।
काव्यस्याङ्गेषु च प्राहुरौचित्यं व्यापि जीवितम्।। १०।।

8-10. They say that propriety, which is the very life of poetry, should be found pervading the word and sentence, the import of the composition, the merits and figures of speech, the falvour, the verb, the case, the gender, the number, the adjective, the prefix, the particle, the tense, the surroundings, the family, the vow or choice, the truth, the force, the purpose, the winding up of sense, in intuition, the stage, the thought, the nomenclature, the benediction and other essentials of poetry.

एतेषु पदप्रभृतिषु स्थानेषु मर्मस्विव काव्यस्य सकलशरीरव्यापि जीवितमौचित्यं स्फुटत्वेन स्फुरदवभासते।। ८-१०।।

In these vital places as it were—words and others— of the poem, priety, the life pervading the entire form of poetry, shines clearly.

तेषूदाहरणानि क्रमेण दर्शयितुमाह–

तिलकं बिभ्रती सूक्तिर्भात्येकमुचितं पदम्।
चन्द्राननेव कस्तूरीकृतं श्यामेव चान्दनम्।। ११।।

(The author) quotes to illustrate these, in order—

11. A beautiful saying looks bright when possessing a single suitable world, as does a moon-faced damsel, bearing the kastūrī-mark on the forehead, or a *'śyāmā'* (a darkcomplexioned) woman bearing a sandla mark.

एकमेवोचितं पदं तिलकायमानं बिभ्राण सूक्तिः समुचितपरभागशोभातिशयेन रुचिरतामावहति।

A beautiful saying, containting just one proper word the counterpart of the mark on the forehead, becomes all the more thriliing on account of imparting excessive charm to the rest of the constituents.

यथा परिमलस्य–

मग्नानि द्विषतां कुलानि समरे त्वत्खड्गधाराकुले
नाथाऽस्मिन्निति बन्दिबाक्ति बहुशो देव! श्रुतायां पुरा।

मुग्धा गुर्जरभूमिपालमहिषी प्रत्याशया पाथसः
कान्तारे चकिता विमुञ्चति मुहुः पत्युः कृपाणे दृशौ।।

अत्र मुग्धापदेनार्थौचित्यचमत्कारकारिणा सूक्तिः शरदिन्दुवदनेव श्यामतिलकेन श्यामेव शुभ्रविशेषकेण विभूषिता सकलकविकुलललामभूतां विच्छित्तिमातनोति।

For example, Parimala's (verse)—

'In the forest, my sire, the innocent queen of the Gurjara king, with a desire to obtain water, casts her glances again and again in amazement on her husband's sword, having heard before, many a time the encomiums sung by bards; namely, 'O Lord, is this battle-field, families of your foes have been drowned in the edge-like stream of your sword'.

Here, with the word 'innocent' which lends charm to propriety in meaning, the stanza exhibits an emotional joy pre-eminently agreable to all poets, just as a woman with her face like the autumnal moon looks beautiful with the black *tilakal* or a dark woman with the white decoration.

न तु यथा धर्मकीर्तेः–

लावण्यद्रविणव्ययो न गणितः क्लेशो महान्स्वीकृतः
स्वच्छन्दस्य सुखं जनस्य वसतश्चिन्ताज्वरो निर्मितः।
एषापि स्वयमेव तुल्यरमणाभावाद्वराकी हता
कोऽर्थश्चेतसि वेधसा विनिहितस्तन्व्यास्तनुं तन्वता।।

अत्र 'तन्व्याः' इति पदं केवलशब्दानुप्रासव्यसनितया निबद्धं न काञ्चिदर्थौचित्यचमत्कारकणिकामाविष्करोति। 'सुन्दर्याः' इत्यत्र पदमनुरूपं स्यात्। अन्यानि वा निरतिशयरूपलावण्यव्यञ्जकानि। तन्वीपदं तु विरहविधुररमणीजने प्रयुक्तमर्थौचित्यशोभां जनयति।

But not as in Dharmakīrti's verse—

'What purpose, indeed, did the creator contemplate at heart when he fashioned the body of this *tanvī* (frail Beauty)? He did not care for the waste of such wealth of loveliness. On the other hand he suffered great toil. Moreover, he created such fever of anxiety in the heart of the free-moving gentry. And, alas the poor lady also was killed for want of a husband befiting her qualities'.

Here the term *tanvī* (frail Beauty) has been put in just for the sake of alliteration and does not display even an iota of the potic (harm in meaning. The word *sundarī* (Lovely maiden) or any other, expressive of exceesive grace and beauty, would have been more appropriate. The word *tanvī* "frail one", on the other hand, can bring out the beauty of propriety in meaning, only when applied to a woman distressed in separation.

यथा श्रीहर्षस्य–

परिम्लानं पीनस्तनजघनसङ्गादुभयत–
स्तनोर्मध्यस्यान्तः परिमलनमप्राप्य हरितम्ः
इदं व्यस्तन्यासं श्लथभुजलताक्षेपवलनैः
कृशाङ्ग्याः सन्तापं वदति बिसिनीपत्रशयनम्।।

अत्र सागरिकाया विरहावस्थासूचकम् 'कृशाङ्ग्याः' इति पदं परममौचित्यं पुष्णाति। ११।

As in Śrī Harṣa's verse—

'This bed of lotus leaves shows the affliction of the slender-limbed girl, since it has faded away on both sides having been in contact with the well-developed thighs and bosom, while (the part) under the middle of the breasts is green, for it does not seem to have been pressed, and this part (of the bed) has its arrangment disturbed by the tossing movments of her languid creeper-like arms'.

Here the term *kṛśāngī* (the slender-limbed girl), which shows Sāgarikā's condtion in separation (from the royal lover), contributes to (its) extreme propriety.

वाक्यगतमौचित्यं दर्शयितुमाह–

औचित्यरचितं वाक्यं सततं संमतं सताम्।
त्यागोदग्रमिवैश्वर्यं शीलोज्ज्वलमिव श्रुतम्।। १२।।

Inorder to show propriety in a sentence (the author) says—

12. A sentence, composed with propriety, always wins the approbation of the good, as does wealth exalted by liberality, or learning brightened by good character.

औचित्यरचितं वाक्यं काव्यविवेकविचलक्षणानामभिमततमम्।

A sentence construed with propriety is most liked by those who are experts in literary criticism.

यथा मम विनयवल्ल्याम्–

देवो दयावान्विजयो जितात्मा यमौ मनः संयममाननीयौ।
इति ब्रुवाणः स्वभुजं प्रमार्ष्टि यः कीचकाकालिककालदण्डम्।।
धीरः स किर्मीरजटासुरारिः कुबेरशौर्यप्रशमोपदेष्टा।
दृष्टो हिडिम्बादयितः कुरूणां पर्यन्तरेखागणनाकृतान्तः।। (युग्मम्)

अत्र भीमस्य भीमचरितोचितकीचकाकालिककालदण्डहिडिम्बादयितादिभिः पदैरुन्निद्ररौद्ररसस्वरूपानुरूपो वाक्यार्थः सजीव इवावभासते।

As in my *Vinayavalī*—

"Your Lordship is all mercy, Vijaya (Arjuna) is self-controlled, and the twins are to be regarded for subduing their mind"—thus shouting does (Bhīma) the Loving Consort of Hiḍimbā pat his arm, which was the untimely rod of Death of Kīcaka. A hero is he, the enemy of the demon Kirmīra, one who ordered truce to Kubera's power (i.e. subduer of Kubera), and one who is the god of Death to the Kurus counting the last lines of their (forces)'./

Here the meaing of the sentence appears as if vivid with epithets like "the untimely rod of Death of Kīckaca", "the Loving Consort of Hiḍimbā", and others appropriate to the dreadful deeds of Bhīma, and suited to the display of the sentiment of terror *(raudra)*.

यथावा राजशेखरस्य–

सम्बन्धी पुरुभूभुजां मनसिजव्यापारदीक्षागुरु-
गौराङ्गीवदनोपमापरिचितस्तारावधूवल्लभः।
सद्योमार्जितदाक्षिणात्यतरुणीदन्तावदातद्युति-
श्चन्द्रः सुन्दरि! दृश्यतामयमितश्चण्डीशचूडामणिः।।

अत्रापि चन्द्रमसः श्रृङ्गारान्तरङ्गैरनङ्गोद्दीपनैः पदैर्निर्वर्तितो वाक्यार्थः सदर्थौचित्यसामर्थ्येनात्यर्थमर्थनीयतां प्राप्तः।

Or, as in Rājaśekhara's (verse)—

'O beauteous one, look at the moon, the crest ornament of the Lord of Caṇḍī—the moon, who is a relation of the kings of Puru family, the preceptor of initiation into the art of making love, familiar to people by his resemblance with the faces of fair-limbed (damsels), the beloved lord of stars and possessed of a bright lustre like that of the newly-brushed teeth of a southern woman'.

Here also, the meaning of the sentence has become very desirable by the power of propriety consisting in giving appropriate sense—the sense, which has been brought to a finish by epithets of the moon, exciting love and therefore, essential to the erotic sentiment.

न तु यथास्यैव–

नाले शौर्यमहोत्पलस्य विपुले सेतौ समिद्वारिधेः
शश्वत्खड्गभुजङ्गचन्दनतरौ क्रीडोपधाने श्रियः।
आलाने जयकुञ्जरस्य सुदृशां कन्दर्पदर्पे परं
श्रीदुर्योधनदोष्णि विक्रमपरे लीनं जगन्नन्दतु।।

अत्रातिशयपरकर्कशसोत्कर्षसुभटभुजस्तम्भस्यासमुचितेन कुवलयनालतुलाधिरोपणेन वाक्यार्थः सोपहासतयेव निबद्धः कुवलयनालतुलाधिरोपणेन वाक्यार्थः सोपहासतयेव निबद्धः परिज्ञायते।। १२।।

But not as in the same (author's verse)—

'May the world reclining on the victorious arm of lustrous Duryodhana enjoy happiness; —the arm, which is the stalk of the eminent lotus of bravery, a massive bridge over the ocean of battle, an eternal sandal tree for the snake in the form of sword; a sportive pillow for the goddess of wealth, a tying post for the elephant of victory, and the source of extreme pride for the god of love in the case of beautiful ones'.

Here, by comparing the extremely hard and pillar like arm of a warrior to an unsuitable (object like the) lotus-stalk, the meaning of the sentence seems to have been intended as a joke.

प्रबन्धार्थौचित्यं दर्शयितुमाह–

उचितार्थविशेषेण प्रबन्धार्थः प्रकाशते।
गुणप्रभावभव्येन विभवेनेव सज्जनः।। १३।।

In order to explain propriety in the meaing of a composition (the author) says—

13. The meaing of a composition becomes charming with a particularly suitable meaning, just as a good person obtains lustre through wealth, made blissful by the strenth of virtues.

अम्लानप्रतिभाप्रकर्षोत्प्रेक्षितेन सकलप्रबन्धार्थाप्यायिपीयूषवर्षेण समुचितार्थविशेषेण महाकाव्यं स्फुरदिव चमत्कारकारितामापद्यते।

By means of approrpiate sense, conceived through the flight of unfading fancy, which acts as sprinkling of nectar which pervades the entire composition, a 'mahākāvya', as if glistening, acquires exquisite charm.

यथा कालिदासस्य–

जातं वंशे भवनविदिते पुष्करावर्तकानां
जानामि त्वां प्रकृतिपुरुषं कामरूपं मघोनः।
तेनार्थित्वं त्वयि विधिवशाद्दूरबन्धुर्गतोऽहं
याच्ञा मोघा वरमधिगुणे नाधमे लब्धकामा।।

अत्राचेतनस्य चेतनाध्यारोपेण मेघस्य दौत्ययोग्यताधानाय प्रथितपुष्करावर्तकपर्जन्य-वंश्यत्वममात्यप्रकृतिपुरुषत्वं च यदुपन्यस्तं तेन समस्तप्रबन्धस्याभिधानतोत्प्रेक्षितेति-वृत्तरुचिरतरस्य निरतिशयमौचित्यमुद्द्योतितम्।

As, for instace in Kālidāsa's (verse)—'

'You were born in the family of Puṣkarāvartaka clouds famous throughout the world. I consider you, who can change your form at will, as the minister of Indra. Therefore, by Providence, I, who am far from my kith and kin, have become a suppliant before you. A request rejected by a highly virtuous person is better than one fulfilled by a mean one'.

Here, by attributing consciousness to an insentient being and by confering (on the cloud) the rank of a minister and a lineage of the well-known Puṣkarāvartaka family in order to make the cloud capable of conveying the message, extreme propriety beams forth from the captivating sense rising from the expression of the entire composition.

यथा वा भवभूतेः–

(नेपथ्ये।)

योऽयमश्वः पताकेयमथवा वीरघोषणा।
सप्तलोकैकवीरस्य दशकण्ठकुलद्विषः।।

लवः–(सगर्वमिव।) अहो सन्तापनान्यक्षराणि। भो भोः! किमक्षत्रिया पृथिवी यदेवमुद्घुष्यते। (विहस्य।) आः, किं नाम स्फुरन्ति शस्त्राणि। (धनुरारापयन्।)

ज्याजिह्वया बलयितोत्कटकोटिदंष्ट्रमुद्गारिघोरघनघर्घरघोषमेतत्।
ग्रासप्रसक्तहसदन्तकवक्त्रयन्त्रजम्भाविडम्बिविकटोदरमस्तु चापम्।।

अत्रार्थे रामायणकथातिक्रमेण नूतनोत्प्रेक्षिता रामतनयस्य सहजविक्रमानुसारिणी शौर्योत्कर्षभूमिः परप्रतापस्पर्शासहिष्णुता प्रबन्धस्य रसबन्धुरामौचित्यच्छायां प्रयच्छति।।

As also in Bhavbhūti's (drama)—

'This horse, this banner or rather this war cry (belongs to) that one supreme hero of the seven worlds, the foe unto the race of the ten-necked one (i.e. Rāvaṇa)'.

Lava—(as if haughtily) O these words are provoking. Ye (people), are there no Kṣatriyas on the face of the earth, that you proclaim thus? (Defiantly) Well, the weapons are flashing (Stringing his bow)—

'Let this bown of mine, with its teeth in the form of the rising ends, encircled by the tongue-like string, and sending forth a deep frightful rumbling roar, become by its deep cavity the yawn of the machine-like mouth of the god of death, gnashing his teeth when engaged in devouring (the world)'.

In this composition, the (fact of) not bearing the ascendency of another's glory, which is a new conception, being a departure from the story of the Rāmāyaṇa, and which shows the climax of power and conforms to the natural glory of Rāma's son, lends grace of propriety to the flavour of the passage.

न तु यथा राजशेखरस्य-

रावणः–यत्पार्वतीहठकचग्रहणप्रवीणे
पाणौ स्थितं पुरभिदः शरदां सहस्रम्।
गीर्वाणसारकणनिर्मितगात्रमत्र
तन्मैथिलीक्रयधनं धनुराविस्तु।।

जनकः–आविरस्तु सममगर्भसंभवया सीतया।

अत्र 'आविरस्तु समं सीतया' इति जनकराजेन यदुच्यते तेनास्य पिशिताशनायतनयाप्रतिपादनमभिमतमिवोपलक्ष्यते। न चैतद्विद्मः कथं भक्ष्यभूता कुसुमकोमलाङ्गी पुरुषादाय प्रतिपाद्यते, इत्यनौचित्येन प्रसिद्धेन वृत्तवैपरीत्यं परं हृदयविसंवादमादधाति।

But not so Rājaśekhara's—

'Ravaṇa—"Let the bow, the price with which Sītā can be bought, be presented,—the bow, which remained for a thousand autumns in Śiva's hand accustomed to forcieble seizing of Pārvatī's hair and which is made up of the essence of the strength of divinities".

'Janaka—"Let it be presented along with Sītā who was not born of human embryo".

Here, as Janaka says, "Let it be presented with Sītā", it shows his desire to give away his daugher to a carrion-eater (Rāvaṇa). We do not know how a woman with limbs delicate as flowers could be given over as food to a cannibal. Thus, this extreme impropriety and the reversal of the event proves disagreeable.

यथा वा कलिदासस्य–

ऊरुमूलनखमागपंक्तिभिस्तत्क्षणं हृतविलोचनो हरः।
वाससः प्रशिथिलस्य संयमं कुर्वतीं प्रियतमामवारयत्॥

अत्राम्बिकासंभोगवर्णने पामरनारीसमुचितनिर्लज्जसज्जनखराजिविराजितोरुमूलहृतविलोचनत्वं त्रिलोचनस्य भगवतस्त्रिजगद्गुरोर्यदुक्तं तेनानौचित्यमेव परं प्रबन्धार्थः पुष्णाति॥ १३॥

And also in Kālidāsa's (verse)—

'Then Śiva at that time, with his eyes attracted by the line of marks of scratches by nails at the upper part of Pārvatī's loins, stopped his beloved (Pārvatī) from tying her loosened garments'.

Here, while describing the amorous enjoyment of Pārvatī, it has been mentioned that the eyes of Śiva, the Lord of the three worlds, were riveted on the loins on which the marks of nail-scratches were prominent. This is surely shamelessness as with ordinary women. An extreme impropriety has resulted on account of this.

गुणौचित्यं दर्शयितुमाह–

प्रस्तुतार्थोचितः काव्ये भव्यः सौभाग्यवान्गुणः।
स्यन्दतीन्दुरिवानन्दं संभोगावसरोदितः॥ १४॥

In order to show the propriety of merits (the author) says—

14. The sublime merit, possessed of charm and relevant to the context, rains down joy, as does the moon that rises in time for amorous sport.

प्रस्तुतस्यार्थस्यौचित्येनौज:प्रसादमाधर्यसौकुमार्यादिलक्षणो गुण: काव्ये भव्य: सौभाग्यवत्तामवाप्त: सहृदयानन्दसन्दोहमिन्दुरिव स्यन्दति ।।

In poetry, a merit, marked with vigour, clarity, sweetness, delicacy *et cetera,* arising from the propriety of the relevant sense and thus obtaining charm, being itself graceful, pours down a shower of joy to the men of taste, as does the moon.

यथा भट्टनारायणस्य–

महाप्रलयमारुतक्षुभितपुष्करावर्तक-
प्रचण्डघनगर्जितप्रतिरवानुकारी मुहुः।
रव: श्रवणभैरव: स्थगितरोदसीकन्दर:
कुतोऽद्य समरोदधेरयमभूतपूर्व: पुर: ।।

अत्रोजस्विन: भटमुकुटमणेरश्वत्थाम्न: स्फूर्जदूर्जितप्रतापानुरूपं वाक्यमोजसा काव्यगुणेनोदग्रतामवाप्तं सहस्त्रगुणमिव विक्रमौचित्यगौरवमावहति ।।

As in Bhaṭṭanārāyaṇa's (verse)—

'Whence has this thundering roar of the ocean of battle, unheard of hitherto and dreadful to ears, has risen—the roar, which has filled the cavity of the earth and the heaven and which imitates the terrible echoing of the rumbling noise of clouds, Puṣkaras and Āvartakas, agitated by the winds on doomsday?

Here, the speech beffing the refulgent and dazzling luster of valiant Aśvatthāman, the crest-jewel of the brave, exhibits thousand-fold prorpriety of grandeur of prowess attaining eminence through the poetic merit of virgour.

यथा वा भट्टबाणस्य–

हारो जलार्द्रवसनं नलिनीदलानि प्रालेयशीकरमुचस्तुहिनांशुभास:।
यस्येन्धनानि सरसानि च चन्दनानि निर्वाणमेष्यति कथं स मनोभवाग्नि: ।।

अत्र विप्रलम्भभरभग्नधैर्याया: कादम्बर्या विरहव्यथावर्णना माधुर्यसौकुमार्यादिगुणयोगेन पूर्णेन्दुवदनेव प्रियंवदत्वेन हृदयानन्ददायिनीं दयिततमतामातनोति।

As also in Bhaṭṭa Bāṇa's (verse)—

'How will that fire of the mindborn be extinguished—one whose fule are the pearl-necklace, garments wet with water, lotus leaves, snow-spraying moon-beams and juicy sandal?'

Here, the description of Kādambarī's affliction in separation, with her firmenss giving way before the acuteness of spearation—(the description) which is full of sweetness, delicacy and other merits, produces a heart-captivating sense of agreeableness, jsut as the full-moon-faced lady does with sweet speech.

न तु यथा चन्द्रकस्य-

युद्धेषु भाग्यचपलेषु न मे प्रतिज्ञा दैवं नियच्छति जयं च पराजयं च।
एषैव मे रणगतस्य सदा प्रतिज्ञा पश्यन्ति यन्न रिपवो जघनं हयानाम्।।

अत्र क्षत्रवृत्तिरिवौजसा काव्यगुणेनास्पृष्टा सुभटोक्तिरुचितार्थापि तेजोजीवितविरहिता दुर्गतगृहदीपशिखेव मन्दायमाना न विद्योतते।

But not as in Candraka's (verse)—

'I make no promise about the result of the battled (whose issue) depends of fate, for it is Destiny that grants victory of defeat; but when in the battle-field, I always make a vow that the enemy shall not see the back of my horses'.

Here, the braggin of a warrior, which is in the manner of a (true) Kṣatriaý, though possessing the propriety of meaning yet bereft of poetic vigour, and lacking the lustrous life, does not look bright like the fading flame of a lamp placed in the house of a poor man.

यथा वा राजशेखरस्य-

एतस्याः स्मरसंज्वरः करतलस्पर्शैः परीक्ष्यो न यः
स्निग्धेनापि जनेन दाहभयतः प्रस्थंपचः पाथसाम्।
निर्वीर्यीकृतचन्दनौषधविधौ तस्मिंस्तडत्कारिणो
लाजस्फोटममी स्फुटन्ति मणयः सर्वेऽपि हारस्रजाम्।।

अत्र विरहविधुररमणीमनोभवावस्थानुरूपं माधुर्यमुत्सृज्य तडत्कारिंणो लाजस्फोटं स्फुटन्तीत्योजःस्फूर्जितोर्जितस्वभावाधिवासिता सूक्तिर्लावण्यपेशलतनुर्ललितललनेव परुषभाषिणी झटित्यनौचित्यं चेतसि संचारयति।। १४।।

Nor as in Rājaśekhara's (verse)—

'Through fear of being burnt, the temperature of the fire of her love cannot be taken (lit. examined) with the touchings of palms by those even who love her—the fire of love which would dry up a 'prastha' of water. That fever has rendered the medicines and the sandal futile and all the jewels in the necklace and the garlands are bursting with a crackling noise of fried rice'.

Here, laying aside the sweetness which befits the state of love of a owman afflicted with separation and (by saying) that (the pearls) burst with lud report like fried rice, the verse, though possessed of lustre, eloquence and force of expression, strikes the mind with impropriety like a beautiful lady having a lovely and tender body, but speaking harshly.

अलङ्कारौचित्यं दर्शयितुमाह–

अर्थौचित्यवता सूक्तिरलङ्कारेण शोभते।
पीनस्तनस्थितेनेव हारेण हरिणेक्षणा।। १५।।

In order to show propriety of the figures of speech (the author) says—

15. A poem becomes bright with a figure of speech which has a propriety of meaning, just as a fawn-eyed lady looks beautiful with a necklace hanging on her well developed bosom.

प्रस्तुतार्थस्यौचित्येनोपमोत्प्रेक्षारूपकादिनाऽलङ्कारेण सूक्तिश्चकास्ति कामिनीवोच्चकुचचुम्बिना रुचिरमुक्ताकलापेन।

A verse looks bright (i.e., becomes lovely) with figures of speech—simile, metaphor, poetic fancy and the rest—having a propreity of relevant sense, just as a woman looks bright with a beautiful pearl-necklace touching her well-developed bosom.

यथा श्रीहर्षस्य–

विश्रान्तविग्रहकथो रतिमाञ्जनस्य चित्ते वसन्प्रियवसन्तक एव साक्षात्।
पर्युत्सुको निजमहोत्सवदर्शनाय वत्सेश्वरः कुसुमचाप इवाभ्युपैति।।

अत्र वत्सेश्वरस्य कुसुमचापेनोपमा शृङ्गारावसरसरसचारुतरतामौचित्येन कामपि चेतश्चमत्कारिणोमाविष्करोति।

As in Śrī Harṣa's (verse)—

'Here comes to witness his great festival, the ever longing Lord of the Vatsas, who has stopped all talk about war, is of erotic mind, and has won the hearts of his people; and thus he (the Lord of Vatsas) imitates Love, that flowerbowed god, with no more talk of his body going about, accompanied by his wife Rati, living in the hearts of men, and dear to his friend spring, and arriving to attned his own festival'.

Here, the suitable comparison of the Lord of Vatsa with the flower-bowed god reveals through propriety an indescribable charm to the mind especially in the love context.

न तु यथा चन्दकस्य–

खगोत्क्षिप्तैरन्त्रैस्तरुशिरसि दोलेव रचिता
शिवा तृप्ताहारा स्वपिति रतिखिन्नेव वनिता।
तृषार्तो गोमायुः सरुधिरमसिं लेढि बहुशो
बिलान्वेषी सर्पो हतगजकराग्रं प्रविशति।।

अत्रानुचितस्थानस्थितायाः पुरुषपिशिततृप्तसुप्तायाः शिवायाः सुरतकेलिक्लान्तकान्तया विच्छाययैयोपमा परं वैपरीत्यं प्रकाशयति।

But not as in Candaka's (verse)—

'The entrails thrown up by birds have made themselves into swings as it were on the tops of trees; a she-jackal having had enough to eat is sleeping like a woman tired of amorous sport; the thirsty jackal licks again and again the swrod besmeared with blood; the snake, searching for an aperture enters into the opening of a dead elephant's trunk'.

Here, the lustreless comparison of a she-jackla, sleeping after having eaten human flesh to its fill, and mentioned at an improper place, with a woman exhausted after the amorous sport, is quite out of place and produces utter disgust.

यथा वा मालवरुद्रस्य–

अभिनववधूरोषस्वादः करीषतनूनपा-
दसरलजनाश्लेषक्रूरस्तुषारसमीरणः।
गलितविभवस्याज्ञेवाद्य द्युतिर्मसृणा रवे-
र्विरहिवनितावक्त्रौपम्यं बिभर्ति निशाकरः।।

अत्र कोमलकामिनोकोपेन करीषकृशानोः सादृश्यं शीतसमयस्वादुतया हृदयसंवादसुन्दरमप्यनुचितत्वेन सहसैव चेतसः सङ्कोचमिवादधाति।

Nor as in Mālavarudra's (verse)—

'The fire of dry cow-dung is plesant like the anger of newly-wedded wife; (the touch of) the frosty wind is piercing like the embrace of a wicked person; the light of the sun has grown mild like command of one who has lost one's riches, and the moon bears resemblance to the face of a woman in separation'.

Here the comparison of the fire of dry cow-dung with the anger of a delicat woman, (simply because we) like (fire) in autumn, even though beautiful, because agreeableness gets to the heart, makes the mind[1] shudder through its impropriety all at once, as it were.

यथा वा राजशेखरस्य–

चिताचक्रं चन्द्रः कुसुमधनुषो दग्धवपुषः
कलङ्कस्तत्रत्यः स्पृशति मलिनाङ्गारकलनाम्।
यदेतत्सज्योतिर्दरदलितकर्पूरधवलं
मरुद्भिर्भस्मैतत्प्रसरति विकीर्णं दिशि दिशि।।

अत्राप्यानन्दिसुधावस्यन्दसुन्दरस्येन्दोश्चिताचक्रत्वमनुचिततया कर्णकटुकमातङ्क-मिवातनोति। योऽर्थस्तु हृदयसंवादी स यद्यनौचित्यस्पर्शलेशरहितस्तदाऽधिकतरामलङ्कारशोभां पुष्णाति।

Nor as in Rājaśekhara's (verse)—

'The moon is the circular funeral pyre of the dead body of the flower-bowed god. The dark spots in it resemble the black charcoal; and since with its light, it looks like camphor slightly cut, (it seems as if) the ahses are blowing in all directions being scattered by wind'.

Here, as the comparison of the moon, lovely on account of raining down delightful nectar, with a funeral pyre, is improper; it is unwelcome to the ears and rouses a sense of awe. A statement, free from all impropriety, and agreeable to the heart, develops beauty of the figures of speech all the more.

यथा कार्पटिकस्य–

शीतेनोद्धूषितस्य माषशिमिवच्चिन्तार्णवे मज्जतः
शान्ताग्निं स्फुटिताधरस्य धमतः क्षुत्क्षामकण्ठस्य मे।
निद्रा क्वापि विमानितेव दयित संत्यज्य दूरं गता
सत्पात्रप्रतिपादितेव वसुधा न क्षीयते शर्वरी।।

1. The difference between heart and mind is very subtle indeed.

अत्रानौचित्यस्पर्शपरिहारेण केवलं हृदयसंवादसौन्दर्यमेव स्वादुतामादधाति।। १५।।

As in Kārpaṭika's (verse)—

'While I, assailed by cold and with my throat parched by hunger, was sinking in the ocean of thoughts like a bean corn, and with my underlip, split by cold, was blowing at the dying fire, sleep somehow deserted me like a neglected mistress and went afar. The nigh, however, like the land which has been bestowed on a worthy person does not get exhausted.

Here, beauty, appealing to the heart and untouched by impropriety, rouses flavour.

रसौचित्यं दर्शयितुमाह–

कुर्वन्सर्वाशये व्याप्तिमौचित्यरुचिरो रसः।
मधुमास इवाशोकं करोत्यङ्कुरितं मनः।। १६।।

In order to show propriety in sentiment, the (author) says—

16. The sentiment, fascinating on account of its propriety, and pervading the entire sense, makes the mind grosw, as does the spring the Aśoka tree.

औचित्येन भ्राजिष्णुः श्रृङ्गारादिलक्षणो रसः सकलजनहृदयव्यापी वसन्त इवाशोकतरुमङ्कुरितं मनः करोति।

The sentiment—Erotic and others—lustrous with propriety, pervading the hearts of all people makes the mind grow just as spring makes the Aśoka tree sprout.

यथा श्रीहर्षस्य–

उद्दामोत्कलिकां विपाण्डुररुचं प्रारब्धजृम्भां क्षणा–
दायासं श्वसनोद्गमैरविरलैरातन्वतीमात्मनः।
उद्योद्यानलतामिमां समदनां नारीमिवान्यां ध्रुवं
पश्यन्कोपविपाटलद्युति मुखं देव्याः करिष्याम्यहम्।।

अत्रेर्ष्याविप्रलम्भरूपस्य श्रृङ्गाररसस्य वासवदत्तायामवेक्ष्यमाणस्य नवमालिकालताया ललितवनितातुल्यतया विरहावस्थारोपणेन नितरामौचित्यरुचिरचसत्कारकारिणी दीप्तिरुपपादिता।

As in Śrī Harṣa's (verse)—

'I shall today make the queen's face glow red with anger by locking at this garden creepr which shows a luxuriant growth of buds, is of palish lustre, is just beginning to grow long, is tormenting itself through exposure to incessant breezes, and which thus closely resembles a passionate woman given to unrestrained dalliance, of palish complexion, yawning for a moment, and languishing through incessant sighs'.

Here, while assigning to Vāsavadattā the sentiment of love in separation mixed with jealousy, attributing to a Navamālikā creeper a state of separation on account of its similarity with a lovely maiden, brings abouot a brilliance resulting in charm which is lovely through propriety.

यथा वा कालिदासस्य–

बालेन्दुवक्राण्यविकासभावाद्बभुः पलाशान्यतिलोहितानि।
सद्यो वसन्तेन समागतानां नखक्षतानीव वनस्थलीनाम्।।

अत्र पार्वत्यां परमेश्वरस्याभिलाषश्रृङ्गारे वक्ष्यमाणे प्रथममुद्दिपनविभावभृतस्व वसन्तरस्य वर्णनायां कामुकाध्यारोपेण वनस्थलीललनानां फुटिललोहितपलाशकलिकामिर्नवसङ्गमयोग्यन-खक्षतान्युत्प्रेक्षितानि परमामौचित्यचारुतां प्रतिपादयन्ति।

As also in Kālidāsa's (verse)—

'The deep Palāśa flowers, not in full bloom, and thus appearing curved like the digit of the young moon, looked like the fresh nail-marks on the woodland tracts coming in contact with spring'.

Here, when narrating the erotic longings of Śiva for Pārvatī, the description of the primary excitant, spring, by ascribing to it the function of a lover, the poet has fancied red and crooked Palāśa buds to be the nail-marks on the damsel-like woodland regions at the time of their first union with spring; and has thus given rise to an extreme beauty of propriety.

न तु यथास्यैव–

वर्णप्रकर्षे सति कर्णिकारं दुनोति निगन्धतया स्म चेतः।
प्रायेण सामग्र्यविधौ गुणानां पराङ्मुखी विश्वसृजः प्रवृत्तिः।।

अत्र केवलकर्णिकारकुसुमवर्णनमात्रेण विधातृवाच्यतागर्भेणैव प्रस्तुतशृङ्गारानुपयोगिना तदुद्दीपनविभावोचितं न किंचिदभिहितम्।

But not as in Kālidāsa's (another verse)—

'Even though endowed with good colour the *harṇikāra* flower Pained one, because it had no fragance. The tendency of the creator generally is not seen to be in favour of happing up all Virtus at one place.' Here by Simply describing the colour of the Karnikāra flower and by censuring the Creator, that being in no way beneficial to the prevailing sentiment of love, nothing has been said which serves as a fitting excitant.

(Propriety) in the sentiment of Humour (is seen), for instance, (in) my (verse) in the poem called *Lāvaṇyavatī.*

'Do you not kiss the mouth for fear of touching wine? Why do you hide your nose? O you show off your unbalanced scriptural scholarship as you appear quite dull without a courtesan,— saying this, Vāsantikā, with her eyes rolling on account of infatuation, sprinkels wine on Atrivasu reclining on Mālatī, as if on a Bakula tree'.

Here, the act of sprinkling wine by the courtesan in order to rouse passion in Atrivasu, the theologican, who is shrinking back for fear of being touched by polluting wine, is just like sprinkling of wine on a dried up Bakula tree in order to produce freshness in it. Here in delightful propreity is produeced by the commingling of humour with a semblance of the Erotic sentimetnt, which is subservient to the former, just as the mixing of wine with mango juice, brings about relish.

हास्यरसे यथा मम लावण्यवतीनाम्नि काव्ये–

सीधुस्पर्शभयान्न चुम्बसि मुखं किं नासिकां गूहसे
रे रे! श्रोत्रियतां तनोषि विषमां मन्दोऽसि वेश्यां विना।
इत्युक्त्वा मदघूर्णमाननयना वासन्तिका मालती
लीनस्यात्रिवसोः करोति बकुलस्येवासवासेचनम्।।

अत्र श्रोत्रियस्यात्रिवसोरपवित्रसीधुस्पर्शशङ्कासङ्कोचनिलीनस्य शुष्कबकुलवृक्षस्येव सरसतापादनाय वेशविलासिन्या यदासवासेचनं तदङ्गभूतशृङ्गाररसाभासस्पशंन हास्यरसस्य वरासवस्येव सहकाररसवेधेन सचमत्कारमौचित्यमाचिनोति।

Or as in my (verse) in the same Lāvaṇyavatī—

'A lovely Kerala woman uttering the sound, (hissing sound), her feet having been pricked with pointed ends of Ketaka flowers on the way, and smiling when importuned by a knaeve thus, "Beautiful! Lovely! Please do it again", methinks, out of shame for stealing a glance on the knave, covers her face with the garment of the moonbeams reflected from her ivory necklace of strings'.

Here also, by the proper facetious expression employed by the crafty rogue, the snetiment of humour, assited by a hint of the sentiment of Love, shows a charming propriety.

न तु यथा श्यामलस्य–

चुम्बनसक्तः सोऽस्या दशनं च्युतमूलमात्मनो वदनात्।
जिह्वामूलप्राप्तं खाडिति कृत्वा निरष्ठीवत् ॥

अत्र हास्यरसस्य बीभत्सरसाधिवासितस्य लशुनलिप्तस्येव कुसुमशेखरस्यातिजुगुप्सितत्वादनीप्सितस्य परमानौचित्येन चमत्कारस्तिरोहितः। वृद्धापरिचुम्बने जिह्वामूलप्राप्तस्य च्युतदशनस्य कण्ठलोठिनः ष्ठीवनेन बीभत्सस्यैव प्राधान्यम्, न तु हास्यरसस्य।

But not so in Śyāmala's (verse)—

'While kissing her, he, with the coughing sound of 'khāḍ' spat out her tooth, which had been loosened from its roots and had reached his very throat'.

Here, the sentiment of Humour, mingled with the undesirable sentiment of Repugnance, has, on account of its utter impropreity, dispeled all charm as in the case of a chaplet of flowers wreathed with garlic blossoms. By spitting out the broken tooth,which has reached the root of the tongue, and was rolling in the throat, while kissing the old lady, it is repulsiveness that becomes conspicuous and not humour.

करुणो यथा मम मुनिमतमीमांसायाम्–

प्रत्यग्रोपनताभिमन्युनिधने हा वत्स हा पुत्रके–
त्यश्मद्राविं सुभद्रया प्रलपितं पार्थस्य यत्तत्पुरः।
येनोद्वाष्पविमुक्तशष्पकवलैः सेनातुरङ्गैरपि
न्यञ्चत्पार्श्वगतैककर्णकुहरैर्निःस्पन्दमन्दं स्थितम्॥

अत्र प्रत्यग्रोपनतप्रियतरतनयवियोगोपजनितशोकाख्यस्थायिभावोचितं दृषदामपिहृदयद्रावणं सुभद्रया यत्प्रलपितं तदर्जुनचेतसि प्रतिफलितं न केवलमुद्दीप्ततामुपगतं यावत्तिरश्चां तुरङ्गमाणाप्यन्तः संक्रान्तमुद्बाष्पविमुक्तशष्पकवलनिः स्पन्दस्थितादिभिरनुभावैरुदीर्णतरुणकरुणरसप्रतिपत्तिं किमप्यादधाति।

(Propriety) in Pathos, as in my *Munimatamīmāṁsā*—

'On hearing that stone-melting bemoaning cry that Subhadrā uttered on Abhimanyu's death, occuring recently saying, "Oh my dear child! Oh my little son", even the horses of the army stood silent and motionless their mouthfuls of grass failling out with the tearful sighs and with their ears sunk low'.

Here, befitting the abiding sentiment of Pathos, arising ont of the recent death of the dearest son, the bewailing of Subhadrā, melting the heart even of stones, has not only become excitant as reflected in Arjuna's heart, but it also shows the development of mature sentiment of Pathos by the ensuants having been transferred into the hearts of animals like horses who stand motionless with the mouthfuls of grass being thrown out along with the tearful sighs.

न तु यथा परिमलस्य–

हा श्रृङ्गारतरङ्गिणीकुलगिरे हा राजचूडामणे
हा सौजन्यसुधानिधान हहहा वैदग्ध्यदुग्धोदधे।
हा देवोज्जयिनाभुजङ्ग युवतिप्रत्यक्षकन्दर्प हा
हा सद्बान्धव हा कलामृतकर! क्वासि प्रतीक्षस्व नः।।

अत्र 'हाहे'ति हतमहीपतिविरहे तद्गुणामन्त्रणपदैर्वक्तृवक्त्रगत एव शोकः केवलमुपलक्ष्यते, न तु विभावानुभावव्यभिचारिसंयोगेन शोकाख्यस्य स्थायिभावस्योचितं रसीकरणं किंचिन्निष्पन्नम्।

But not as in parimala's (verse)—

'Alas! O you the chief mountain from which flows the stream of love. Alas! you the crest jewel of kings! Alas! you the repository of the ambrosia of nobility! Alas! you the ocean of the milk of erudition. Alas! O King! Lord of Ujjayinī! Alas! you the personified god of Love for young damsels! Alas, true friend! Alas, you the god of nectar rays for art! Where are you? Just cast a look upon us'.

Here, by uttering (the word) 'Alas' and by counting the king's virtues at his death, the grief of the speaker seems to be restricted to his speech only. The abiding feeling of grief has not even a whit been developed into a sentiment, by means a combination of excitants, ensuants and accessories.

रौद्रे यथा भट्टनारायणस्य–

यो यः शस्त्रं बिभर्ति स्वभुजगुरुमदः पाण्डवीनां चमूनां
यो यः पाञ्चालगोत्रे शिशुरधिकवया गर्भशय्यां गतो वा।
यो यस्तत्कर्मसाक्षी चरति मयि रणे यश्च यश्च प्रतोपं
क्रोधान्धस्तस्य तस्य स्वयमपि जगतामन्तकस्यान्तकोऽहम्।।

अत्र क्रूरक्रोधस्थायिभावात्मकस्योन्निद्ररौद्ररस्योचिता शिशुस्थविरगर्भगतविशसन-निस्त्रिंशकर्माध्यवसायाधिरोहणसंवादिनी द्रोणवधविधुरामर्ष्जविषविषमव्यथा कश्मलशिथिलमश्वत्थाम्नः स्थेमानं प्रतिज्ञापयति।

(Propriety) in the Furious sentiment as in Bhaṭṭanārāyaṇa's (verse)—

'Of him, whosoever, pround of his arms (i.e. valour), wields weapons in the army of Pāṇḍu's sons; of him, whosoever, (born) in the tribe of Pāñcālas has passed into childhood or youth or even taken his natal sleep; of him, whosoever witnessed that (heinous) act; of him, who soever opposes me on the battlefield, I, blind with rage, am the Destroyer, even if he be the world's god of Death himself'.

Here, teh extreme distress arising from the deadly poison of anger at Droṇa's cruel murder, the distress which fits in with the sentiment of Fury, based on the abiding feeling of ruthless rage, and which foreshadows the doing of the cruel act of murdering, children, the aged and (even) those in womb, shows Aśvatthāman's firmness unnerved by ths sense of foul deeds.

न तु यथा श्रीप्रवरसेनस्य–

दणुइन्दरुहिरलग्गे जस्स फुरन्ते णहप्पहाविछड्डे।
गुप्पन्ती विवलाआ गलिअब्बथणंसुए महासुरलच्छी[1]**।।**

अत्र क्रोधव्यञ्जकपदविरहिततया 'दनुजेन्द्ररुधिरलग्ने यस्य नरसिंहस्य स्फुरति नखप्रभासमूहे व्याकुलीभवन्ती विपलायिता गलितस्तनांशुका महासुरलक्ष्मीः' इति वर्णनया रुधिरलग्न इति बीभत्सरसर्स्पर्शे व्याकुलीभवन्ती दैत्यश्रीः पलायितेति भयानकरससङ्करेण प्रकृतोचितप्रधानभूतस्य रौद्ररसस्य क्वचिन्मुखमपि न दृश्यते।

But not as in Śrī Pravarasena's (verse)—

1. दनुजेन्द्ररुधिरलग्ने यस्य स्फुरति नखप्रभासमूहे।
व्याकुलीभवन्ती विपलायित्ता गलितस्तनाशुका महासुरलक्ष्मीः।। इति छाया।

'As the flood of lusture from the finger-nails lit up the (gushing) blood of the Demon-Lord, the swollen Glory of the Demons, in great distress, took to flight, with her breast-garment slipping off'.

Here, by the absence of words showing anger and by the description that the swollen Glory of the demons, distressed at the flood of lustre of the finger-nails of God Narasimha lighting up the gushing blood of the Demon-Lord, took to flight with the breast-garment slipping off, there is rather a touch of the sentiment of Repulsion referring to gushing blood and a contaminiation of the Dreadful one referring to guishing blood and a contaminationof the Dreadful one referring to the Demon-Glory fleeing in distress etc; the sentiment of Terror, which is the main sentiment in point, nay even the face of it, is not seen anywhere.

वीरे यथा मम नीतिलतायाम्--

शौर्याराधितभर्गभार्गवमुनेः शस्त्रग्रहोन्मार्गिण।
संक्षेपेण निवार्य संक्षयमयीं क्षत्रोचितां तीक्ष्णताम्।
आकर्णायतकृष्टचापकुटिलभ्रूभङ्गसंसगिणा
येनान्यायनिषेधिना शममयी ब्राह्मी प्रदिष्टा स्थितिः ।।

अत्र 'सोऽयं रामः' इति रावणाग्रे शुकसारणाभ्यां दूरान्निर्दिश्यमानस्य रामस्य निःसंरम्भगम्भीरावष्टम्भसंभाव्यमानप्रभावोचितायां शस्त्रसंग्रहोन्मार्गगामिनो भार्गवस्य मुनेः स्वजातिसमुचितस्थित्युपदेशे सति प्रभविष्णुतायां चापरूपभङ्ग्या भ्रूभङ्गः प्रदर्शितः, न तु स्वाभाविकः वीरस्य क्रोधे विकारासंभवात्। प्रसन्नमधुरधीरा हि वीरवृत्तिः, तदुचितमत्राभिहितम्, भार्गवाभिभवेन च प्रधाननायकस्योत्कर्षः प्रतिपादितः।

(Propriety) in the Heroic sentiment as in my *Nītilatā*—

'He who prevented injustice and who, having warded off summarily the warrior-like all-destructive severity of the Bhārgava sage, who had taken up arms and had obtained glory through valour, showed him the peaceful state of a Brāhmaṇa with a twist of his brows which had become crooked at the stretching of his bow to his ear'.

Herein, while Śuka and Sāraṇa are describing to Rāvaṇa from a distance "Such is Rāma" the twisting of Rāma's eyebrows has been shown in his breaking of the bow, which act conforms to

Rāma's prowess, whose majesty can be inferred from his demeanour,which is sober, serene and steady and especially so when this twisting of the eybrows was displayed at the time of admonishing Paraśurāma, who had gone astray by taking to arms and was asked not to leave the boundaries of his own caste. This twisting of the eyebrows is not natural with Rāma, for a hero in rage would not give way to excitement. A warrior's way must suits such a warrior's behavior, and the superiority of the hero has been confiremed by the defeat of Paraśurāma.

यथा वा राजशेखरस्य–

स्त्रीणां मध्ये सलीलं भ्रमितगुरुगदाघातनिर्नष्टसंज्ञः
सद्यो वध्योऽभवस्त्वं पशुरिव विवशस्तेन राज्ञाऽर्जुनेन।
तस्य च्छेत्तापि योऽसौ सकलनृपरिपुर्जामदग्न्यो भुजानां
जित्वौच्चैः सोऽपि येन द्विज इति न हतस्तापसस्त्वेष रामः।।

अत्र रावणकार्तवीर्यजामदग्न्योत्कर्षोत्कर्षतरसोपानपरम्पराधिरोहणक्रमेण प्रधाननायकस्य प्रतापः परां कोटिमारोपितः।

Or as in Rājaśekhara's (verse)—

'You wre easily reduced to unconsciousness in the midst of women, by the blows of the moving great mace and became helpless and liable to be killed like an animal byKing Arjuna (i.e. Sahasārjuna). The son of Jamadagni, the enemy of all kings, cut down the arms of that king even (viz. Sahasrārjuna). This is that ascetic (called) Rāma, who conquered easily even him (i.e. Paraśurāma) but did not kill him simply because he was a Brāhmaṇa.

Here, by the gradual ascendancy in superiority over Rāvaṇa Kārtavīrya and Paraśurāma, the prowess of the principal hero reaches the highest point.

न तु यथा भवभूतेः–

वृद्धास्ते न विचारणीयचरितास्तिष्ठन्तु हु वर्ततां
युद्धं स्त्रीदमनेऽप्यखण्डयशसो लोके महान्तो हि ते।
यानि त्रीणि कुतोमुखान्यपि पदान्यासन्खरायोघने
यद्वा कौशलमिन्द्रसूनुदमने तत्राप्यभिज्ञो जनः।।

अत्राप्रधानस्य रामसूनोः कुमारलवस्य परप्रतापोत्कर्षासहिष्णोर्वीररसोद्दीपनाय

सकलप्रबन्धजीवितसर्वस्वभूतस्य प्रधाननायकगतस्य वीररसस्य ताडकादमनखररणापसरणान्यरणसंसक्तवालिव्यापादनादिजनविहितापवादप्रतिपादनेन स्ववचसा कविना विनाशः कृत इत्यनुचितमेतत्।

But not as in Bhavabhūti's (verse)—

'They are elderly people, their actions need not be criticised. Mum is the word. Their glory remains untarnished even when a battle ensues and a woman is subdued, for they are great in the world. The three steps, however, that were taken in some direction (not facing the enemy) in the fight with Khara and the dexterity which was shown in killing the sone of Indra i.e. Vālin, are indeed well-known to people'.

Here, in order to excite the sentiment of Heroism in Rāma's son, prince Lava, who is a minor character and who cannot brook another's prowess, the poet in his own words has undone the effect of Heroic sentiment pertaining to the chief hero (Rāma) and the very life of his composition, by referring to the murder of Tāṭakā, the withdrawal in his fight with Khara, the murder of Vālin while he was fighting with another person, and similar other deeds, which have provoked public censure. This is improper.

भयानके यथा श्रीहर्षस्य–

कण्ठे कृतावशेषं कनकमयमधः श्रृङ्खलादास कर्ष
न्क्रान्त्वा द्वाराणि हेलाचलचरणरणत्किङ्किणीचक्रवालः।
दत्तातङ्कोऽङ्गनानामनुसृतसरणिः संभ्रमादश्वपालैः
प्रभ्रष्टोऽय प्लवङ्गः प्रविशति नृपतेर्मन्दिरं मन्दुरायाः।।

अपि च–

नष्टं वर्षवरैर्मनुष्यगणनाभावादकृत्वा त्रपा–
मन्तः कञ्चुकि कञ्चुकस्य विशति त्रासादयं वामनः।
पर्यन्ताश्रयिभिनिजस्य सदृशं नाम्नः किरातैः कृतं
कुब्जा नीचतयैव यान्ति शनकैरात्मेक्षणाशङ्किनः।।

अत्राङ्गनानां निशितदशननखशिखोल्लेखातङ्कदानेन प्रचुरतरवानराभिसरणभयसंभ्रान्तान्तःपुरिकवृद्धवामनकिरातकुब्जादीनां पुरुषगणनाविहीनतया धैर्यविरहकातराणामुचितचेष्टानुभाववर्णनया भयानकरससंवादिरुचिरौचित्यमाचकास्ति।

(Propriety) in the sentiment of Terror as in Śrī Harṣa's verses—

'On its neck a part of the broken necklace, dragging with its feet a string of golden chain, crossing so many doors, with tinkling bells resounding at its feet moving sportively, spreading awe among women folk and pursued on its track by grooms in great confusion—there enters a monkey into the king's palace escapting from the stable.'

Moreover—

'The eunuchs have run away, as they feel no shame for they have no place among men, the dwarf in fear hides himself behind the cloak of the chamberlain, the Kirātas have proved true to their name since they have retired to the extreme ends of the palace (for 'Kirāta' literally means *kiranti aṭanti ca,* i.e. those who lead a nomadic life), and the hunchback lady walks stooping and slowly, dreading to look at herself'.

Here, indeed, does propriety shine forth—charming on account of its conformity with the sentiment of Terror—arising from the description of resultant behaviour suitable to those who are destitute of courage and hence timid. It is the behaviour of those who find no place among the manly folk, such as aged chamberlain, dwarfs, kirātas and hunchbacks, who are terrified by the close chase of a monkey, which does havoc by giving scratches with its sharp teeth and pointed nails.

न तु यथा राजपुत्रमुक्तापीडस्य–

नीवारप्रसराग्रमुष्टिकवलैर्यो वर्धितः शेशवे
पीतं येन सरोजपत्रपुटके होमावशेषं पयः।
त दृष्ट्वा मदमन्थरालिवलयव्यालोलगल्लं (ण्डं) गजं
सानन्दं सभयं च पश्यति मुहुर्दूंर स्थितस्तापसः।।

अत्र गजस्याघातकविकृतचेष्टानुवर्णनाविरहिततया स्थायिभावस्य भयानुभाववर्जितस्य केवलं नाममात्रोदीरणेन च भयानकरसाचितसंभ्रमाभावादुपचितमौचित्यं न किंचिदुपलभ्यते।

But not as in Prince Muktāpiḍa's (verse)—

'The ascetic standing at a distance looks again and again with fear as well as joy, at the elephant, whom he has reared in his childhood by giving mouthfuls in the form of handfuls of wild grain, who has drunk the water remaining after the sacrifice (dropped) in the cavity of the vessel of lotus leaf, and whose temples are constantly in motion to shake off the hovering bees intoxicated with his rut'.

Here, there is no desirable propriety forthcoming because of the absence of confusion proper to the sentiment of Terror; (more over), the Various strange acts of the dephemt, at the time of attacking, have not been mentioned and the main sentiment (is) unassisted by the excitant 'terror', which is mentioned in name only.

बीभत्से यथा मम मुनिप्रतमीमांसायाम्–

सर्वापायचयाश्रयस्य नियतं कुत्सानिकायस्य किं
कायस्यास्य विभूषणैः सुवसनैरानन्दनैश्चन्दनैः।
अन्तर्यस्य शकृद्यकृत्कृमिकुलक्लोमान्त्रमालाकुले
क्लेदिन्यन्तदिने प्रयान्ति विमुखाः कौलेयकाका अपि।।

अत्र वैराग्यवासनाच्छुरितबीभत्सरसस्य जुगुप्साख्यस्थायिभावोचितकायगतकुत्सित-तरान्त्रतन्त्रादिसमुदीरणेन परा परिपुष्टिनिःसारशरीराभिमानवैरस्यजननी प्रतिपादिता।

(Propriety) in the Repulsive sentiment as in my *Munimatamīmāṁsā*—

'Of what avail to this body, which is the repository of all that is evil and an associate of contempt, are the fine ornaments, rich raiment, and the delightful sandal unguents,—the body, the interiror of which contains ordure, liver, worms, bladder and network of intestines and on the last day of whoe decay even dogs and crows turn away from it?'

Here, by mentioning the foul net-work of intestines etc. in the body, a feeling of disgust proper for the main sentiment, has been prouduced and thus the Repulsive sentiment combined with the desire for renunciation, has been developed to the highest point it and leads to aversion to the vanities of the body which is so unreal.

न तु यथा चन्दकस्य–

कृशः काणः खञ्जः श्रवणरहितः पुच्छविकलः
क्षुधाक्षामो रूक्षः पिठरककपालर्दितगलः।
व्रणैः पूतिक्लिन्नैः कृमिपरिवृतैरावृततनुः
शुनीमन्वेति श्वा तमपि मदयत्येष मदनः।।

अत्राशुचिचर्वणरुचेरुपचितविचिकित्सकुत्सानिकायस्य स्वभावजुगुप्सितयोनेः शुनकस्य किमेतर्बीभत्सविशेषणैरतिशयनिर्बन्धानुबद्धैरधिकमुद्भासितम्। एतैरेव पुरुषगतैर्जुगुप्सा परं गौरवमावहति।

But not as in Candaka's (verse)—

'Even a lean, one-eyed, lame dog, bereft of ears, deformed at the tail, extremely hungry, dreary with hollow cheeks and bruishe neck, with his body covered with wounds emitting purulent matter and worms, follows the bitch. Verily the god of Love excites him also'.

Hre, it is no used bringing into prominence the repulsive epithets, put together with great persistence, of a dog, which by its very nature, belongs to an abominable stock, given to eating loathsome things and has its person deep immersed in contemptible things. With these (epithets) applied to a person, the feeling of disgust would have commanded greater attention.

अद्भूते यथा चन्दकस्य–

कृष्णेनाम्ब! गतेन रन्तुमधुना मृद्भक्षिता स्वेच्छया
सत्यं कृष्ण! क एवमाह मुसलीमिथ्याम्ब! पश्याननम्।
व्यादेहीति विकासितेऽथ वदने दृष्ट्वा समस्तं जग-
न्माता यस्य जगाम विस्मयपद पायात्स व केशवा।।

अत्र पाण्डुराङ्गकरसाक्षिलक्षितमृद्भक्षणाक्षेपोद्यतजननीभयचकितस्यापहवकारिणः शिशोविकासितास्यस्यान्तः समस्तजगद्दर्शनेन मातुश्च तत्प्रभावानभिज्ञतया वात्सल्यविह्वलाया विस्मयगमनेनात्युचितोऽयमद्भुतातिशयः।

(Propriety) in the sentiment of Wonder as in Candaka's (verse)—

'Mother just now Kṛṣṇa, when he went out to play, ate clay at his will. "It is true, O Kṛṣṇa?" "Who says so?" "Balarāma". "It is untrue, mother. Look into my mouth". "Open it to me". Saying thus, as he yawned, his mother was struck with wonder on seeing the entire universe in the cavity of his mouth. May that Keśava protect you'!

Here, the climax of the sentiment of wonder is highly made proper by making the mother, not knoiwng his (Kṛṣṇa's) prowess and restless with filial affection, feel astonished on seeing the entire universe in the open mouth of the child, concealing the truth and afraid of the mother who was about to scold him for eating clay, the evidence for which was provided by his own dusty hands and body.

न तु यथा मम मुनिमतमीमांसायाम्–

समस्ताश्चर्याणां जलनिधिरपारः सवसति–
स्ततोऽप्याश्चर्यं यत्पिबति सकलं तं किल मुनिः।
इदं त्वत्याश्चर्यं लघुकलशजन्मापि यदसौ
परिच्छेत्तुं को वा प्रभवति तवाश्चर्यसरणिम्।।

अत्रापारसरित्पतिप्रभावेण मुनिना तस्यैकचुलकाचमनेन मुनेश्च लघुकलशजन्मना क्रमाक्रान्तिसमारूढोऽप्यसमविस्मयमयोऽयमद्भुतप्रसरः संसारस्यैवंविधैवाश्चर्यसरणिरपरिच्छिन्ना न किंचितेदतत्कौतुकमित्यर्थान्तरन्याससामर्थ्येन सहसैवावरोपित इव तिरोभूततामुपगतः।

But not as in my *munimatamīmāṁsā*—

'The boundless ocean in the object of great wonder with all the abodes in its interior; but it is still more wonderful that, as has been heard, a sage drinks it up; but it is the most wonderful that he was born of a small pitcher. Or rather, who can fathom your long series of wonderful deeds?'

Here, by (the act of) the sage drinking the coean in (jsut) one draught as hapossessed the splendour of a boundless ocean, and by (the fact that) the sage was born of a small pitcher, this devlopment of the sentiment of Wonder, though getting deeper and deeper at every step, vanishes as if obscured by the fact of the intoduction of the figure of Corroboration, for there is no end to such series of wonders in the world.

शान्ते यथा मम चतुर्यर्गसंग्रहे–

भोगे रोगभयं सुखे क्षयभयं वित्तेऽग्निभूभृद्भयं
दास्ये स्वामिभयं गुणे खलभयं वंशे कुयोषिद्भयम्।
माने म्लानिभयं जये रिपुभयं काये कृतान्ताद्भयं
सर्वं नाम भवे भवेद्ध यमहो राग्यमेवाभयम्।।

अत्र सकलजनाभिमतभोगसुखवित्तादीनां भयमयतया हेयतां प्रतिपाद्य वैराग्यमेव सकलभयायासशग्नमुपादेयतया यदुपन्यस्तं तेन शान्तरसस्य निरर्गलमार्गावतरणमुचिततरमुपदिष्टं भवति।

(Propriety) in the sentiment of Tranquility as in my *Caturvargasaṅgrahu*—

'In the enjoyment of pleasures (there is) the fear of disease and the fear of decay attends happiness; (there is) the fear of king and fire to riches; in services is the feart of the master; to the virtuous, of the wicked; to one born in a high family, of a bad wife. In one's self-pride is the fear of decline, in victory is the fear of enemy, and in the body is the fear of death. In regard to everything in the world, there is fear. (But) ah! renunciation alone knows no fear'.

Here, having first exposed the inferiority of enjoyments, comfort and wealth which are dear to people, by showing that they are full of fear, the unimpeded growth of the sentiment of Tranquillty is properly shown by mentioning in a suitable manner that renunciaton alone is acceptable as it puts to rest all fears and sufferings.

यथा वा मम मुनिमतमीमांसायाम्–

कुसुमशयनं पाषाणो वा प्रियं भवनं वनं
प्रतनु मसृशस्पर्शं वासस्त्वगप्यथ तारवी।
सरसमशनं कुल्माषो[1] वा धनानि तृणानि वा
शमसुखसुधापानक्षैब्ये समं हि महात्मनाम्।।

अत्र सकलविकल्पतल्परहिताभेदावभासमानात्मतत्त्वविश्रान्तिजनितसर्वसाम्य-समुल्लसितशमसुखपीयूषपानोदितनित्यानन्दपूर्णमानमानसानां प्रियाप्रियसुखदुःखादिषु महतां सदृशी प्रतिपत्तिरिति जीवन्मुक्तिसमुचितमभिहितम्।

Or as in my *Munimatamīmāṁsā*—

'A bed of flowers or stones, a beautiful house or a forest, extremely fine clothes of delightful touch or barks of trees, tasty food or sour gruel, wealth or blades of grass—all these are of equal value to the high-souled ones, who are intoxicated with the wine of the dlelihg ot tranquillity'.

The remarks herein become of those emancipated while still alive, viz. the great, who harbour the same feelings towards friends or foes, in weal or woe; for their minds reel in an unending delight which arises from drinking deep the ambrosia of the pleasures of composure, which results from a sense of

1. यवपिष्टम्।

equanimity produced by the knowledge of the Self, and which dispels all ideas of seeming differences relying on concepts of duality.

नतु यथा श्रीमदुत्पलराजस्य–

अहो वा हारे वा बलवति रिपौ वा सुहृदि वा
मणौ वा लोष्टे वा कुसुमशयने वा दृषदि वा।
तृणे वा स्त्रैणे वा मम समदृशो यान्ति दिवसाः
क्वचित्पुण्यारण्ये शिवशिवशिवेति प्रलपतः।।

अत्र जीवन्मुक्तोचितं प्रियाप्रियरागद्वेषोपशमलक्षणमोक्षक्षमं सर्वसाम्यमहिहारसुहृदरिसमदृष्टिरूपमभिदधता क्वचित्पुण्यारण्ये यदभिहितं तद्विकल्पप्रतिपादकमभेदवासनाविरुद्धमनुचितमवभासते। धाराधिरूढसर्वसाम्यविगलित-भेदाभिमानग्रन्थेर्हि सर्वत्र सर्वं शिवमयं पश्यतस्तपोवने नगरावस्करकूटे[1] च विकलात्मलाभतृप्ततया समानदृशः क्वचित्पुण्यारण्यादिवचनमनुचितोच्चारणमेव।। १६।।

But not as in Śrī Utpalarāja's (verse)—

'Making no difference between a snake and a necklace, a powerful enemy and a friend, a jewel and a clod of clay, a stone and a bed of flowers, a blade of grass and women folk my days pass in a holy forest as I utter, "Śiva, Śiva, Śiva".

Here, while speaking of a sense of equanimity for everything, which is proper for one who is liberated even before death from all liabilities of future births, which is capable of bringing emancipation marked by cessation of any sense of likes and dislikes or of love and hate, and which amounts to the absence of any discrimination between a snake and a necklace, a friend and a foe, the mention of "some holy forest" diverts one's attention and looks improper being contrary to the statement of indifference (towards everything, as already mentioned). For one, who has got into the habit of regarding everything equal, and whose egoism and sense of differentiation have vanished, and who, being satisfied by realizing his pure self, regarding everything equal and seeing good everywhere, looks upon a penance grove and a heap of night soil of a city as the same, the utterance of the words 'holy forest' etc. is highly unbecoming.

---

1. पुरस्थविष्ठासमुदाये।

यथा मधुरतिक्ताद्या रसाः कुशलयोजिताः।
विचित्रास्वादतां यान्ति श्रृङ्गाराद्यास्तथा मिथः।। १७।।

17. Just as the sweet, bitter and other flavours, when mixed cleverly, taste wonderfully, similarly the erotic and other sentiments. When put together in a clever way, provide indescribable (lit. strange) joy.

तेषां परस्पराश्लेषात्कुर्यादौचित्यरक्षणम्।
अनौचित्येन संस्पृष्टः कस्येष्टो रससङ्करः।। १८।।

18. One should maintain propriety when putting together the sentiments, (for) to whom is the mixture of sentiments, touched by impropriety, welcome?

रसाः कटफकमधुराम्ललवणाद्याः कुशलसूदेन वेसवार[1] पानादिषु योजिता विचित्रास्वादतामुपयान्ति तथैव परस्परमविरुद्धाः श्रृङ्गारादय इति तेषामन्योन्यमङ्गभावयोजनायामौचित्यस्य जीवितसर्वस्वभूतस्य रक्षां कुर्यात्। अनौचित्यरजसा रससंयोगः स्पृष्टो न कस्यचिदभिमत इत्यर्थः।

Sweet, bitter, sour, saltish and other tastes mixed in the 'veśavāra' (a kind of drink) seasoned with coriander, mustard, pepper, ginger etc., by a clever cook, taste wonderful; similarly do the Erotic and other sentiments when mixed together but no inconsistent with one another. One should preserve propriety, the very life (of poetry), when putting these together as constituents and the constituted. Touched with (even a particle of) the dirt of impropriety the mixture of sentiments is not liked by anyone. That is the idea.

रससङ्करौचित्ये शान्तश्रृङ्गारयोरङ्गाङ्गिभावो यथा भगवतो महर्षेर्व्यासरय–

सत्यं मनोरमा रामाः सत्यं रम्या विभूतयः।
किन्तु मत्ताङ्गनापाङ्गभङ्गिलोलं हि जीवितम्।।

अत्र भगवता जन्तुहिताभिनिविष्टेन मोक्षक्षमोपदेशेऽङ्गिनः शान्तरसस्य रागिजनानिष्टत्वात्सकल जनमनःप्रह्लादने बालगुडजिह्विकया शङ्गारेऽङ्गभावमुपनीते पर्यन्ते शान्तस्यैव लोलं जीवितमित्यनित्यताप्रतिपादनपरिनिर्वाहेण परममौचित्यमुच्चैः कृतम्।

In regard to the propriey of mingling together the sentiments

1. शुण्ठ्यादिचूर्णपानादौ।

e.g., the mixing of Quietism and Eroticism as the principal and subordiate constituents, just refer to sage Vyāsa—

'Verily damsels are heart-bewitching, verily the riches are enjoyable; but life is as unsteady as the twinkling of the eye-corner of an infatuated woman'.

Here the Illustrious One, devoted to do good to all the living beings, (while advising for emancipation, which constitutes the sentiment of Quietism, which is not longed for by the amorous people), has made the erotic sentiment as a subordinate constituent, just as (one puts) unrefined sugar on the tongues of the child (before giving him medicine); and in the end, by firmly establishing that life is fickle, he has brought into prominence the propriety of the sentiment of Quietism.

बीभत्सश्रृङ्गारयोरङ्गाङ्गिभावो यथा मम बौद्धावदानकल्पलतायाम्–

श्रीबस्येवाचलस्य दुतहृतहृदया जम्बुकी कण्ठसक्ता
रक्ताभिव्यक्तकामा कमति नखमुखोल्लेखमासूत्रयन्ती।
आस्वाद्यास्वाद्य यूनः क्षणमधरदलं दत्तदन्तव्रणाङ्कं
लग्नानङ्गक्रियायामियमतिरभ्सोत्कर्षमाविष्करोति।।

अत्र श्लेषोपमया तुल्यकक्षाधिरूढयोरपि परस्परविरुद्धयोरर्थयोर्बीभत्सश्रृङ्गाराङ्गाङ्गिभावयोजनायां जम्बुकी तरुणशवस्य क्षीबस्येव निश्चलस्थितेः सहसैव हृतहृदयपद्मा कृष्ठचित्ता वा, कण्ठे लग्ना शोणिते भृशमभिव्यक्तस्पृहा रक्ताभिव्यक्तकामा वा, नखोल्लेखमासूत्रयन्ती दत्तंदन्तवणमधरमास्वाद्याङ्गच्छेदक्रियायामनङ्गभोगक्रियायां वा, लग्ना गात्राणामूर्ध्वगतं कर्षणं रतकौशलोत्कर्षं वा, प्रकाशयतीति समानयोर्बीभत्सश्रृङ्गारयोः कामिनीपदपरित्यागेन केवलं जम्बुक्याः कर्तृ त्वेन बीभत्सस्यैव प्राधान्ये श्रृङ्गारेऽङ्गतामपुगते वक्तुबाधिसत्त्वस्यान्तर्गतगाढवैराग्यवासनाधिवासितचे तसः कुत्सार्हजुगुप्सया नितम्बिनीरतिविडम्बनमौचित्यरुचितरामादधाति। यद्यप्यत्र महावाक्ये शान्तस्यैव प्राधान्यं तथाप्युदाहरणश्लोकवाक्ये बीभत्सस्यैव।

The Repulsive and the Erotic in relation as principal and subordinate constituents are (illustrated) as in my *Bauddhāvadānakalpalatā*—

'Quickly seizing the heart of (a dead body) lying still like an intoxicated person, clinging to its neck, showing its craving for blood, producing scratches on its face with its nials, a she-jackal looks charming, having tasted again and again the sprout-like lower lip of (the dead) young man; and giving a scar-mark of teeth-bite, it is busy in hacking its (the dead body's) limbs and in lifting them up with great vehemence'.

Here, by means of a simile containing double entendre, a mixture of the Erotic and the Repulsive sentiments both of equal importance, but contradicting each other, has been shown, the Repulsive being the principal and the Erotic the subordinte one. A she-jackal (or a lady on the other hand) is represented as 'snatching away the heart' of a fresh corpse lying still or 'attracting the mind of an intoxicated one', 'clinging to its neck' or 'embracing him', 'exhibiting its great desire for blood' or 'showing her passion', 'making scratches with the nails and tasting the lower lip, leaving its marks there while cutting off the limbs' or 'doing the same thing in amorous sport', 'dragging the limbs' or 'showing excellence in erotic pleasures', while (the verb) "exhibits" can be applied to both the Erotic or Repulsive sentiments. By simply omitting the word woman and making the she-jackal the subject of the sentence the Repulsive has become the main sentiment (while) the Erotic (occupies) a subordinate position. The speaker being a Bodhisattva with his mind full of strong (feeling) for renunciation, the mockery of the enjoyment of woman's love, through abominable disgust, carries charming propriety with it. Though in the principal sentence the sentiment of Quietism is predominant as a whole, yet in the illustrative sentence in the stanza, the sentiment of Repulsiveness is made definitely prominent.

चीरकरुणयोर्यथा मम मुनिमतमीमांसायाम्–

गाण्डीवस्त्रुवमार्जनप्रणयिनः स्नातस्य बाष्पाम्बुभि–
श्चण्डं खाण्डवपावकादपि परं शोकानलं बिभ्रतः।
जिष्णोर्नूतनयौवनोदयदिनच्छिन्नाभिमन्योश्चिरं
हा वत्सेति बभूव सैन्धववधारब्धाभिचारे जपः।।

अत्र त्रिगर्तसङ्ग्रामगतस्य गाण्डीवधन्वनः शत्रुभिर्नवयौवनोदयसमयनिहत–तनयस्यकार्मुकस्त्रुवमुन्मार्जयतः प्रसरदश्रुस्नातस्य शोकाग्निमुद्वहतश्चिरं हा पुत्रेति जयद्रथवधारब्धाभिचारे जपो बभूवेति यदुपन्यस्तं, तेनारिक्षये दीक्षासमुचितव्रतवर्णनया शोकाग्नेश्चण्डत्वेन खाण्डवपदोदीरणेन वीररसस्याङ्गिनः सहसैवागन्तके करुणरसे प्रज्वलिते सैन्धववाधारब्धाभिचाराभिधानेन पर्यन्ते शौर्यनिर्वाहेण परममौचित्यमुज्जृम्भते।

The mixture of the sentiments of Heroism and Pathos as in my *Munimatamīmāṁsā*—

'The victorious one, whose (son) Abhimanyu had departed from him from all time in his fresh youth, who was busy cleansing the ladle of (his bow) Gāṇḍīva, who was bathed in tears and was bearing the fire of grief more intense than the great conflagration of the Khāṇḍava forest, was uttering to himself : "Alas, my son"; and it became his preliminary incantation for conjuring up the death of the king of the Sindhus (i.e. Jayadratha)'.

Here, Arjuna (lit. one wielding the Gāṇḍīva) bow whose son was killed by his enemy in the bloom of youth, while he himself was fighting with the Trigartas, and who was batehd in a torrent of tears was cleansing the ladle of his bow, and was bearing the fire of grief, repeated continuously, 'Alas' my son', which was a preliminary incantation to kill Jayadratha. This statement shows great propriety of the sentiment of Heroism which is the principal one here, by describing the vow which is proper to one initiated into the act of destroying one's foes, by the mention of the word khāndana and there by hinting at the fero city of the fire of grief, even though the introducing sentiment of Pathos had been flared up all at once by the mention of the magic spell to bring about the death of Jayadratha.

शान्तश्रृङ्गारकरुणबीभत्सानां यथा मम तत्रैव–

तीक्ष्णान्तस्त्रीकटाक्षक्षतहृदयतया उयक्तसंसक्तरक्ताः
क्रोधादिक्रूररोगव्रणगणगणनानीततीव्रव्यथार्ताः ।
स्नेहक्लेदातिळग्नैः कुमिभिखि सुतेः स्वाङ्जैर्भक्ष्यमाणाः।
स्नेहक्लेशशय्यानिपतिततनवः पश्य सीदन्ति मन्दाः।।

अत्र मुख्यस्याङ्गिनः शान्तरसस्यैवोद्दीपने कारणीभूतास्तीक्ष्णान्तस्त्रीकटाक्षक्षतहृदयव्यथार्तस्नेहक्लेदातिलग्नकृमितुल्यतनयादिपदोपादानेन श्रृङ्गारकरुणबीभत्साः शान्तमुखप्रेक्षिणः संलीनतया स्तिमितवृत्तयो भृत्या इव परममौचित्यं दर्शयन्ति।

(A proper combination of) the sentiments of Quietism, Eroticism, Pathos and Repulsion, as in the same work of mine—

'Look at these unlucky folks suffering distress, with their bodies lying on the bed of affliction of this world, exhibiting attachment and passion, their hearts being pierced with the extremely sharp sidelong glances of women, afflicted with countless tortures cause by the wounds of anger and other tormenting maladies, being eaten up by their own progeny to whom they are greatly attached on account of affection for them like worms born of one's own body, and eating it up with fondness for its grease'.

Here, the Erotic, Pathetic and Repulsive sesntiments exhibited by the phrases, e.g., 'hearts distressed with the affliction of being pierced with sharp side-long glances of women', and 'worm them'—all act as the means of exciting the Quietistic sentiment which is the principal one. These (Erotic, Pathetic and Repulsive sentiments) being secondary (in the sentence) and subordinate to the Quietistic sentiment look extremely proper like assiduous servants with gentle and respectful behaviour.

रससङ्करस्यानौचित्मुद्भावयितुमाह। श्रृङ्गारशान्तयोर्यथाऽमरकस्य–

गन्तव्यं यदि नाम निश्चितमहो गन्तासि केयं त्वरा
द्वित्राण्येव पदानि तिष्ठतु भावन्पश्यामि यावन्मुखम्।
संसारे घटिकाप्रणालविगलद्वारा समे जीविते
को जानाति पुनस्त्वया सह मम स्याद्वा न वा संगमः।।

अत्र प्रकरणवर्तिनः श्रृङ्गाररसस्य पश्यामि यावन्सुखमित्युत्कण्ठोत्कण्ठासमुज्जृम्भ माणस्य स्वभावविरोधिनि शान्तेऽङ्गभावमुपनीते विस्तीणैतरानित्यतावर्णनया वैराग्येण रतेर्न्यग्भावमापादयन्त्या प्रधानरससंबन्धेनाधिकमनौचित्यमुत्साहितम्। निःसारसंसाराचारुताश्रवणेन हि कठिनक्रियाक्र रचेतसामप्युत्साहभङ्गादङ्गान्यलसीभवन्ति, किमुत कुसुमसुकुमारश्रृङ्गाररसकोमलमनसां विलासवताम्। प्रान्ते च शान्तपरिणेषनिर्वाहेण रागवैरस्यमेव पयवस्यति।

Now in order to make the reader apphrehend the impropriety in the combination of sentiments, (the author) says. (An improper) combination of the Erotic and the Quietistic as inAmaruka's (verse)—

'Well, if you have to go, you will go; where is the (need for) hurry? Stay just for a while (lit. padāni etc. i.e. the time in taking three steps or so), that I may see your face. Who knows whether I will meet you again or not, in this world, where life is passing away like the trickling of water from a water-pot dial?'

An extreme impropriety has been ventured here by making the

Quietistic sentiment, naturally opposed to the sentiment of Love, a dependent constituent of the Erotic sentiment which pervades the composition and which was rising higher and higher (with the words) "while I see" etc., and by the detailed descritpion, harping for a long time on the fickleness of the world and ranking passion lower than renunciation and thus associating an irrelevant sentiment. On hearing the ugliness of the transitory world, even those whose minds have been hardened with cruel deeds give way to languidness, their courage being broken down, much less the coquettish people whose minds are already softened by the sentiment of Eroticism, tender like a flower. In the end, by developing the Quietistic sentiment, the insipidity of flavour alone pervades (the composition).

तदुक्त मानन्दवर्धनेन–

विरोधी वाऽविरोधी वा रसोऽङ्गिनि रसान्तरे।
परिपोषं न नेतव्यस्तेन स्यादविरोधिता।।

तदेवात्र वैपरीत्येनोपलभ्यते। परिपोषविपरीते स्वभावविरोधिन्यपि प्रधानानुपरोध एव।

Ānandavardhana has also remarked—

'A sentiment, whether opposite (to the main flavour)or not, should not be developed into another sentiment which in itself is a principal sentiment. By that means alone there can result non-contradiction'.

The same rule has not been observed here. (The subordinate sentiment) which is naturally opposed (to the main flavour) has even been developed as if unconflicting with the principal sentiment.

यथा राजशेखरस्य–

[1]माणं मुंचध देह वल्लहजणे दिट्ठिं तरंगुत्तरं
तारुण्णं दिअहाइं पञ्च दह वा पीणत्थणत्थंभणं।
इत्थं कोइलिमंजुसिंजिणमिसाद्देवस्स पंचेसुणो
दिण्णा चित्तमहूसवेण सहसा आणब्व सब्वंकसा।।

1. मानं मुञ्चत दत्त वल्लभजनेदृष्टिं तरङ्गोत्तरां तारुण्यं दिवसानि पञ्च दश वा पीनस्तनस्तम्भनम्। इत्यं कोकिलमञ्जुरिञ्चितमिषाद्देवस्य पञ्चेषोर्दत्ता चैत्रमहोत्सवेन सहसाऽऽज्ञेव सर्वकषा।। इति छाया

अत्र 'मानं' मुञ्चत ददत वल्लभजने दृष्टिं तरङ्गितां तारुण्यं दिनानि पञ्च दश वा पीनस्तनस्तम्भनमित्थं काकिलमधुरध्वनिव्याजेन देवस्य पञ्चेषोश्चैत्रमहोत्सवेनाज्ञेव सर्वंकषा दत्ता' इति वाक्ये मुख्यः श्रृङ्गाररसः प्रारम्भपर्यन्तव्याप्तिशाली कतिपयदिवसस्थायि यौवनमित्यनित्यतारूपशान्तरसबिन्दुना मध्यब्रुडितेनेव स्थायी कुञ्जर इव श्वभ्रपातितः पुनरुत्थातुं नोत्सहत इत्यल विस्तरेण। अनया दिशा रससङ्करे भेदप्रपञ्चौचित्यं विपश्चिद्भिः स्वथं विचार्यम्।। १८।।

As in Rājaśekhara's (verse)—

'Give up arrogance. cast your tremulous glance on your beloved. Youth, stiffening the well-developed breasts, endures for five or ten days'. Thus under the guise of the lovely cooings of the cuckoo, the Festival of Spring issued the irresistible commands of the god of Love.

Here, in the statement, 'leave aside your arrogance, cast the tremulous glance on your beloved; youth which stiffens the well-developed breasts (lasts) for (just) five or ten days, through those lovely cooings of the cuckoo, the Spring Festival issued, as it were, the order of the god of Love which affects all'—the predominant Erotic sentiment, pervading the whole of the composition from beginning to end, does not grow insipid with a drop of the Quietistic sentiment which flounders in the mid-way having been hinted by the bare mention showing the transient character (of the world), 'youth stays for a few days'. (This is so) because the (opposite) sentiment has not been developed. By the impropriety arising out of the description of the opposite (sentiment) the main sentiment cannot rise to its full height, just as an elephant, fallen in a pit, cannot rise again; so enough of it. In like manner, the learned (readers) should themselves discern the different varieties of propriety in the process of mixing them (i.e. the sentiments).

रसौचित्यविचारानन्तरमुद्देशानुसारकमेण क्रमोपगतं क्रियापदौचित्यं दर्शयितमाह–

सगुणत्व सुवृत्तत्वं साधुता च विराजते।
काव्यस्य सुजनस्येव यद्यौचित्यवती क्रिया।। १९।।

Having dealt with the propriety of sentiment, (now), in order to show propriety in the verb, which comes next in order, (the author) remarks—

19. The excellence, the lovely metre, and the goodness of a poem become prominent (lit. shine) if the verb is proper, just as the virtues, the behaviour and the noblity of a person shine, if his deeds are good.

काव्यस्य माधुर्यादिगुणवत्ता वसन्ततिलकादिसुवृत्तता परिपूर्णलक्षणसाधुता च विराजते, यद्यौचित्ययुक्तं क्रियापदं भवति। सुजनस्येवेति तत्तुल्यत्वं स्पष्टार्थमेव।।

Being possessed of merits such as sweetness and others, having good metres like vasantatilakā and the rst, full of exquisiteness in the form of possessing all the good points, a poem beams with brightness if the verb is proper. (The phrase) "as of a noble person" etc. needs no explanation as the comparison is obvious.

क्रियापदौचित्यं यथा मम नीतिलतायाम्–

यः प्रख्यातजवः सदा स्थितिविधौ सप्ताब्धिसंध्यार्चने
दोर्दर्पेण निनाय दुन्दुभिवपुर्यः कालकङ्कालताम्।
यः पातालमसृङ्मयं प्रविदधे निष्पिष्य मायाविनं
सुग्रीवाग्र्यविभूतिलुण्ठनपटुर्वाली स किं स्मर्यते।।

अत्र सप्ताब्धिसंध्यार्चनप्रख्यातजवो महिषरूपदुन्दुभिदानवोन्माथी मायाविदानव-निष्पेषाद्भूतशोणितपूरितपातालतलः स किं वाली स्मर्यत इति क्रियापदेन शुकासारणाभ्यां रावणस्य दुर्नयाभिनिवेशिनस्तद्विरामाग हितोपदेशेन भवान्वसनक्रोणनियमिततनुः कक्षायां निःक्षिप्त इत्युचितयुक्तमुक्तं भवति।।

Propriety in the verb as in my *Nītilatā*—

'Do you remember Vālin who was famous for his speed in regularly performing Sandhyā at the seven oceans, morning and evening, and who by the force (lit. pride) of his arms reduced the body of Dundubhi to the state of a lifeless (or dreadful) skeleton, who by pounding Māyāvin filled the nether world with gore, and who was clever (i.e. powerful) enough to spoil the splendour of Sugrīva'.

Here, by means of the verb in the sentence—'do you remember that Vālin, whose speed is well-known by his worshipping the seven oceans at twilight, who was the killer of the demon Dundubhi (appearing) in the form of a buffalo, and who filled the nether world with blood coming out of (the body) of the domon Māyāvin when killed'—the sense has been properly conveyed by Śuka and Sāraṇa giving a wholesome piece of advice to check Rāvaṇa intent on evil ways viz., You were thrown under his armpit, your body having been squeezed in the corner of his garment.

न तु यथा श्रीप्रवरसेनस्य–

सग्गं अपारिजाअं कोत्थुहलच्छिरहिअं महुमहस्स उरं।
सुमिरामि महणपुरओ समुद्धअन्दं हरअडापब्भारं।।

अत्र जाम्बुवतामिधोयमाने 'स्वर्गमपारिजातं कौस्तुभलक्ष्मीभ्यां विरहितं मधुमधनस्योरः, स्मराम्यमृतमथनपुरतोऽप्यबालचन्द्रं हरजटाप्राग्भारम्' इति प्रगुणगुणाख्यानप्रसङ्गे क्रियापदेन जराजर्जरशरीरत्वमात्रमेव प्रतिपादितम्। न तु पौरुषोत्कर्षविशेषातिशयः कश्चिदुचितः संसूचितः।।१९।।

But not as in Śrī Pravarasena's (verse)—

'I well remember the mass of Hara's matted hair bereft of the bright moon before the churning of the ocean, when even the heavens had no desire-yielding celestial tree (Pārijāta) and Viṣṇu had neither the Kaustubha jewel nor the goddess of Wealth.'

Here, in the staement of Jāmbavān, viz., I have in my memory the mass of Hara's matted hair bereft of the moon before the churning of the ocean, when the heavens had no Pārijāta tree, and neither was there Kaustubha nor Lakṣmī on the bosom of Viṣṇu, concerning the narration of the virtues of the Exalted One,—the verb simply signifes a body broken with age. Nothing becoming has been said which raises to any excellence the prowess (of Jāmbavān).

कारकौचित्यं दर्शयितुमाह–

सान्वयं शोभते वाक्यमुचितैरेव कारकैः।
कुलाभरणमैश्वर्यमौदार्यचरितैरिव ।।२०।।

Now in order to show the propriety of cases, it is remarked—

20. The sentence with all its constituents looks bright with proper syntactical cases, just as riches, which are an ornament to a high family, look lustrous with deeds of magnanimity.

उचितैरेव कारकैः सदन्वयवद्वाक्यं विराजते सद्वंशभूषितमैश्वर्यं सच्चरितैरिव।।

A sentence, syntactically suitable, looks charming as the wealth of a high family (looks bright) with noble deeds.

कर्तृपदौचित्यं यथा भट्टाबाणस्य–

स्तनयुगमश्रुस्नातं समीपतरवर्ति हृदयशोकाग्नेः।
चरति विमुक्ताहारं व्रतमिव भवतो रिपुस्त्रीणाम्।।

अत्र शत्रुस्त्रियो व्रतं चरन्तीति वक्तव्ये, स्तनयुगं वाष्पसलिलस्नातं शोकाग्निसमीपचर्तिं विमुक्तभोजनं विगतमुक्ताहारं च सद्व्रतं चरतीत्युक्ते कर्तृपदमौचित्यमुपचितं जनयति।।

Propriety in the nominative case as in Bhaṭṭa Bāṇa's (verse)—

'The pair of the breasts of your enemies' wives is observing a vow, as it were, like one who has given up taking food, as these (breasts) are bathed in tears, remain close to the fire of grief burning in the heart, and are bereft of pearl-necklaces'.

Here, (the poet had simply) to say that the wives of the enemies are observing a vow; but the agent noun enhances the propriety when it is said that the breasts are bathed in the water of tears that remain claose to the fire of grief, and are bereft of pearl-necklaces, so they observe a vow.

न तु यथा परिमलस्य–

आहारं न करोति नाम्बु पिबति स्त्रैणं न संसेवते
शेते यत्सिकतासु मुक्तविषयश्चण्डातपं सेवते।।
त्वत्पादाब्जरजःप्रसादकणिकालोभोन्मुखस्तन्मरौ
मन्ये मालवसिंह! गुर्जरपतिस्तीव्रं तपस्तप्यते।।

अत्र गुर्जरपतिर्विद्रुतो मरुगहनं प्रविष्टः परित्यक्ताहारादिसमस्तविषयश्चण्डातपोपसेवी तपश्चरतीति यदुक्तं तत्कर्तृपदस्य विशेषाभिप्रायोचितं न किञ्चिदुपलक्ष्यते शत्रुत्रासतरलतया मरुकान्तारान्तरावसन्नः सकलविषयसुखभोगपरिभ्रष्टः किमन्यत्कुरुताम्। स्तनयुगचत्कर्तृपदस्य चमत्कारोचितं न किंचिदभिहितम्।।

But not as in Parimala's (verse)—

He does not take food, nor does he drink water. He does not mix with his women. Forsaking (the pleasure of) the senses, he sleeps on sands and suffers scorchign heat. I think, O Mālavasiṁha! that the lord of the Gurjaras, with a desire to obtain an atom of the dust of your lotus-like feet, is practising hard penance in the desert'.

Here, while saying that the lord of the Gurjaras, who had taken to flight and had entered desolate wilderness, had given up taking food and entertaining other desires and was bearing unbearable heat, and was thus practising severe penance, nothing has been said specailly worthy of the subject, for, what other experience could he have when he was in utter bewilderment at the harassment by the enemy and had taken shelter in a desolate wilderness and was deprived of all sensual enjoyment? Nothing charming and proper has been said of the subject unlike the previous verse "bathed in tears" etc.

कर्मपदौचित्यं यथा मम लावण्यवत्याम्–

सदा सक्तं शैत्यं विमलजलधारापरिचितं
घनोल्लासः क्ष्माभृत्पृथुकटकपाती वहति यः।
विधत्ते शौर्यश्रीश्रवणनवनीलोत्पलरुचिः
स चित्रं शत्रूणां ज्वलदनलतापं भवदसिः।।

अत्र निश्चलममलजलधारागतं शैत्यं तैक्ष्ण्यं शीतलत्वं व, घनोल्लासो निबिडात्साहः पर्जन्यतुल्योदयश्च, क्षमाभृतां सानुसैन्यनिपाती वहति स शौर्यश्रीश्रवणनवनीलोत्पल-तुल्यस्त्वत्सङ्गश्चित्रं शत्रूणां संतापं करोतीति यदुक्तं तत्कर्मभूतस्य तापस्य शिशिरतरसामग्रीजन्मनः परं वैचित्र्यं रुचिरमौचित्यमासूत्रितम्।।

Propriety in the accusative case as in my *Lāvaṇyavatī*—

'Your sword of the lusture of clouds smiting armies of the kings has always a coldness of the stream of limpid water (i.e. sharpness of its edge). (It) possessing the hue of the ear lotus of the goddess of valour', causes an affliction, cas if of blazing fire, to your enemies. It is strange indeed.'

Here, the Phruses, viz, Permanent Sharpness of the edge of the sword or coldness of water', of firm determination, or of the exaltation of the clouds, the Peaks or the armies; 'having the lustre of the ear lotus of the goddress 'the sword gives a strange affliction of heat to your enemies', impart a unique and charming propriety to the heat, which is said to have its sources in things which are cool by nature.

न तु यथा ममंवावसरसारे–

भग्नाहितश्वसितवातविबोध्यमानः काष्ठाश्रयेण[1] सहसैव विवृद्धिमासः।
तापं तनोति निहतारिविलासिनीनां वह्निद्युतिर्भुवननाथ! भवन्प्रतापः।।

1. दिग्रूपदारुसग्बन्धेन।

अत्र विद्रुतारातिनिःश्वसितानिलप्रबोध्यमानः काष्टाश्रयेण दिक्चक्रपूरणेन प्रौढतां प्राप्तः पावकतुल्यस्त्वत्प्रतापः शत्रुकान्तानां तापमात्रं तनोतीति तत्समुचितमाश्चर्यं न किंचित्।

But not as in my *Avasarasāra*—

'O lord of the world, your glory of fiery glow being kindled with the wind in the form of sighs of your defeated foes, and growing in flames all of a sudden having come in contact with the wood (in the form of directions), causes pain (or heat) to the wives of your dead foes.'

Hre, the statement viz. your glory resembling fire, being kindled by the wind of the sighs of foes who have been defeated and increasing by obtaining fuel in the form of quarters, causes only pain to the wives of the enemies—is usaul and contains nothing charming.

करणौचित्यं यथा गौडकुम्भकारस्य–

लाङ्गूलेन गभस्तिमान्वलयितः प्रोतः शशी मौलिना
व्याधूता जलदाः सटाभिरुडवो दंष्ट्राभिरुत्तम्भिताः।
प्रोत्तीर्णो जलधिर्दृशैव हरिणा स्वैराट्टहासोर्मिभि–
र्लङ्केशस्य च लङ्घितो दिशि दिशि प्राज्यः प्रतापानलः।।

अत्र हरिणा हनुमता जलनिधितरणे तरणिलाङ्ग्‌गूलेन वलयितः किरीटप्रान्तेन शशी प्रोतः सटाभिमेघा व्याधूतास्तारा दंष्ट्राभिरायासितास्तीर्णोऽब्धिर्दृष्ट्यैवाट्टहासतरङ्गैर्लङ्केशस्य विस्तीर्णः प्रतापाग्निः शमित इति बहुभिः करणपदैरुत्साहाधिवासितैर्विस्मय-शिखरारोहणसोपानैरिव रघुपतिप्रभावारम्भविजयध्वजायमानस्य पवनसूनोरौचित्यातिशयः प्रकाशितः।

Propriety in the instrumental case as in Gauḍakumbhakāra's (verse)—

'With his takl the sun was encircled; the moon was eclipsed by his crown; by his hair the clouds were scattered; thte stars were made to stay by his teeth; the ocean was crossed by his very gaze. and with the rippling series of his loud laughter, the extensive fire of glory of the king of Laṅkā was surpassed on all sides by the monkey'.

Here, the monkey Hanumān (at the time of) crossing the ocean, encircled the sun with his tail, eclipsed the moon with the edge of his crown, scattered the clouds with his hair, tortured the stars with his teeth, crossed the ocean with his gaze and extinguished the vast fire of Rāvaṇa's glory with the ripples of his loud laughter; the many words full of vigour, are as if steps to ascend the height of wonder; put in the instrumental case, they show the grat propriety of Hanumān (lit. son of wind) who acts as the banner of victory for the exalted power of Rāma.

जयत्युपेन्द्रः स चकार दूरतो बिभित्सया यः क्षणलब्धलक्ष्यया।
दृशैव कोपारुणया रिपोरुरः स्वयं भयाद्भिन्नमिवास्नपाटलम्।।

अत्र भगवतो नृसिंहस्य कोपरक्तया दृष्ट्यैव क्षणलब्धलक्ष्यया हिरण्यकशिपोर्वक्षः स्वयं भयाद्भिन्नमिवेति यदुक्तं तन्महोत्साहपराक्रमस्य प्रतिनायकस्य रिपोः प्रधाननायकप्रतापोद्दीपनोपकरणीभूताधिकधैर्यस्य स्वयं भयविह्वलतया हृदयस्फुटनमित्युपचितमनौचित्यं 'दृशैव' इति करणपदस्य शिरसि विश्रान्तम्।

But not as in Bhaṭṭa Bāṇa's (verse)—

'Victorious is Viṣṇu, who with the desire of striking his enemy from afar, catching sight of his mark for a moment with his wrath-inflamed eye, made his enemy's chest red as if it had burst of itself in terror'.

Here, in the sentence—Hiraṇyakaśipu's breast burst by itself by the mere glance of great Nṛsiṁha, red with rage, and catching sight of the mark for a moment, the bursting itself, out of fear, of the heart of the opponent of great steadiness and valour, whose great courage is to serve as the excitant towards the glory of the hero (has been described). The impropriety can be attributed to (lit. placed on the head of) the phrase 'by the mere sight' (dṛśaiva) put in the instrumental case.

सम्प्रदानौचित्यं यथा भट्टप्रभाकरस्य–

दिङ्मातङ्गघटाविभक्तचतुराघाटा मही साध्यते
सिद्धा सापि वदन्त एव हि वयं रोमाञ्चिताः पश्यत।
विप्राय प्रतिपाद्यते किमपरं रामाय तस्मै नमो
यस्मादाविरभूत्कथाद्भुतमिदं यत्रैव चास्तं गतम्।।

अत्र दिग्गजचतुरस्रा भूः साध्यते, सा च सिद्धा हेलवैयात्रमुष्टिरिवैकस्म विप्रमात्राय प्रतिपाद्यत इति निरतिशयौदार्याश्चर्यचमत्काररुचिरौचित्यचर्वणया क्यं रोमाञ्चाञ्चिताः पश्यत, रोमाञ्चस्य प्रत्यक्षपरिदृश्यमानत्वात्, किमपरमपूर्वत्यागिने भार्गवाय तस्मै नम इति विप्रायेति सम्प्रदानपदगत एवोत्कर्षविशेषः प्रकाशते।

Propriety in the (use of) the dative as in Bhaṭṭa Prabhākara's (verse)—

'The earth bounded on four sides by the mass of the quarter-elephants is subdued, while simply saying that it is subdued, look, we are horripilated. Even when subdued it is given to a Brāhmaṇa. What more (shall we say)? Salutations to that Rāma (i.e., Paraśurāma) with whom this wonderful deed began and with whom it ended too'.

Here, by dwelling on the charming propriety arisig from the amazing and extreme liberality expressed in (the statement), viz., the earth bounded by four quarter-elephants is subdued, and when subdued it is given away sportively to a mere Brāhmaṇa; look, our hair are standing on end—(the word 'look' has been used) because the horripilation could be clearly seen. "What else shall we say; our homage to that extremely charitable Bhārgava". Here, (it is only) in the expression "for the Brāhmaṇa" (viprāya) put in the dative that the acme is to be found.

न तु यथा राजशेखरस्य–

पौलस्त्यः प्रणयेन याचत इति श्रुत्वा मनो मोदते
देयो नैष हरप्रसादपरशुस्तेनाधिकं ताम्यति।
तद्वाच्यः स दशाननो मम गिरा दत्ता द्विजेभ्यो मही
तुभ्यं ब्रूहि रसातलत्रिदिवयोर्निर्जित्य किं दीयताम्।।

अत्र रावणदू तेन परशुं याचितो भार्गवो ब्रूते–'नैषहरप्रसादलब्धः परशुर्दानयोग्यः। तत्तस्मादस्मद्वसा स दशग्रीवो वाच्यः–पृथ्वी मया कश्यपाय प्रतिपादिता, तुभ्यं पातालत्रिदिवयोर्मध्यात्किं निर्जित्य दायताम्' इत्यनुचितं मुनेर्लोकहितप्रवृत्तस्य त्रैलोक्यकण्टकभूताय राक्षसाय भुवनप्रतिपादनम्।

But not as in Rājaśekhara's (verse)—

'My mind is filled with delight on hearing that Rāvaṇa (lit. son of Pulāstya) begs for something humbly, (but I feel distressed very much (when I think) that this battle-axe obtained through the pleasure of Śiva, is not to be given away. So, tell Rāvaṇa on my behalf that the earth has been given to the Brāhmaṇas (by me); which of the (remaining) two—the nether world or the heavens should I give to him after conquering it.'

When Rāvaṇa's messenger asked for the battle-axe, Paraśurāma says, "This battle-axe obtained by the favour of Śiva is not to be given away. So tell Rāvaṇa on my behalf that I have given the earth to Kaśyapa. Of the nether world or the heavens, which one should I conquer and bestow on you?" Here, it is improper for the sage, given to the welfare of the world to give a region to a demon who is a thorn of the three worlds.

अपादानौचित्यं यथा मालवरुद्रस्य–

एतस्माज्जलधेर्मिताम्बुकणिकाः काश्चिद्गृहीत्वा ततः
पाथोदाः परिपूरयन्ति जगतीं रुद्धाम्बरा वारिभिः।
भ्राम्यन्मन्दरकूटकोटिघटनाभीतिभ्रमत्तारकां
प्राप्यैकां जलमानुषीं त्रिभुवने श्रीमानभूदच्युतः।।

अत्र यदुक्तमेतस्मान्महोदधेः परिमिताम्बुकणिकाः प्राप्य जलदा जगत्पूरयन्ति, तथा भ्रमन्मनदरकूटकोटिसङ्घट्टत्रासतरलतारकामेकां जलमानुषीं श्रियं प्राप्य श्रीमानच्युतोऽभूदिति तेन सासरगतनिरतिशयोत्कर्षविशेषः प्रदर्शितः। तत्र एतस्माज्जलधेरित्येतत्पदमौचित्यस्य मूलभूमिः।

Propriety in (the use of) ablative, as in Mālavarudra's (verse)—

'Having taken a limited number of water-drops from this ocean, the clouds covering the firmament fill the whole world with waters. Obtaining just one nymph with her eyes still rolling for fear of striking against the millions of pinnacles of the moving Mandara (mountain), the Great One has become 'infallible' *(acyuta)* in all the three worlds'.

Here, by the statement—having taken a few drops of water from this ocean, the clouds fill the world (with water), and having obtained just one nymph, the Goddess of Wealth, with her eyes rolling in fear of striking against the millions of the pinnacles of Mandra (mountain), the Great One has become infalliable—(the poet) has shown the great glory of the ocean. Here the expression 'from this ocean' (= etasmāj jaladheḥ) is the basis of all propriety in the verse.

न तु यथा भट्टेन्दुराजस्य–

आदाय वारि परितः सरितां मुखेभ्यः किं नाम साधितमनेन महार्णवेन।
क्षारीकृतं च वडवादहने हुतं च पातालमूलकुहरे विनिवेशितं च।।

अत्र महार्णवव्यपदेशेनाऽन्यायोपार्जितद्रविणदुर्व्ययकारिणः सत्संविभागविमुखस्य कस्यचिदुच्यते। सरितां मुखेभ्यः समन्तात्तोयमादायापात्रेभ्यः प्रतिपादतं दूषितम्। यत्त्वत्र सरिद्भ्यः समादायेति वक्तव्ये सरिन्मुखेभ्य इति यदुक्तं मुखशब्दस्य नैरर्थक्यादत्रानौचित्यमेव पर्यवस्यति।

But not as in Bhaṭṭendurāja's (verse)—

'What purpose has this vast ocean served by taking water out of the mouths of the rivers all round? (It has either) made it sour or has poured it into the submarine fire or has placed it in the deepest caverns of the nether world'.

Here, the above remarks have been made under the pretext of addressing the ocean about one, who , having collected wealth unjustly, uses it improperly and does not distribute among suitable persons. (The statement)—having taken water from the mouths of the rivers, (it has) given to those not worthy of it—is defective. Here, (the poet) instead of saying "having taken from the rivers", has said, "from the mouths of the rivers", there is therefore impropriety here, because the word mouth is redundant.

अधिकरणौचित्यं यथा कुन्तेचरदौत्ये कालिदासस्य–

इह निवसति मेरुः शेखरः क्ष्माधराणामिह विनिहितभाराः सागराः सप्त चाऽन्ये।
इदमहिपतिभोगस्तम्भविभ्राजमानं धरणितलमिहैव स्थानमस्मद्विधानाम्।।

अत्र महाराजदूतोऽपि सामन्तास्थाने स्वप्रभुसमुचितगौरवपूजार्हमासनमनासाद्य कार्यवशेन भूमावेवोपविष्टः प्रागल्भ्यगाम्भीर्यणैवं ब्रूते–यथास्मद्विधानां वसुधातल एव भुजगपतिभोगस्तम्भप्राग्भारनिष्कम्पे धरासने स्थानं युक्तं यस्मादिहैव मेरुरचलचक्रवर्ती समुपविष्टः सप्तमहाब्धयश्च, तत्तुल्यतैवास्माकमित्यौचित्यमधिकरणपदसम्बद्धमेव।

Prorpiety in (the use of) the locative case as in Kālidāsa's (verse) in the *Kunteśvaradautya*—

On this lies the Meru, the crest-jewel of all the mountains; and, moreover, here lie the seven oceans with heavy loads inside; and here is the surface of the earth supported by the pillar-like hoods of the lord of snakes. This is the place (fit for) sitting for people like us'.

Here, even the embassy of the great king, not getting the seat, worthy of the pride and respect of his lord, consequently sits on the earth in the assembly hall and speaks eloquently and with serenity. "it is proper for people like us to sit on the ground, immovable with the mass of the pillar-like hoods of the lord of snakes (i.e. *śeṣanāga);* since it is here that the lord of mountains—Meru—stays, as also the seven oceans, and I am like them". Here the propriety lies in the word in the locative case.

न तु यथा परिमलस्य–

तत्र स्थितं स्थितिमतां वर देव! दैवाद्भृत्येन ते चकितचित्तमियन्त्यहानि।
उत्कम्पिनि स्ततनटे हरिणेक्षणानां हारान्प्रवर्तयति यत्र भवत्प्रतापः।।

अत्र त्वद्भृत्येन मया तत्र तस्तिन्देशे स्थितं यत्र भवत्प्रतापः कम्पतरलस्तनतटे हरिणदृशां हारान्प्रवर्तयतीति यदुक्तं तेन शौर्यशृङ्गारगुणोत्कर्षस्तुतौ सर्वतो दिग्गमनाविच्छिन्नप्रसरः प्रतापः पारिमित्यं प्राप्तः। एकत्र परिच्छिन्ने देशे मया तत्र स्थितं यत्र त्वत्प्रतापस्तरुणीस्तनतटेषु हारतरलनं करोत्यन्यदेशे विलक्षणमुपलक्षणम्। सर्वयत्र त्वत्प्रतापस्तरुणीस्तनतटेषु हारतरलनं करोत्यन्यदेशे विलक्षणमुपलक्षणम्। सर्वगतश्चेत्प्रतापस्तत्सर्वत्रैव मया स्थितमिति वक्तव्ये तत्रेत्येकदेशाभिधायायि पदं नोपपद्यते, दस्युमात्रस्याप्येकदेशे जृम्भाणप्रतापत्वात्। तदत्राधिकरणपदगतमनौचित्यमुपलभ्यते। तत्र तत्र मया स्थितं यत्र यत्र भवत्प्रताप इत्येव स्तुत्युचिंत युक्तमुक्तं स्यात्।। २०।।

But not as in Parimala's (verse)—

'O my lord best of those possessed of stability as luck would have, (this) servant (of yours), with his mind filled with wonder, stayed all those days there, where your glory even turns round the necklaces on the bank-like throbbing breasts of the fawn-eyed ladies (of your enemies)'.

Here, the statement viz. your servant (i.e. I) lived in that country where your glory makes the necklace roll on the throbbing declivity of breasts of the fawn-eyed ladies of your enemies, though highly commendable because of the (combination) of the sentiments of heroism and eroticism, has set a limit to glory, though its extension cannot be checked even when it reaches the ends of the quarters. (It amounts to saying), "In a certain out of the way country I lived at a place where your glory makes the necklace toss about on the declivity of the breasts of the enemies ladies, (while) in other countries, (this act) is (thought to be) a strange observation'. If the glory pervades every part of the country, the expression, "I stayed everywhere" ought to have been used, and thus the word "there" (tatra) is improper as it refers to only one particular country because even a robber may be flourishing in his own province. Here we find impropriety in the locative case. "I satyed in all the places where your glory existed" would be well-said in an eulogy.

लिङ्गौचित्यं दर्शयितुमाह–

उचितेनैव लिङ्गेन काव्यमायाति भव्यताम्।
साम्राज्यसूचकेनेव शरीरं शुभलक्ष्मणा।। २१।।

In order to show propriety in gender, (the author) says—

21. A composition becomes beautiful by the use of proper genders; just as the body looks beautiful with auspicious marks indicative of sovereignty.

प्रस्तुतार्थोचितेन लिङ्गेन काव्यं भव्यतामुपयाति, राजलक्षणेनेव शरीरम्।

By the gender suiting the context, the composition becomes beautiful, as the body does with royal insignia.

यथा मम ललितरत्नमालायाम्–

निद्रां न स्पृशति त्यजत्यपि धृतिं धत्ते स्थितिं न क्वचि-
द्दीर्घां वेत्ति कथां व्यथां न भजते सर्वात्मना निर्वृतिम्।
तेनाराधयता गुणस्तवजपध्यानेन रत्नावलीं
निःसङ्गेन पराङ्गनापरिगतं नामापि नो सह्यते।।

अत्र वत्सेश्वरस्य रत्नावलीविरहविधुरचेतसः स्मरावस्थासमुचितं विदूषकेण सुसङ्गतायै यदभिहितम्–निद्रां न स्पृशति, धृतिं त्यजति, स्थितिं न धत्ते, दीर्घां कथां व्यथामिव वेत्ति, निर्वृतिं भजते, तां विना तेन तद्गुणजापिना तद्ध्याननित्येन जनसङ्गत्यागिनाऽन्यासामङ्गनानां नाममपि न सह्यत इति। तत्र स्थितिधृतिकथानिर्वृतीनां स्त्रीलिङ्गाभिधानेनाङ्गत्वाध्यारोपेण परममौचित्यं प्रतिपादितम्।

As in my *Lalitaratnamālā*—

'He does not enjoy (lit. touch) sleep, has forsaken his courage, does not stay for long anywhere, considers a long story boring, finds solace nowhere. Thinking of Ratnāvalī and concentrating on her by repeating the praise of her virtues, he, avoiding all company, cannot bear even the name of another woman (uttered before him)'.

Here, the Jester speaks to Sausaṅgatā (these words) befitting the state of the love-sick king of vatsa, with his mind grieved at his separation from Ratnāvalī. "He gets no sleep, has forsaken all courage, is restless, considers a long story boring, finds no peace, and without her, always repeating her virtues and thinking of her, and leaving all company, does not bear even the name of other women"—here, in putting constancy, courage, story and composure in the feminine gender, and by conforming (their gender) to (that of) the main (object of the verse i.e. Ratnāvalī), extreme propriety is shown.

न तु यदा मम नीतिलतायाम्–

वरुणरणसमर्था स्वर्गभङ्गैः कृतार्था यमनियमनशक्ता मारुतोन्माथसक्ता।
धनदनिधनसज्जा लज्जते मर्त्ययुद्धे दहनदलनचण्डा मण्डली मद्भुजानाम्।।

अत्र रावणः कपिनिकारामर्षविषमविकाराविष्कारोचितं ब्रूते– 'वरुणादिलोकपालविशालबलावलेपविप्लवकारिणी मर्त्यमात्रयुद्धे लज्जते प्रचण्ड मद्भुजमण्डली'ति स्त्रीलिङ्गेन निर्देशस्त्रैलोक्यविजयोचितस्य प्रतापस्य कठोरतामपहरन्ननोचित्यं सूचयित।। २१ ।।

But not as in my *Nītilatā*—

'This cluster of my arms is ashamed to fight with a mortal. This cluster of arms is powerful enough to go to war with Varuṇa, has accomplished its object by ruining the heaven, has the power to subdue Yama, is busy uprooting Marut, is prepared to destroy Kubera, and is frightful in tearing and burning (the foes)'.

Here, Rāvaṇa speaks words suited to display the furious temper at the insult offered by the monkey. (He says,), "The frightful circle of my arms, which has humiliated the pride of the quarter-guardians in their supreme strength, Varunaạ, and the rest, is ashamed to fight with a mere mortal. "Here the use of femine gender (in *maṇḍalī*) takes away the severity of the alory, amassed after the conquest of the three worlds, and shows inappropriateness.

वचनौचित्यं दर्शयितुमाह–

उचितैरेव वचनैः काव्यमायाति चारुतम्।
अदैन्यधन्यमनसां वदनं विदुषामिव।। २२ ।।

To show the propriety of numbers, (the author) says—

22. A poem becomes lovely through (the use of) proper

numbers, just as the faces of the learned people, whose minds are blessed with fortitude, look bright with proper speech.

उचितैरेकवचनद्विवचनबहुवचनैः काव्यं चारुतामायाति। अदैन्योदारचेससां विदुषामिव वदनमयाच्ञाचारुचिरौचित्यचारुभिर्वचोभिः।

> A poem becomes beautiful through the appropriate (use) of singular, dual, and plural numbers, just as the faces of learned people with high magnanimous minds are bright with no look of supplication and charming with gracefully appropriate words.

यथा मम नीतिलतायाम्–

> **त्रैलोक्याक्रमणैर्वराहविजयैर्निःसंख्यरत्नाप्तिभिः**
> **प्रख्यातः स्वरसस्वयंवरशतैर्युद्धाब्धिमध्ये श्रियः।**
> **साश्चैर्यर्बलिबन्धनैश्च बहुभिर्नित्यं हसत्युत्थितः**
> **पौलस्त्यः सकृदुद्यमश्रमवशाद्व्यासक्तनिद्रं हरिम्।।**

अत्र शुकसारणाभ्यां रघुपतेरग्रे दशग्रीवपराक्रमेऽभिधीयमाने यदुक्तं पौलस्त्यः शेषशायिनं हरिमेकवारोद्योगश्रमवशेन संसक्तालस्यनिद्रमेकत्रैलोक्याक्रमणैर्वराहविजयिनां सुभटानां जयैरनेकरत्नप्राप्तिभिः समरसमुद्रमध्ये बहुवारविहितैः श्रियः स्वयम्वरशतैर्बलिनां च लोकपालानां बन्धनैः प्रख्यातः सदोत्थितः सात्साहः सततं हसतीति बहुवचनैरेव हरिवैलक्षण्यलक्षणमुपचितमौचित्यमुद्रञ्चितम्।

> As in my *Nītilatā*—
>
> 'By stepping over the worlds, with the victories of the Great Boar, by obtaining innumerable jewels, growing famous when chosen by Lakṣmī in the middle of the ocean of battle (in the ceremony of the choice of a husband according to one's own inclination), and by wondrous deeds of binding the mighty—with these words Rāvaṇa, being wakeful, laughts at Hari, who having performed the above-mentioned (acts) just once, sleeps through the weariness of their undertaking'.
>
> Here, Śuka and Sāraṇa, while praising Rāvaṇa's valour before Rāma, speak thus :"By stepping over the three worlds, by the victories over the great warriors, capturing boars, by acquiring many jewels, by the hundred of the ceremonies of the goddess of Glory choosing by herself her husband in the ocean of battle, and by binding the quarter-guardians, Rāvaṇa, becoming famous, full of lustre and courage, is constantly laughing at Hari who is sleeping lazily on the Śeśanāga due to the fatigue of trying all

this just once". Here, the suitable propriety implying Hari's embarrassment (lit. strangeness) has been shown by means of the plural number.

न तु यथा मातृगुप्तस्य–

नायं निशामुखसरोरुहराजहंसः कीरीकपोलतलकान्ततनुः शशाङ्कः।
आभाति नाथ! तदिदं दिवि दुग्धसिन्धुडिण्डीरपिण्डपरिपाण्डु यशस्त्वदीयम्।।

अत्र नायं शशी, त्वदीयमिन्दुदुग्धाब्धिफेनपिण्डपाण्डुरं यश इति यदभिहितं तद विच्छिन्नप्रसराणां यशसां बहुवचनेन वर्णनायां समुचितायामेकवचनोपन्यासश्चन्द्रबिम्बाकारेण पिण्डमात्रपरिच्छिन्नतया सङ्कोचरूपमनौचित्यमुद्भावयति।। २२।।

But not as in Mātṛgupta's (verse)—

'This is not the moon, which is the royal swan of the lotus of the face of night, whose body is beautiful like the cheek of a lady of the country of Kīra (i.e., Kashmir). My lord, it is your glory that is shining in the sky—(the glory), which is white like a heap of the foam of the milky ocean".

Here, in the statement—"this is not the moon that your glory white like the heap of the foam of the milky ocean'—by the use of singular number with the (word) 'glory' (yaśas) which ought to have properly been put in the plural number, because of its unchecked diffusion, an impropriety arises in the form of the limitation (of glory) by its way of contraction into a ball in the form of the moon.

विशेषणौचित्यं दर्शयितुमाह–

विशेषणैः समुचितैर्विशेष्योऽर्थः प्रकाशते।
गुणाधिकैर्गुणोदारः सुहृद्भिरिव सज्जनः।। २३।।

In order to show propriety of adjectives, (the author) says—

23. The meaning defined by proper adjectives shines like a virtuous and large-hearted gentleman, who is made to shine by friends excelling in virtues.

काव्ये विशेष्योऽर्थः समुचितैरेव विशेषणैः शोभां लभते, गुणोदारः साधुर्यथाभ्यधिकगुणैः सुहृद्भिः।

The defined meaning appears bright only with proper adjectives, as does a virtuous and large-hearted man with friends excelling in virtues.

यथा मम मुनिमतमीमांसायाम्–

चैत्रे सूत्रितयौवनान्युपवनान्यामोदिनी पद्मिनी
ज्योत्स्नाप्रावरणानि रत्नवलभीहर्म्याणि रम्याः स्त्रियः।
सर्वं चारुतरं न कस्य दयितं यस्मिस्तु तद्भुज्यते
तन्मृन्निर्मितनाभभाजनमिव क्षिप्रक्षयं जीवितम्।।

अत्र युधिष्ठिरस्यासादितमहाविभूतेर्मयनिर्मितमणिमयसभाभिमानिनो विभवप्रभावे वर्ण्यमाने सकलभावाभावस्वरूपभावस्वरूपभाववादोपदेशिनो महामुनेराशयविचारवसरे यदुक्तं कुसुमसमयसमुपचिततौवनान्युपवनानि मकरन्दामोदसुन्दरारविन्दिनीज्योत्स्नापटप्रावृतानि रत्नवलभीहर्म्याणि रमणीया रमण्श्चेति सर्वमेतच्चारुतरं सर्वस्याभिमतम्, किन्तु यस्मिन्भुज्यते तज्जीवितमाममृत्पात्रनिः सारं क्षिप्रक्षयमिति तद्विशेष्यपदोत्कर्षकारिविशेषणपदोदितसौन्दर्येण पर्यन्तानिःसारतानिर्वेद संवादि स्फुरदौचित्यमातनोति।

As in my *Munimatamīmāṁsā*—

'In the Caitra month, gardens invested with youth (i.e. spring), lotus-beds full of fragrance, the roofs of jewelled palaces wrapped in moon-light, and ladies enjoyable—in short, to whom is all that is deliguful not dear? But life in which all this is to be enjoyed does soon decay (i.e. end) like a pot of unbaked clay'.

Here, while describing the splendour of the wealth belonging of Yudhiṣṭhira, who had acquired great wealth and was pround of the jewelled assembly hall made by Maya, the statement is made at the time of reflecting on the underlying sense by the great sage, who exposes the reality of the nature (lit. form) of all beings, animate or inanimate, namely, the gardens invested with the youth of spring, the lotus-beds lovely on account of their fragrance, the roofs of the houses studded with jewels, and covered with the cloth of moon-light, and charming ladies—all these which are beautiful appeal to everyone, but the life in which all (these are) to be enjoyed is easily destructible and is hollow like an unbaked pot. (In this statement) propriety conforming to this remorse brought out in the end is made prominent by the beauty arising out of the epithets heightening the excellence of the object qualified.

न तु यथा भट्टलट्टनस्य–

ग्रीष्मं द्विषन्तु जलदागममर्थयन्तां ते सङ्कटप्रकृतयो विकटास्तडागाः।
अब्धेस्तु मुग्धशफरीचटुलाचलेन्द्रनिष्कम्पकुक्षिपयसो द्वयमप्यचिन्त्यम्।।

अत्र ग्रीष्मं द्विषन्तु, मेघागमं सङ्कटस्वभावा विकटा विस्तीर्णांश्च तटाकाः प्रार्थयन्ताम्, महालब्धेस्तु बालशफरीलोलात्तलेन्द्रनिश्चलकुक्षिपयसो ग्रीष्मघनागमावप्यगणनीयावितियदुक्तम्, तत्र तडागविशेषणयोः सङ्कटविकटपदयोः परस्परविरुद्धार्थयोरनौचित्यं स्पष्टमवभासते, सङ्ककटस्वभावस्य हि विकटत्वं विस्तीर्णत्वं नोपपद्यते। अथ स्वभावे सङ्कटत्वमाकारे विकटत्वम्, तदपि तटाकस्य निश्चेतनस्य स्वभावाभावादनुपपन्नमेव।। २३।।

But not as in Bhaṭṭa Laṭṭana's (verse)—

'May the extensive or narrow puddles (or pools) hate summer and supplicate for the coming of the rains (lit. clouds), but none of the two (summer and rainy season) matters for the oceans, the waters in whose fissures (lit. belly) are motionless though everything from the smallest fish to the biggest mountain is moving in it'.

Here (in the sentence)—'the extensive and narrow pools hate summer but pray for the rainy season; but the advent of summer of the rainy season does not matter for the ocean, the waters in whose caverns are motionless though (everything beginning with) the small *śapharī* fish and (ending with) the great mountain is moving within it'—the adjectives of the tanks 'extensive' and 'narrow' being contradictory are obviously inappropriate. Extensiveness does not fit in with narrowness. Here, the expression 'narrowness' in mind' and 'extensiveness in size' is improper for an inanimate pool since it has no feelling.

उपसर्गौचित्यं दर्शयितुमाह–

योग्योपसर्गसंसर्गैर्निरर्गलगुणोचिता।
सूक्तिर्विवर्धते सम्पत्सन्मार्गगमनैरिव।। २४।।

To show propriety in the use of prepositions, (the author) says—

24. (The charm of) a stanza having an unimpeded excellence increases by means of suitable prepositions just as wealth increases by following the virtuous paths.

उचितैः प्रादिभिरुपसर्गैः सूक्तिरुन्नतिमासादयति, विभूतिरिव सन्मार्गगमनैः।

A verse attains greater excellence when proper prepositions—'pra' and others—are used, just as wealth increases by following the virtuous path.

यथा मम मुनिमतमीमांसायाम्–

आचारं भजते त्यजत्यपि मदं वैराग्यमालम्बते
कर्तुं वाञ्छति सङ्गभङ्गगलितोत्तुङ्गाभिमानं तपः।
दैवन्यस्तविपर्ययैः सुखशिखाभ्रष्टः प्रणष्टो जनः
प्रायस्तापविलीनलोहसदृशीमायाति कर्मण्यताम्।।

अत्र दुर्योधनस्य घोषयात्रायां गन्धर्वबन्धपराभवभग्नाभिमानस्य प्राज्यसाम्राज्यमुत्सृज्य तपःप्रयत्नाभिनिविष्टस्य दुर्ग्रहे वर्ण्यमाने यदुक्तं–सर्वो जनः सुखभ्रष्टः प्रणष्टविभवः सदाचारं भजते, मदं त्यजति, वैराग्यमाश्रयति, सङ्गभङ्गेन विगलितोत्तुङ्गाभिनं तपः कर्तुं वाञ्छतिः, प्रायो बाहुल्येन तापविगलितलोहपिण्डसदृशीं कर्मण्यतामायातीति, तत्रोत्पूर्वतया सोपसर्गस्य तुङ्गशब्दस्य स्वभावोम्नतिर्द्विगुणतामुपयातादुर्भदाभिमानार्थौचित्यमुच्चैः करोति।

As in my *Munimatamīmāṁsā*—

'People suffering a fall from the heights of pleasures through the reverses of fate, become mannerly, give up haughtiness, take to asceticism, want to practise penance, which melts away height of arrogance by doing away with attachment. Generally they become manageable like mineral ore heated and melted in fire'.

Here, while describing the obstinacy of Duryodhana, who, having suffered humiliation (lit. his pride broken) at the hands of the Gandharva, who caught him at the time of his march against the habitation of herdsmen, and who wanted to renounce his vast kingdom and practise penance, it has been said, "Everyone deprived of his comfort becomes mannerly, gives up haughtiness, takes to asceticism, and wants to practise penance in which the obstinate pride is melted away by (doing away) with attachment, generally becomes manageable like the ore melted in fire". In this statement by the use of the preposition 'ut' (meaning high) the height indicated by the word 'tuṅga' (meaning 'high') is doubled and the appropriate sense of the pride of the haughty is enhanced.

न तु यथा कुमारदासस्य–

अयि! विजह्रीहि दृढोपगूहनं त्यज नवसङ्गमभीरु! वल्लभम्।
अरुणकरोद्गम एष वर्तते वरतनु! सम्प्रवदन्ति कुक्कुटाः।।

अत्राभिवानङ्गसङ्गमगाढमालिङ्गननिश्चलाङ्गच्छन्नाङ्गनाप्रबोधने संख्या यदुक्तं वल्लभं मुञ्च प्रभातसंध्यायामरुणकिरणोद्गमो वर्तते, कुक्कुटाश्च सम्प्रवदन्तीति, तच्च सम्प्रोपसर्गशून्यशब्दापूरणमात्रेण निरर्थकत्वादनुचितमेव।। २४।।

But not as in Kumāradāsa's (verse)—

'Ah, loosen the close embrace, O you, who are timid at the first meeting; leave your beloved, O beautiful one, here come (lit. rise) the rays of the sun and the cocks are crowing'.

Here, the friend waking up the girl, whose limbs are motionless in her passionate embrace of her beloved on her first meeting says, "Leave your beloved. The rays of the sun are shooting (forth) in the morning twilight. The cocks are crowing". Here, the prefixes 'sam' 'pra' are inappropraite because they convey no meaning and are merely expletive.

निपातौचित्यं दर्शयितुमाह–

उचितस्थानविन्यस्तैर्निपातैरर्थसङ्गतिः ।
उपादेयैर्भवत्येव सचिवैरिव निश्चला।। २५।।

To show propriety in the use of particles (the author) says—

25. The sense becomes fixed by means of useful particles, well-placed, as the accumulation of wealth is assured by means of good counsellors well-placed.

उपादेयैश्चादिभिर्निपातैरुचितपदविनिवेशितैः काव्यस्यार्थसङ्गतिरसन्दिग्घा सत्स हायैरिव भवति।

The meaning of a poetic composition becomes confirmed by means of lovely particles, 'ca' and others placed in the proper place, just as wealth accrues in abundance by having good dallies.

यथा मम मुनिमतमीमांसायान्–

सर्वे स्वर्गसुखार्थिनः क्रतुशतैः प्राज्यैर्यजन्ते जडा
स्तेषां नाकपुरे प्रयाति विपुलः कालः क्षणार्धं च तत्।
क्षीणे पुण्यधने स्थितिर्न तु यथा वेश्यागृहे कामिनां
तस्मान्मोक्षसुखं समाश्रयत भोः! सत्यं च नित्यं च यत्।।

अत्र स्वर्गसुखस्य वेश्याभोगवदवसानविरसचपलतायां प्रतिपादितायां निश्चलमोक्षसुखस्य निःसन्देहनिश्चिता प्रतिपत्तिर्निपातपदोपबं हिता वाक्यार्थौचित्यं जनयति।

As in my *Munimatamīmāmsā*—

'All foolish people desiring the comfort of heaven perform

hundreds of sacrifices with lavish offerings. They live for a long time in the heaven, but it is by no means more than half a second; then their wealth of merit being exhausted, they cannot stay there like libertines in a courtesan's house. So, ye, have recourse to the joy of emancipation which indeed is true (joy) as well as eternal'.

Here, while establishing the enjoyments of the heaven as transitory and tasteless in the end like the amorous enjoyment of a courtesan, the satement of the indisputable happiness arising from unalterable pleasure of emancipation, being made forceful by the use of particles ('ca' and 'ca'), gives rise to propriety in the meaning of the sentence.

न तु यथा श्रीचक्रस्य–

देवो जानाति सर्वं यदपि च तदपि ब्रूमहे नीतिनिष्ठं
सार्धं सन्धाय जालान्तरधरणिभुजा निर्वृतो बान्धवेन।
म्लेच्छानुच्छिन्धि भिन्धि प्रतिदिनमयशो रुन्धि विश्वं यशोभिः
सीदन्वन्मेखलायां परिकलय करं किञ्च विश्वम्भरायाम्।।

अत्र क्षितिपतिस्तुतिप्रस्तावे 'देवो जानानि सर्वं यदपि च तदपि' इति यदुक्तं तत्र पूर्वापरपदयोरसम्बद्धत्वेन निरर्थक एव निरुपयोगश्चकारः प्रततोत्सवबहुजनभोजन-पङ्क्तावपरिज्ञातः स्वयमिव मध्ये समुपविष्टः पश्चादभिव्यक्तः परं लज्जादुर्मनौचित्यं प्रतनोति।। २५।।

But not as in Śrī Cakra's (verse)—

'Though your lordship knows this, that and everything, still do we say what constitutes proper policy. Having made peace with the king of Jālāntara (Jullundur) (or with the king in your captivity) and thus pleased with your kinsmen, wipe out the infidles, remove you infamy, make your glory pervade the whole world, and extend your hand towards winning over the sea-girdled earth'.

Here, while praising the king, the expression 'Your lordship knows this, that and everything, and even then do we say this' (has been used). In it the word 'and' (='ca') has no sense because the two phrases (it joins) are not correlated. The particle 'ca' shows immodesty and unmannerliness like a stranger who sits uninvited in the middle of the line of many people taking food but is found out at last and proves himself a source of shame and disgust.

कालौचित्यं दर्शयितुमाह–

कालौचित्येन यात्येव वाक्यमर्थेन चारुताम्।
जनावर्जनरम्येण वेषेणेव सतां वपुः।। २६।।

To show propriety of tense, (the author) says—

26. With the meaning having propriety of tense, the sense attains charm just as the body of the virtuous (looks beautiful) with dress which is agrreable to people.

कालकृतौचित्ययुक्तेनार्थेन वाक्यं चारुतामेति वेषपरिग्रहेणेव कालयोग्येन सतामवसरज्ञानां वपुः।

By the meaning having the propriety of tense, the sentence becomes beautiful just as the body of the virtuous, knowing the proper occasion, looks beautiful by wearing the dress befitting the time.

यथा मम मुनिमतमीमांसायाम्–

योऽभूद्गोपशिशुः पयोदधिशिरश्चौरः करीषङ्कष–
स्तस्यैवाद्य जगत्पते खगपते शौरे मुरारे हरे।
श्रीवत्साङ्क! जडैरितिस्तुतिपदैः कर्णौ मृणां पूरितौ
ही कालस्य विपर्ययप्रणयिनी पाकक्रियाश्चर्यभूः।।

अत्रामर्पविषविषमाविष्कारमुमूर्षुणा शिशुपालेनाभिधीयमाने यत्किल गोपा द्बबालः पयोदधिशिरश्चौरः करीषङ्कषोऽभूत्तस्यैवाद्य जगन्नाथादिभिः स्तुतिदैर्नृणां कर्णौ पूरितौ ही बत कालस्य विपर्ययकारिणी पाकक्रियाऽऽश्चर्यैभूमिरिति वाक्येऽभूदिति भूतकालेनाश्चर्यपरिपोष–रुचिरमारब्धाधिक्षेपलक्षणं वाक्यौचित्यं कृतम्।

As in my *Munimatamīmāṁsā*—

'Of the same person, who was the son of a herdsman and used to steal away the cream of milk and curd, and was a sweeeper of cow-dung, the epithets to-day viz. "O Lord of the world! O Lord of Garuḍa! O brave warrior! O foe of Mura! O Hari! O Viṣṇu! piled up by foolish people,fill the ears of men. The ripening process of time which favours vicissitudes is surely the cause of great wonder'.

Here, Śiśupāla with a desire to dies by manifesting the venom of jealousy says, "The son of a herdsman, who used to steal the cream of curd and milk, and was a sweeper of cow dung; but the ears of the people have been filled with words of praise—'O Lord of the world' and others. Verily the ripening process of time which favours vicissitudes is an object of wonder". In this sentence, by the verb 'was' (abhūt) in the past tense, the propriety of the sentence has been brought out, marked with the taunt which is made charming by developing the sense of wonder.

यथा वा मालवकुवलयस्य–

च्युतसुमनसः कुन्दाः पुष्पोद्गमैरलसा द्रुमा
मनसि च गिरं गृह्णन्तीमे किरन्ति न कोकिलाः।
अथ च सवितुः शीतोल्लासं लुनन्ति मरीचयो
न च जरठतामालम्बन्ते क्लमोदयदायिनीम्।।

अत्र शिशुतरवसन्तकान्तोपवननवरसोल्लाससूच्यमानम नसिजोत्कण्ठावर्णनायामृतुसन्धिसमुचिताः कुन्दाः कुसुमानसानशून्यतनवः, किंशुकाशोकाः कलिकोद्गमभरालसाः, मनसि कोकिलाः कलकूजितान्यनुसन्दधति, रवेर्मरीचयः शीतोल्लासमथ च निवारयन्ति न च सन्तापदायिनीं प्रौढतामालम्बन्ते, इत्युक्ते वर्तमानकालपदेष्वेव हृदयसंघादसुन्दरमौचित्यं किमप्यामोदते।

Or as in Mālavakuvalaya's (verse)—

'The jasmine plants have their flowers fallen down; the trees are languid through their putting forth luxuriant growth of flowers. The cuckoos do not coo but check their voice within themselves. And the rays of the sun dispel the bite of the cold, but they do not resort to severity giving rise to languidness'.

Here, in the description of the eagerness of love shown by the fresh exuberance of the erotic sentiment in the garden, beautiful with early spring, it has been said, "the jasmine creepers, proper (to be mentioned) in connection with the advent of spring, are bare, their flowers having withered away, the Kiṁśuka and the Aśoka trees are languid with the buds coming out, the cuckoos restrain their beautiful cooings in their hearts, the rays of the sun dispel the biting cold, but do not become violent as to afflict". Here, it is the verbs (put) in the present tense alone that an indescribable propriety, dear to the heart, delight us.

यथा वा भट्टभल्लटस्य–

मृत्योरास्यमिवाततं धनुरिदं मूर्च्छद्विषाश्चेषवः
शिक्षा सा विजितार्जुना प्रतिलयं सर्वाङ्गलग्ना गतिः।
अन्तः क्रौर्यमहो शठस्य मधुनो हा हारि गीतं मुखे
व्याधस्याऽस्य यथा भविष्यति तथा मन्ये वनं निर्मृगम्।।

अत्र लुब्धकस्य धनुःसायकशिक्षागतिक्रौर्यगीतानि तथा यथा वनं निर्मृगं भविष्यतीति भविष्यत्कालः प्रकृतार्थपरिपोषेण हृदयसंवादौचित्यमादधाति।

Or as in Bhaṭṭa Bhallaṭa's (verse)—

'This bow is wide like the yawning mouth of Death; the arrows make the victims faint away; his skill (lit. learning) excels that of Arjuna; agility is perceptible in every limb. Alas! This fowler, a rogue, who looks sweet, has cruelty at heart, and has an enchanting song on his lips. So I think the forest will be bereft of all animals'.

Here, "the fowler's bow, arrow, skill, agility, cruelty and song, all these are such that the forest will be bereft of animals". The future tense brings out the heart-bewitching propriety by developing the relevant sense.

न तु यथा वराहमिहिरस्य–

क्षीणश्चन्द्रो विशति तरणेर्मण्डलं मासि मासि
लब्ध्वा काञ्चित्पुनरपि कलां दूरदूरानुवर्ती।
सम्पूर्णश्चेत्कथमपि तदा स्पर्धयोदेति भानो-
र्नो दौर्जन्याद्विरमति जडो नापि दैन्याद्व्यरंसीत्।।

अत्र रवेर्मण्डलं क्षीणः शशी प्रतिमासं प्रविशति ततः काञ्चिदाप्यायिकां कलां प्राप्य दूरे दुरे भुवति, परिपूर्णश्च तस्यैव स्पर्धयाऽभ्युदेति, दौर्जन्यान्न विरमति न च दैन्याद्यरंसोदित्येतद् 'विरमति' 'व्यरंसीत' इति परस्परासङ्गत्तं कालपदद्वयं चन्द्रस्य सदृशयोर्दौर्जन्यदैन्ययोः सर्वकालमभिनिर्वृत्तयोर्यदुपन्यस्तं तत्र व्यरंसीदिति विरुद्धार्थत्वादनुचितमेव।। २६।।

But not as in Varāhamihira's (verse)—

'The emaciated moon enters the solar orb month after month receding farther and farther; and after obtaining a few digits, it somehow becomes full and rises in envy of the sun. A fool does not give up his wickedness, nor did his shake off his humility'.

The fading moon enters the solar orb everey month and gaining a digit, causing fullness, recedes farther and farther, and when complete, it rises incompetition with the same (sun); it does not shake off its rougery or it did not desist from humiliation. Here 'does not shake off' and 'did not stop' these two verbs whose tenses are different (refer to) the ever presence of roguery and humiliation in the moon. (The tense in the verb) 'did not stop' is inappropriate because it conveys a contrary sense.

देशौचित्यं दर्शयितुमाह–

देशौचित्येन काव्यार्थः ससंवादेन शोभते।
परं परिचयाशंसी व्यवहारः सतामिव।। २७।।

To show propriety in (the description of) a country, (the author) says—

27. The meaning of a poem becomes bright by means of propriety in the agreeable description of the country, like the conduct of the virtuous people showing intimacy.

देक्षविषयौचित्येन हृदयसंवादिना काव्यार्थः सतां व्यवहार इव परिचयसूचकः शोमते।

By suitable propriety as regards the country, the meaning of the composition looks beautiful like the conduct of the virtuous showing intimacy.

यथा भट्टभवमृतेः–

पुरा यत्र स्रोतः पुलिनमधुना तत्र सरितां विपर्यासं यातो घनविरलभावः क्षितिरुहाम्।
बहोर्दृष्टं कालादरपमिव मन्ये वनमिदं निवेशः शैलानां तदिदमिति बुद्धिं द्रढयति।।

अत्र बहुभिर्वर्षसहस्रैरतिक्रान्तैः शन्बुकवधप्रसङ्गेन दण्डकारण्यं रामः पूर्वपरिचितं पुनः प्रविष्टः समन्तादवलोक्यैवं ब्रूते–'पुरा यत्र नदीनां प्रवाहस्तत्रेदानीं तटम्, वृक्षाणां घनविरलत्वे विपयेयश्चिराद्दृष्टं वनमिदमपूर्वमिव मन्ये, पर्वतसन्निवशस्तु। तदेवैतदिति बुद्धिं स्थिरीकरोति' इत्युक्ते चिरकालविपर्ययपरिवृत्तसंस्थानका ननवर्णनयाहृदयसंवादी देशस्वभावः पग्ममौचित्यमुद्द्योतयति।

As in Bhaṭṭa Bhavabhūti's (verse)—

'Formerly where there was the stream, now there is a sandy bank; the density and sparseness of trees have exchanged places. Seeing after a long time, I take this forest to be another, but the position of the mountains lends conviction to the idea that it is the same'.

Here, in connection with the killing of Śambūka, Rāma enters the familiar forest after many thousands of years, and looking all round says, "Where formerly there were streams now there are sandy banks, there is change in the density and sparseness of trees. Seeing after a long time, I think this to be a forest not seen before, but the position of the mountains strengthens the idea that it is the same". In this statement the heart-bewitching physical nature of the country. (pictured) in the description of the forest with its situations changed in the course of a long time, shows extreme propriety.

न तु यथा राजशेखरस्य–

कर्णाटीदशनाङ्कितः शितमहाराष्ट्रीकटाक्षाहतः
प्रौढान्ध्रीस्तनपीडितः प्रणयिनीभ्रूभङ्गवित्रासितः।
लाटीबाहुविवेष्टितश्च मलयस्त्रीतर्जनीतर्जितः
सोऽयं सम्प्रति राजशेखरकविर्वाराणसीं वाञ्छति।।

अत्र कर्णाटमहाराष्ट्रान्ध्रलाटमलयललनासम्भीगसुभगः कालेन गलितरागमोहः सम्प्रति राजशेखरकविर्वाराणसीं गन्तुमिच्छतीत्युक्ते श्रृङ्गाररसतरङ्गितवराङ्गनाप्रसङ्गेऽनङ्गनिरर्गल-दक्षिणापथदेशोद्देशमध्ये प्रणयिनीभ्रूभङ्गवित्रासित इति देशोपलक्षणबिरहितकेवलप्रणयिनीपदेत देशौचित्यमुपचितमप्यनुचिततां नीतम्।। २७।।

But not as in Rājaśekhara's (verse)—

'Bearing the scars of the bitings of the teeth of women of Karṇāṭa country, pierced with the sharp glances of the Mahārāṣṭra women, embraced closely by the bosoms of grown-up Āndhra women, frightened by the knitting of the eye-brows of the beloveds, encircled by the arms of the women of Lāṭa country, and threatened with the index finger of the Malaya women, the poet Rājaśkhara now seeks Vārāṇaśī'.

'The poet Rājaśekhara fortunate (enough) to enjoy the women of Karṇāṭa, Mahārāṣṭra, Āndhra, Lāṭa and Malaya and with his delusion of love gone, now wants to go to Vārāṇasī". In this statement in the talk ladies filled with the passion about of love, and (showing) the middle region of the southern country as (the place for) his unimpeded love, the expression, 'frightened with the knitting of eye-brows (in anger) of the beloved" meders inappropriate, the otherwise appropriate description, as it does not mention the name of a country, and contains only the world 'beloved'.

कुलौचित्यं दर्शयितुमहा–

कुलोपचितमौचित्यं विशेषोत्कर्षकारणम्।
काव्यस्य पुरुषस्येव प्रियं प्रायः सचेतसाम्।। २८।।

To show propriety of the dynasty (to be described, the author) says—

28. The propriety surrounding a family lends special excellence to the charm of the poetry, just as the propriety of the lineage of a person is generally dear to those who have a heart to feel.

पुरुषस्येव काव्यस्य कुलोन्नतमौचित्यं सविशेषोत्कर्षजनकं प्रायेण बाहुल्येन सहृदयानामभिमतम्।

The propriety of the dynasty leading to special charm in the poetry, is dear to those who possess a heart that feels, just as the propriety of the dynasty of a person, leading to great respect is dear to people who have a heart that appreciates.

यथा कालिदासस्य–

अथ स विषयव्यावृत्तात्मा यथाविधि सूनवे नृपतिककुदं दत्वा यूने सितातपवारणम्।
मुनिवनतरुच्छायां देव्या तया सह शिश्रिवे गलितवयसामिश्वाकूणामिदं हि कुलव्रतम्।।

अत्र 'अथ स राजा वृद्धस्तरुणाय सूनवे राज्यं प्रतिपाद्य तथा देव्या सह तपोवनं भेजे, विरक्तचेतसाभिक्ष्वाकूणामन्ते हि कुलव्रतमिदमेव' इत्यक्ते भूतवर्तमानभाविनां तद्वंश्यानामौचित्यमुन्मीलितम्।

As in Kālidāsa's (verse)—

'Then, having given according to rites the white umbrella (the emblem of royalty), the very insignia of kings to the young (son), he, whose mind was averse to enjoyment, resorted to the shade of the trees in ascetic grove with his queen. This verily is the traditional vow of the descendents of the Ikṣvāku family, who are advanced in age'.

Here, in this statement—'then that old king having given his kingdom to his young son, went to the hermitage with his queen; this is the traditional vow of the descendents of the Ikṣvāku race, whose minds are indifferent to enjoyment—the propriety of behaviour of past, present, and future scions of that dynasty has been shown.

न तु यथा यशोवर्मदेवस्य–

उत्पत्तिर्भण्डकुले यदभीष्टं तत्पदं समाक्रान्तम्।
भोगास्तथापि दैवात्सकृदपि भोक्तुं न लभ्यन्ते।।

अत्र ममोत्पत्तिर्भण्डकुले समोहितपदाक्रम्रणं च निष्पन्नं तथापि दैवापिंतग्रियावियोगाद्भोगा भोक्तुं न लभ्यन्त इत्यभिहिते स्वसंवेद्यमेव भण्डकुलमन्यत्राप्रसिद्धं स्वयमेव निर्दिश्यमानमुत्कर्षविशेषणविरहित केवलपदोपादानेन निरर्थकतया निरौचित्यमेव। इक्ष्याकुकुलस्य तु निर्विशेषणत्वमुपपद्यत एव, त्रिभुवनप्रसिद्धौचित्यचरित्रत्वात्।। २८।।

But not as in Yaśovarmadeva's (verse)—

'Born in the dynasty of the Bhaṇḍas, (I) rose to (my) desired position; but, as ill luck would have it, I have not even once had pleasures to enjoy'.

Here, it has been said, "I am born in the dynasty of the Bhaṇḍas and have risen to the desired position,but I have not been able to enjoy myself through the separation of my beloved, as ill luck would have it". Here, the Bhaṇḍa dynasty mentioned by him is not known anywhere and has to be told about by one's own self, as it is known to the speaker alone; and impropriety is quite evident because of its meaninglessness, as the word alone is mentioned without any epithets. In the case of the Ikṣvāku dynasty the absence of epithets is but proper, because its deeds are well-known in all the three worlds.

व्रतौचित्यं दर्शयितुमाह–

काव्यार्थः साधुवादार्हः सद्व्रतौचित्यगौरवात्।
सन्तोषनिर्भरं भक्तया करोति जनमानसम्।। २९।।

To show propriety of the mode of vow, (the author) says—

29. The sense of a composition deserving praise on account of its worthiness due to the propriety of a sensible vow, fills the minds of the people with satisfaction by its charm.

काव्यार्थः समुचितव्रतगौरवात्साधुवादयोग्यः सन्तोषपूर्ण जनमनः करोति। भक्तिर्विच्छित्तिः।

The meaning of a composition worthy of praise fills the mind of people with satisfaction on account of the excellence of the virtuous vow. 'Bhakti' means charm.

यथा मम मुक्तावलीकाव्ये–

अत्र वल्कलजुषः पलाशिनः पुष्परेणुभरभस्मभूषिताः।
लोलभृङ्गवलयाक्षमालिकास्तापसा इव विभान्ति पादपाः।।

अत्र तपोधनोचितव्रतव्यञ्जकवल्कलभस्माक्षसूत्रप्रणयिपादपवर्णनायामवेतनानामपि शमसमयविमलचित्तवृत्तिरौचित्यमुपजनयति।

As in my poem *Muktāvalī*—

'Here the 'palāśa' trees clad in the bark, decorated with the massive pollen dust of the flowers, and possessing the rosary beads in the form of lines (lit. circles) of hovering bees, look like ascetics'.

Here, in the descritpion of the trees longing for bark, ashes and rosary beads which show the mode of life proper for ascetics, the fact that purity of mind proper for restraint is seen even among inanimate objects, gives rise to propriety.

न तु यथा दीपकस्य–

पुण्ये ग्रामे वने वा महति सितपटच्छन्नपालोकपाली-
मादाय न्यायगर्भद्विजहुतहुतभुग्धूमधूम्रोपकण्ठम्।
द्वारं द्वारं प्रवृत्तो वरमुदरदरीपूरणाय क्षुधार्तो
मानी प्राणी सनाथः स पुनरनुदिनं तुल्यकुल्येषु दीनः।।

अत्र 'वैराग्यनिरर्गलवर्णनायां भिक्षाकपालीमादाय क्षुत्क्षामः कुक्षिपूरणाय प्रवृत्तो मानी वरं द्वारं द्वारं यष्टिनिविष्टपाणिः परिभ्रान्तो न पुनरनिशं तुल्यकुल्येषु दीन' इत्युक्ते। सहजप्रशमविमलमानसविश्रान्तिसन्तोषमुत्सृज्य तुल्यकुल्यद्वेषविजिगीषापरमेव वाक्यं भृशमनौचित्यमुद्भावयति। वरमेतत्तीव्रव्रतकष्टं न तु स्वजनदैन्ययाचनमिति संसारग्रन्थिबन्धाभिमानोपन्यासः।। २९ ।।

But not as in Dīpaka's (verse)—

'A self-possessed person, afflicted with hunger but holding his honour high. should better, in order to fill the carity of his belly, wander from door to door with a begging bowl in his hand, coverd with a white scarf in a village or a pious forest, the vicinity of which is darkened with the smoke of the fire in which oblations are offerd by Brāhmaṇas versed in logic, rather than feel humble day after day before his own kinsmen'.

Here, while describing renunciation in an unimpeded manner, the statements—'rather than feeling humiliated always before those born of the same family, a self respecting person emanciated with hunger, supported by a stick in hand, taking a beggar's bowl, had better wander about from door to door to fill his belly'—display extreme impropriety resting on the desire to vanquish one's kinsmen and feel jealous of them instead of feeling contented as a result of restraint, pure-mindedness, and a paceful temperament. The phrase, 'the hardship of the difficult vow is better than the act of helplessly begging before one's own kinsmen', shows stub bornness and attachment with wordly ties.

तत्त्वौचित्यं दर्शयितुमाह–

काव्यं हृदयसंवादि सत्यप्रत्ययनिश्चयात्।
तत्त्वोचिताभिधानेन यात्युपादेयतां कवेः।। ३०।।

To show propriety of the real import, (the author) says—

30. A poet's heart-bewitching composition appeals (all the more) by its containing (lit. by the mention of) the proper sense, the truth of which has been ascertained.

तत्त्वोचिताख्यानेन कवेः सूक्तं सत्यप्रत्ययस्थैर्यात्संवादि गृह्यतां याति।

By containing a saying full of proper meaning (or sense) a poet's composition appeals when its truth has been ascertained.

यथा मम बौद्धवदानलतिकायाम्–

दिवि भुघि फणिलोके शैशवे यौवने वा जरसि। निधनकाले गर्भशय्याश्रये वा।
सहगमनसहिष्णोः सर्वथा देहभाजां नहि भवति विनाशः कर्मणः प्राक्तनस्य।।

अत्र प्राक्तनस्य कर्मणस्त्रैलोक्ये शैशवयौवनवृद्धत्वावस्थासु देहिनां सह गमने समर्थत्वान्न विनाशोऽस्तीत्युक्ते निःसंशयसकलजनहृदयसंवादितत्त्वाख्यानमौचित्यं ख्यापयति।

As in my *Bauddhāvadānalatikā*—

'Whether in the celestial regions or in the mortal world or in the abode of the snakes, whether in childhood, youth or dotage, whether at death-bed or in the womb, the acts of persons, done in previous births, and powerful enough to pursue one in the next birth, are not destroyed at all'.

Here, in the statement—viz. deeds done in previous existences do not perish even in any of the three worlds as they have the power to follow embodied beings in all the stages (of life, namely) childhood, youth, and old age,—propriety has been brought out by its conveying a sense which undoubtedly appeals to all hearts.

न तु यथा माघस्य–

बुभुक्षि तैर्व्याकरणं न भुज्यते न पीयते काव्यरसः पिपासितैः।
न विद्यया केनचिदुद्धृतं कुलं हिरण्यमेवार्जय निष्फलाः कलाः।।

अत्रार्यार्थार्थितापरत्वेन धनमेवार्जय, क्षुधितैर्व्याकरणं न भुज्यते, न च काव्यरसः पिपासितैः पीयते, न च विद्यया कुलं केनचिदुद्धृतमित्युक्ते सर्वमेतद्दारिद्र्यदैन्यविद्रुत-धैर्यकातरतया तत्त्वविरहितं विपरीतमुपन्यस्तमनौचित्यं सुयुक्तमेव। विद्यानामेवसर्व-सम्पत्प्रसविनीनां कुलोद्धारक्षमत्वं नान्यस्य।। ३०।।

But not as in Māgha's (verse)—

'Hungry (stomachs) cannot eat (live upon) grammar nor can thirsty (mouths) drink the juice of poetry. Nobody ever rescued a family by learning. Hence gold alone do you earn; for useless are all the arts'.

here, while asking for amassing wealth, the remarks viz. grammar is not eaten by the hungry, nor is the liquor of poetry drunk by the thirsty, nor has learning resuced any family, have no sense, and are actuated by cowardice, the firmness (of the speaker) having vanished through the humility (brought on him) by poverty; and are quite meaningless and highly improper. It is only learning that can improve (the condition) of a family, because it is the source of all kinds of wealth, and nothing else can improve the condition of a family.

सत्त्वौचित्यं दर्शयितुमाह–

चमत्कारं करोत्येव वचः सत्त्वोचितं कवेः।
विचाररुचिरोदारचरितं सुमतेरिव।। ३१।।

To show propriety of spirit, (the author) says—

31. A poet's composition, (containing) proper spirit shows charm, like the magnanimous acts of the wise made agreeable with thoughtfulness.

सत्त्वोचितं ककेर्वचश्चमत्कारं करोति, सुमतेरिव विचार्यमाणं रुचिरमुदारचरितम्।

A poet's composition made agreeable with the right spirit becomes charming, like the lbhael deeds of a wise man united to thoughtfulness.

यथा मम चित्रभारते नाटके–

नदीवृन्दोद्दामप्रसरसलिलापूरिततनुः
स्फुरत्स्फीतज्वालानिबिडवडवाग्निक्षतजलः।
न दर्पं नो दैन्यं स्पृशति बहुसत्त्वः पतिरपा-
मवस्थानां भेदाद्भवति विकृतिर्नैव महताम्।।

अत्र पयाधिव्यपदेशेन युधिष्ठिरस्य सत्त्वोत्कर्षेऽभिधीयमाने सरित्पूरप्रवर्धिततनुर्वड-वाग्निनिष्पीतश्च नोत्सेकं न सङ्कोचमब्धिर्विपुलसत्त्वः स्पृशति, न ह्यवस्थानां भेदान्महाशयानां विकारो भवतीयुत्क्ते गम्भीरधीरा सत्त्ववृत्तिरौचित्यमातनोति।

As in my drama *Citrabhārata*—

'The large-hearted lord of waters (i.e. the ocean) on the one hand with its body swelled with unlimited water flowing into it from a number of rivers and on the other hand its water being dried up by the submarine fire furious with its blazing, thriving flames, does neither feel proud nor humiliated. In the case of the great, a change in spirit does not result from a change in circumstances'.

Here, while the greatness of Yudhiṣṭhira's character is being praised under the pretext of the ocean, in the statement viz. the ocean, with its body swelled up by the flow of rivers, and being drunk (i.e. dried up) by the submarined fire, out of its immense strength, does neither feel pride nor humility, because by a change in the circumstances the great do not change, the profundity and firmness of character show propriety.

नतु यथा भट्टेन्दुराजस्य–

आश्चर्यं वडवानलः स भगवानाश्चर्यमम्भोनिधि-
र्यत्कर्मातिशयं विचिन्त्य मनसः कम्पः समुत्पद्यते।

एकस्याशयघस्मरस्य पिबतस्तृप्तिर्न जाता जलै-
रन्यस्यापि महात्मनो न वपुषि स्वल्पोऽपि जातः श्रमः।।

अत्र वडवानलसमुद्रयोः सत्त्वमहत्त्वे वक्ष्यमाणे नातिविपुलाशयत्वादेकस्य पिबतः पयोभिस्तृप्तिर्न जाता, द्वितीयस्य तदुपजीव्यमानस्य न मनागपि खेदः, तदेतदुभयमाश्चर्यमित्युक्ते निःसन्तोषतया सततथा च कस्य न वडवाग्नेर्लज्जा, न च जलनिधेराश्रितैकार्थि-पूरणसामर्थ्यमित्यसत्त्वे सत्त्वस्तुतिरनौचित्यमावहति।। ३१।।

But not as in Bhaṭṭendurāja's (verse)—

'Wonderful is the submarine fire,and still more wonderful is the great ocean, thinking of whose great deeds the mind shivers. One, eating up its own means of stay, is not satiated with waters it has drunk, and the other great being does not feel any exhaustion in its body of waters'.

Here, while describing the greatness of the character of the submarine fire and that of the ocean, it has been said that the first, its stoamch not being very big, is not satiated with drinking water, and the other, on whom the first is living, does not experience any exhaustion : so both are wonderful. (In this statement) who does not (cry) shame on the submarine fire on account of its constant greed? The ocean also is not shown to have the capaticty of satisfy (just) one needy person depending on him : so the praise of one, who does not possess the virtue worth the priase, is improper.

अभिप्रायौचित्यं दर्शयितुमाह–

अकदर्थनया सूक्तमभिप्रायसमर्पकम्।
चित्तमावर्जयत्येव सतां स्वस्थमिवार्जवम्।। ३२।।

To show the propriety of purpose, (the author) says—

32. A saying whose purpose is exhibited without (much) difficulty pleases the mind, like the self-abiding innocence of the virtuous.

अक्लेशेनाभिप्रायसमर्पकं काव्यं हृदयमावर्जयति सज्जनानां निर्मलमार्जवमिव।

A composition conveying (to the reader) its import without any difficulty captivates the mind like the untarnished straight forwardness of the virtuous.

यथा दीपकस्य–

श्येनाङ्घ्रिग्रहदारितोत्तरकरो ज्याङ्कप्रकोष्टान्तर
आताम्राधरपाणिपादनयनप्रान्तः पृथूरःस्थलः।
मन्येऽयं द्विजमध्यगो नृपसुतः कोऽप्यम्ब! निःशम्बलः
पुत्र्येवं यदि कोष्ठमेतु सुकृतैः प्राप्तो विशेषातिथिः।।

अत्र 'स्वैररमणी रमणीयं दिनावसाने युवानं पथिकमालोक्याभिप्रायसूचकं जननीमेवं ब्रूते–यदसौ राजपुत्राकृतिः श्येनग्रहनाराचपरिचयोचितः सायं समये प्राप्तः इत्युक्ते मात्राप्यभिप्रायपूरकमभिहितम्– पुत्रि यद्येवं तत्कोष्ठाङ्कं प्रविशतु सुकृतैर्विशेषोऽतिथिः प्राप्तः पूज्य इत्येतेन स्फुटाभिप्रायसूचकमौचित्यमुपचितमाचकास्ति।

As in Dīpaka's (verse)—

"O mother, I think this person among these Brāhmaṇas is some prince; the upper side of his hand is scratched by the hawk's clutches, his forearm is marked on the inner side with the (rubbing of the) bow-string his lower lip, hands and feet and the corners of the eyes are copper red and he is braod-chested; but he has no provision for the journey'. 'Daughter, it be so, let him enter the house; through meritorious deeds have (we) obtained this special guest".

Here, a wanton lady, seeing a young agrreable, traveller, one fine evening, purposely says thus to her mother, "Here has arrived this (person) of princely appearance, accustomes to hawking and using arrows". Spoken thus the mother also intentionally says, "Daughter, if it be so, let him enter the house. Through (great) merit have we obtained this special guest who ought to be honoured". By this statement indicative of the purpose, the propriety becomes prominent.

न तु यथाऽस्यैव–

अयि विरहविचित्ते! भर्तुरर्थे तथार्ता सणदि निपतिता त्वं पादयोश्चण्डिकायाः।
स्वयमुपहितधूपस्थालकच्छत्रश्रृङ्गोद्दलितमपि ललाटं येन नैवाललक्षे।।

अत्र 'विनयवत्याः सुचिरात्पत्यावागते ललाटनखोल्लेखापह्नववचने सख्या समुपदिश्यमाने हे विरहोन्मत्ते भर्तुरर्थे चण्डिकापादपतनेस्वयंस्थापितधूपस्थालकोटिक्षतमपि न लक्षितं भवत्या ललाटमि'त्युक्तौ स्वैरापह्नवशिक्षामात्रमेवोपलक्ष्यते, न तु तस्याः सख्या वा कश्चिदभिप्रायविशेषः।। ३२।।

But not as in another (verse) of his—

O you, whose mind is unsteady on account of separation (from your husband), you were so much distressed for the sake of your husband, that you did not notice your forehead which, when you bowed all at once at the feet of Caṇḍikā was scratched with the bulging edge of the plate which contained the incense and which you yourself had placed'.

Here, pointing to the nail-scratches on the forehead of Vinayavatī whose husband had come after a long time, the female friend, in a dissimulatory manner speaks thus, "O you, frantic in separation, while bowing at Caṇḍika's feet for (the safe return of) your husband, you did not notice your forehead which had been scratched by the edge of the plate containing burning incense and which you yourself had placed". In this statement a mere training in dissimulatory speech is displayed; there is no special purpose either of the friend or of the heroine in these remarks.

स्वभावौचित्यं दर्शयितुमाह–

स्वभावौचित्यमाभाति सूक्तीनां चारुभूषणाम्।
अकृत्रिममसामान्यं लावण्यमिव योषिताम्।। ३३।।

To show the propriety of naturalness, (the author) says—

33. Propriety of naturalness appears like a beautiful ornament for compositions, just as natural (lit. inartifical) and unequalled beauty is a lovely ornament for women.

स्वभावोचितत्वं कविवाचामाभरणमाभाति, अकृत्रिममनन्यसामान्यं लावण्यमिव ललनानाम्।

Prorpiety of naturalenss looks like an ornament for the sayings of poets, as does the natural and unequalled beauty for women.

यथा मम मुनिमतमीमांसायाम्–

कर्णोत्तालितकुन्तलान्तनिपतत्तोयक्षणासङ्गिना
हारेणेव वृतस्तनी पुलकिता शीतेन सीत्कारिणी।
निर्धौताञ्जनशोपकोणनयना स्नानावसानेऽङ्गना
प्रस्यन्दत्कबरीभरा न कुरुते कस्य स्पृहार्द्रं मनः।।

अत्र 'व्याससूनोः शुकस्य गाढवैराग्यनिःसङ्गस्य गगनगङ्गातीरे स्नातोत्तीर्णत्रिदशयोषितो विवसनास्तद्दर्शननिःसङ्कोचाः पश्यतः प्रशमविमलमनसः स्मरव्यतिकरनिर्विकारतायां प्रतिपाद्यमानायां कर्णमूलोत्क्षिप्तालकपर्यन्तनिपतत्तोयकणसन्तानेन स्तनयोः कृतमुहूर्तहारविभ्रमा, शीतेन रोमाञ्चसीत्कारिणी, धौताञ्जनारुणनयनान्ता, प्रस्त्रवन्मुक्तकेशललापा, स्नानोत्तीर्णा तरुणी कस्य स्पृहार्द्रे न मनः कराती'त्युक्ते स्वयमाद्रेस्वभावः परमप्यार्द्रीक्रोतीत्युचितमेतत्।

As in my *Munimatamīmāṁsā*—

'Whose mind does not the lady make moist (so to speak) with passion at the end of her bath—the lady, whose bosom is covered as it were with the necklace (in the form of) the water dripping for the moment from the end of the tresses flung over her ears, whose hair are standing on end through cold, and who is thus producing a hissing sound, the corners of whose eyes are red, their collyrium being washed off, and whose braid is dripping (with drops of water)'.

Here has been established the unchanged (mental) state even (in the presence of excitants) for love in the case of Vyāsa's son, Śuka, indifferent on accouont of extreme renunciation, with his mind pure on account of (the power of) restraint, hesitation when being looked at by her. It has been said, "Whose mind does a beautiful woman not melt with passion—a woman from the ends of whose hair, flung back over the ears, is dripping a continuous chain of water-drops, which can be mistaken for the moment for a necklace on her breasts, and who is horripilated and is producing a hissing sound on account of cold, who has the corners of her eyes red, their collyrium being washed away, and whose hair is dripping and flowing loosely? Here it is quite appropriate when we say a thing already moist makes others also wet.

न तु यथा मम तत्रैव–

भक्तिः कातरतां क्षमा सभयतां पूज्यस्तुतिर्दीनतां
धैर्यं दारुणतां मतिः कुटिलतां विद्याबलं क्षोभताम्।
ध्यानं वञ्चकतां तपः कुहकतां शीलव्रतं षण्ढतां
पैशुन्यव्रतिनां गिरां किमिव वा नायाति दोषार्द्रताम्।।

अत्र 'पिशुनस्वभावे वर्णमाने भक्त्यादीनां गुणानां वैपरोत्ये प्रतिपादिते पिशुनानां वचसां किं वा दोषार्द्रतां नायाती'त्यभिहिते स्वयमनार्द्रस्वभावस्य परार्द्रीकरणमनुचितमेव।। ३३।।

But not as (in my verse) in the same work—

'Devotion is interpreted as cowardice, forgiveness as fear, the praise of the worthy as helplessness, firmness as cruelty, forethought as unscupulousness, power of learning as perturbance, meditation as deception, austerities as hypocrisy and vow of noble character as unmanliness. What is not tarnished (lit. moistened) with faults in the mouth of those who have taken a vow of wickedness?''

Here, while describing the character of the wicked and showing the contrary sense ascribed to virtues like devotion and others, the phrase, viz. what is not tarnished (lit. soaked) with calumny in the words of the wicked, is improper because of (the impossibility of) a dry object making something else wet.

सारसङ्ग्रहौचित्यं दर्शयितुमाह–

सारसंग्रहवाक्येन काव्यार्थः फलनिश्चितः।
अदीर्घसूत्रव्यापार इव कस्य न संमतः।। ३४।।

To show propriety of peroration, (the author) says—

34. To whom is not the meaning of a composition dear, (when its) sense has been determined by a perorative sentence and resembling thereby a transaction which is promptly carried out?

सारसंग्रहवाक्येत काव्यार्थः सुनिश्चितफलः शीघ्रकारिण इव व्यापारः कस्य नाभिमतः।

Who does not approve of the meaning of a composition, whose object has been established by means of a perorative sentence, like a transaction promptly carried out?

यथा मम मुनिमतमीमांसायाम्–

विविधगहनगर्भग्रन्थसम्भारभारैर्मुनिभिरभिनिविष्टैस्तत्त्वमुक्तं न किञ्चत्।
कृतरुचिरविचारं सारमेतन्महर्षेरहमिति भवभूमिर्नाहमित्येव मोक्षः।।

अत्र 'भगवद्गीतार्थविचारे सारसंग्रहोऽभिहितः–यत्किल मुनिभिरनेकभेदभिन्नशास्त्र-जडैरभिनिविष्टमतिभिस्तत्त्वमुपादेयं न किञ्चित्कथितम्। भगवतो महर्षेर्व्यासस्य सुमतेर्विमलविचारोत्तीर्णे निश्चितमेतदेव–यदहङ्कारः संसारमूलभूमिर्ममतापरित्याग एव मोक्ष' इति तत्सङ्क्षेपेण भयक्षयोपदेशः प्रकृतार्थस्य परममौचित्यं पुष्णाति।

As in my *Mūnimatamīmāṁsā*—

'The sages applying heart and soul have said nothing of reality in (their) manifold heaps of unfathomable books. After due deliberation; this is the essence of the great sages' (sayings) viz., egoism brings existence and the absence of its emancipation'.

While considering the meaning of the Bhagavadgītā, it has been summarised and expressed (thus), "No true principle worthy of note has been expounded by the sages whose minds have grown dull by (studying) the various dry śastras, and who are still applying themselves (to study). Verily this is the essence of the pure thoughts of the gifts of the revered sage Vyāsa that egoism is the cause of existence and the absence of is that of emancipatioṅ. Here, the summary of the advice for putting an end to existence develops the already full propriety of the context.

न तु यथा परिव्राजकस्य–

तपो न तप्तं वयमेव तप्ता भोगा न भुक्ता वयमेव भुक्ताः।
जरा न जीर्णा वयमेव जीर्णास्तृष्णा न याता वयमेव याताः।।

अत्र 'वयमेव तप्ता भुक्ता जीर्णा याता' इत्युक्ते निःसाराचारुत्वादपर्यवसितो वाक्यार्थः फलशून्यतया सारसंग्रहोचितं न किञ्चित्प्रतिपादयति।। ३४।।

But not as in Parivrājaka's (verse)—

'Penance hasnot been practised, rather it is we who have been afflicted, objects of delight have not been enjoyed (exhausted), rather it is we who have been exhausted; old age has not worn out, rather it is we who are worn out; our desires have not gone, but we ourselves are gone'.

Here, while saying, "It is we who have been afflicted, exhausted, worn out, and gone", the meaning of the sentence does not convey anything; it has no charm and fulfils no motive and nothing worth a summary has been said.

प्रतिभाभरणं काव्यमुचितं शोभते कवेः।
निर्मलं सुगुणस्येव कुलं भूतिविभूषितम्।। ३५।।

To show propriety of poetic fancy, (the author) says—

35. A Poet's composition properly ornamented with poetic

brilliance shines like the spotless family of a virtuous person gifted with fotrunes.

प्रतिभालङ्कृतं कवेः काव्यमुचितं गुणवतः कुलमिव विमलं लक्ष्म्या प्रकाशितं शोभते।

A poet's composition, properly ornamented with poetic brilliance shines like a virtuous person's spotless family made lustrous with wealth.

यथा मम लावण्यवत्याम्–

अदय! दशसि किं त्वं बिम्बबुद्ध्याधरं मे भव चपल निराशः पक्वजम्बूफलानाम्।
इति दयितमवेत्य द्वारदेशासमन्या निगदति शुकमुच्चैः कान्तदन्तक्षतौष्ठी।।

अत्र 'कयापि द्वारदेशाप्तं प्रियं ज्ञात्वा अन्यकामुकदशनखण्डितौष्ठ्या सम्प्रति तदागमनानभिज्ञयेव शुकमुद्दिश्य यदुक्तं–निर्दय, किं त्वं बिम्बफललोभादधरं मम विदारयसि, पक्वानां जम्बूफलानामिदानीं चपल निराशो भव कुपिता तुभ्यं नो दास्यामीति तेनोच्चैः प्रत्यायनापह्नवनवोन्मेषप्रज्ञाचातुर्यचारुवचनमौचित्यचमत्कारं करोति।

As in my *Lāvaṇyavatī*—

'O cruel one, do you bite my lower lip mistaking it for a 'bimba' (fruit)? O capricious one, now be despaired of (getting) the ripe 'jambū' fruit. Thus another seeing that her husnband had reached the foor loudly spekas to the parrot with her lip bitten by her paramour'.

Here, with her lips bitten by another uxorious, lover, and knowing that her husband had reached the door, a lady speaks to the parrot (posing) as if ignorant of his (i.e. her husband's) arrival, "O cruel one, why do you bite my lip thinking it to be a 'bimba' fruit? Now be despaired, O capricious one, of getting the 'jambū' fruit; I being angry, will not give it to you". The above remarks uttered loudly and made lovely through the cleverness, the wit, the novelty of thought and the convincing dissimulative way of saying, exhibit the beauty of propriety.

यदाह भट्टतौतः–'प्रज्ञा नवनवोन्मेषशालिनी प्रतिभा मता' इति।।

And Bhaṭṭa Tauta remarks, "Power to (create) ever novel thoughts is known as *(Pratibhā)* ingenuity".

न तु यथा मम तत्रैव–

निर्याते दयिते गृहे विशयने निर्माल्यमाल्ये हृते
प्राप्ते प्राप्तरसह्यरागिणि परे वारावहारे[1]ऽन्यथा।
द्वारालीनविलोचना व्यसनिनी सुप्ताहमेकाकिनी–
त्युक्त्वा निविविकर्षणैः स चरणाघातैरशोकीकृतः।।

अत्र वेश्या व्यालग्नकामुकस्य वारावहारं विधाय नवकामुकेन सह क्षपायां नीतायां प्रभाते तस्मिन्निर्याते शय्याकुसुमादिसम्भोगलक्षणे निवारिते वारवरञ्चनकुपिते गाढानुरागग्रहग्रस्तमतौ पूर्वकामुके प्राप्ते त्वदालोकनकाङ्क्षिणी व्यसनिनी द्वारन्यस्तनयनाहमेकाकिनी सुप्तेति प्रत्यायनावचनविलीनमन्युसरभससरसनी– विकर्षणोद्यता– कृतिकृतेर्ष्याकोपया चरणनलिनप्रहारैरशोकीकृतः शङ्कशल्योन्मूलनान्निःशोकः सम्पादितः सन्ततपुलाकाङ्कुरत्वादशोकतरुतुल्यतां नीत इति वा वाक्यार्थः केवलसत्यविप्रलम्भ– प्रालभ्यमात्रमेव गणिकाया गाढरागमूलतां च प्रतिपादयति, न तु प्रतिनोद्भूतामोचित्यकणिकां सूचयति।। ३५।।

But not as in the same work of mine—

'The lover having departed, the bedding having been removed from the room, the stale garlands having been put aside, when the one of intense passion whose day of appointment she had not kept had arrived in the morning, the wanton lady dispelled his grief by kicking him too when about to loosen her girdle-string, and saying, "Ah! with my eyes fixed at the door, I had to sleep all alone".

Here, not keeping her appointment with the man already in love with her and spending the night with a fresh paramour, and removing all the signs of amorous sport viz., the bedding,the flowers and the rest, when he had left in the morning, the prostitute, at the arrival of the former, angry at his breaking the appointment, and with is mind caught in love for her, dispelled his greif (or else by removing the shaft of his doubt made him resemble the Aśoka tree with his hair-like sprouts standing on their ends), as she kicked him with her lotus-like foot through (posed) jealousy and anger, when he was about to loosen her girdle-string quickly and assuaged his anger with words arrousing confidence, namely, "With my eyes fixed at the door, in my longing to meet you, I slept all alone! This sentence shows

१. तद्दि ने दू रीकृते।

the base character of a courtesan's lust and only conceals the truth in an eloquent manner. It does not show an atom of propriety arising from ingenuity.

अवस्थौचित्यमाद्यत्ते काव्यं जगति पूज्यताम्।
विचार्यमाणरुचिरं कर्तव्यमिव धीमताम्।। ३६ ।।

To show propriety of the circumstances described, (the author says)—

36. A composition (containing) the propriety of circumstances (described) becomes an object of worship of the world, like the captivating deeds of the wise done after due deliberation.

अवस्थोचिततया काव्यं जगति श्लाव्यतामायाति, मतिमतामिव कृत्यं विचारनिर्घर्षरुचिरम्।

Through propriety of circumstances described, a composition is honoured in the world like the lovable acts of the wise done after due deliberation.

यथा मम लावण्यवत्याम्–

मुक्तः कन्दुकविभ्रमस्तरलता त्यक्तैव बाल्योचिता
मौग्ध्यं निर्धुतमाश्रिता गजगतिर्भ्रूलास्यमभ्यस्यते।
यन्नर्मोर्मिषु निर्मितं मृगदृशा वैदग्ध्यदिव्यं वच–
स्तद्विद्मः सुभगाभिमानलटभाभावे निबद्धो भरः।।

अत्र यदुक्तं–कन्दुकक्रीडा त्यक्ता, बलचापल्यं परिहृतम्, मौग्धयं निरस्तम्, गजगतिरङ्गीकृता, भ्रूलतालास्याभ्यासः क्रियते, नर्मोर्मिषु वचनवैचित्र्यमासूत्रितम्, तेन जानीमहे शैशवावस्थां समुत्सृजन्त्या यौवनमाश्रयन्त्या प्रौढतामनारूढयापि नवसम्भोगगौरवगर्भेण सुभगाभिमानेन लटभाभावे बालया भरो निबद्धः, इत्यभिहिते स्फुटधिया वयोवस्थामध्यसन्धिवर्णनायामौचित्यं स्फुरदिवावभासते।

As in my *Lāvaṇyavatī*—

'Playing with the ball has been abandoned, restlessness befitting childhood has been given up, artless loveliness has vanished, a gait like that of an elephant has been resorted, to the elegant play of the eye-brows is being practised, and since the fawn-eyed one has developed sparkling wit in her amorous talk, we presume that she has amassed a good load of elegant charms, a source of pride to young ladies'.

Here, it has been said, "Playing with the ball has been left off, restlessness befitting childhood has vanished, artless loveliness has disappeared, the gait of an elephant has been accepted, a practice in the wanton play of the creeper-like eyebrows has been resorted to, and an amazing with has been developed in amorous talk. So we know that having left her girlhood and passing over to youth, but not fully embracing it, the maiden in her pride of beauty implying the urgency of approaching union, has amassed (so to speak) a heap of elegant charms which go to make a young damsel". In these words, propriety shines forth prominently, it being portrayed clearly in the description of the middle stage of youth.

न तु यथा राजशेखरस्य-

ज्यायान्धन्वी नवधृतधनुस्ताम्रहस्तोदरेण
क्षत्रक्षोदव्यतिकरपटुस्ताटकाताडकेन।
कर्णाभ्यर्णस्फुरितपलितः क्षीरकण्ठेन सार्धं
योद्धुं वाच्छन्न कथममुना लज्जते जामदग्न्यः।।

अत्र 'भार्गवः स्थविरावस्थास्थितः स्थिरतरपराक्रमकर्कशप्रौढो धनुर्धरः शिशुनारामेण धनुर्ग्रहणारुणितकोमलकरकमलतलेन क्षत्रियक्षयसंरम्भप्रगल्भस्ताटकाताडकेन स्फुरदाकर्णपलितः सम्भाव्यमानजननीस्तनक्षीरकण्ठेनामुना युयुत्सुः कथं न लज्जत' इत्युक्ते पेशलतया राधवावस्थायां जामदग्न्यावस्थाविपरीतायां प्रतिपाद्यमानायां ताटकाताडकेनेति विरुद्धाधिबाऽसोर्थः किमप्यनौचित्पेन चेतसि सङ्कोचमादधाति।। ३६।।

Not as in Rājaśekhara's (verse)—

'Is not Jamadagni's son ashamed of desiring to fight with this (boy) whose palms are red becuae of lack of practice in holding the bow, who has killed only Tāṭakā and whose throat still has in it the milk[1] (from his mother's breasts i.e. who is very young);—Jamadagni's son who is a great archer, clever enough to kill all the Kṣatriyas, and who has white hair flowing over his ears?'

Here, in the statement, viz. is not aged Bhārgava, a fine arhcer

1. Cf. the phrase दूधमूंहा in Hindi.

and powerful (lit. grown) enough to do horrible deeds of valour, ashamed of his desire to fight with the child Rāma, whose delicate, lotus-like palms have grown red by catching the bow; —Bhārgava, who has the power to kill all the Kṣatriyas while Rāma has killed only Tāṭakā. Bhārgava has grey hair flowing up to his ears, while Rāma's throat possibly has yet in it the milk from the breasts of his mother. While artificially describing the difference between the ages of Rāma and one of the son of Jamadagni, the phrase "killer of Tāṭakā" has a contrary effect (i.e. shows Rāma's valour) and brings about some indescribable impropriety which makes the mind shrink.

विचारौचित्यं दर्शयितुमाह–

उचितेन विचारेण चारुतां यान्ति सूक्तयः।
वेद्यतत्त्वावबोधेन विद्या इव मनीषिणाम्।। ३७।।

To show propriety of thought, (the author) says—

37. The composition becomes beautiful by proper thought just as the education of the wise becomes charming on account of learning what really ought to be learnt.

विचारौचित्यनेन सूक्तयश्चारूतां यान्ति, ज्ञेयस्वरूपज्ञानेन विद्या इव विदूषाम्।

By the propriety in thought a composition attains beauty, just as the knowledge of the learned attains beauty by knowing that which is worth knowing.

यथा मम मुनिमतमीमांसायाम्–

अश्वत्थामवधाभिधानसमये सत्यव्रतोत्साहिना
मिथ्या धर्मसुतेन जिह्मवचसा हस्तीति यद्याहृतम्।
सा सत्यामृतरश्मिवैरमसमं संसूचयन्त्याः सदा
शङ्के पङ्कजसंश्रयेण मलिनारम्भा विजृम्भा श्रियः।।

अत्र 'द्रोणनिधनाख्याने सत्यवतोत्साहवता धर्मतनयेनापि मिथ्या लघुवचसा कुञ्जर इति यदुक्तं, सा सततं सत्यचन्द्रद्वेषं सूचयन्त्याः श्रियः शङ्के पङ्कजसंश्रयेण मलिनव्यापारा विजृम्भे'त्यभिहिते ससंवादलक्ष्मीस्वभारिभावनतया तत्त्वावबोधेन मूलविश्रान्त्या फलपर्यवसायी विचारः सहृदयसंवेद्यमौचित्यं व्यनक्ति।

As in my *Munimatamīmāṁsā*—

'The word that Yudhiṣṭhira, the zealous observer of the vow of truth, uttered falsely, viz., "Elephant" in a crooked manner at the time of announcing the death of Aśvatthāman, was nothing but the delusive display (lit. yawn) of Royal Glory sullied on account of her association with the mud born lotus[1] disclosing her deadly enmity towards the moon of truthfulness:

Here, in the story of Droṇa's death, the statement is, "(On account of) the fact that even Yudhiṣṭhira, son of Dharma and observer of the vow of truth, told a lie and spoke the word 'elephant' in a low voice, I think the Goddess of Wealth (shows) her enmity towards the moon by her display (lit. yawn) of disgust for her lotuses (closing at the rise of the moon)". (In this statement) the thought results in the final agreeable propriety made prominent by revealing the reality of the nature of the Goddess of Wealth in an appropriate manner.

न तु यथा मम तत्रैव–

प्रग्लाने चिरकालवृत्तदयिताकेशाम्बराकर्षणे
क्रूरं राक्षसवैशसं यदि कृतं भीमेन दुःशासने।
तत्कालक्षमिणा कुशाश्मपरुषारण्यप्रवासे चिरं
किं पीतं तततापमग्ननहिषस्वेनम्बुपृक्तं पयः।।

अत्र भीमसेनचरिते विचार्यमाणे त्रयोदशदवर्षपर्युषिते कृष्णाकेशाकर्षणपराभवे भीमेन भीमं राक्षसकर्म दुःशासने यदि कृतं तत्सद्यःकृतार्द्रापराधकालक्षमिणा सुचिरं दर्भसूचीविषमाश्मपरुषवनवासे किं ग्रीष्मतापनिमग्नमहिषस्वेदस्रुतिपृक्तं पयः पीतमित्यनुपपन्नकृत्येऽभिहिते कारणविचाराभावान्निर्मूलोपालम्भमात्रमनौचित्यमनुबध्नाति।। ३७।।

But not as in (another verse) in the same work of mine—

'If Bhīma had to commit that demoniac deed of cruelly murdering Duśśasana, when that crime of Duśśasana in pulling his (Bhīma's) beloved Draupadī's clothes and hair had been perpetrated long ago and even faded in memory, why did he, Bhīma in the forest exile, hard on account of kuśa grass and stones, drink for a long time the water mixed with the sweat drops of buffaloes plunged therein being afflicted with heat, when he could do the same act instantly?'

---

1. The splendour of the moon (श्रीः) is inimical towards the lotus.

Here, while pondering over Bhīmasena's exploits (it has been said) "If Bhīma had to commit that demon-like cruel deed of Duśśasana on account of his pulling Kṛṣṇa's hair and clothes thirteen years back, then why did he, who could avenge the newly performed act, even then drink water mixed with this flowing sweat of baffaloes lying therein on account of the heat of summer, while in exile where life was hard on account of the pricking kuśa blades and difficult on account of stones"? In this sentence in discribing the deplorable deed, the author has displayed inappropriateness, because it is a mere taunt and the real cause of Bhīmasena's not killing Duśśāsana then has not been brought out.

नामौचित्यं दर्शयितुमाह–

नाम्ना कर्मानुरूयेण ज्ञायते गुणदोषयोः।
काव्यस्य पुरुषस्येव व्यक्तिः संवादपातिनी।। ३८।।

To show propriety of names, (the author) says—

38. By the significant term, conforming to the motive, the merits and demerits of a composition are shown, just as the name worthy of the acts of a person shows his virtues and defects.

The object of poetry is 'Propriety' and it is by means of suitable names that the merits and demerits of a poem are exposed in an elegant manner, just as a man's name shows his virtues and defects.

यथा कालिदासस्य–

इदमसुलभवस्तुप्रार्थनादुर्निवारः प्रथममपि मनो मे पञ्चबाणः क्षिणोति।
किमुत मलयवातान्दोलितापाण्डुपत्रैरुपवनसहकारैर्दर्शितेष्वङ्कुरेषु ।।

अत्र 'प्रारम्भ एव ममेदं मनः पञ्चबाणः सुदुर्लभवस्तुप्रार्थनादुर्निवारः शकलीकरोति, किमु त लीलाद्यानसहकारैर्मलयानिलान्दोलितबालपल्लवैरङ्कुरेषु दर्शितेष्वि'त्युक्ते मदनस्य पञ्चबाणभिधानमुचितमेन।

As in Kālidāsa's (verse)—

'The five-arrowed god, whom it is difficult to resist because of yearnings for an object difficult to obtain, already afflicts this my heart; nothing to say when the mangoes in the orchard, with their yellowish leaves moving in the Malaya breeze, show their blossoms'.

Here, in the statement, viz. 'the god of love, having five arrows and difficult to stop from longing for scarce objects, has already torn my heart into shreds; what (will happen) when the mango trees or the sport garden, with their fresh leaves being shaken by the Malaya breeze, put forth their blossoms', the epithet five-arrowed one for the god of love is proper.

यथा वा मम बौद्धावदानलतायाम्–

तारुण्येन निपीतशैशवतया साऽनङ्गश्रृङ्गारिणी
तन्वङ्ग्या सकलाङ्गसङ्गमसखी भङ्गिर्नवाङ्गकृता।
निःसंरम्भपराक्रमः पृथुतरारम्भाभियोगं विना
साम्राज्ये जगतां यथा विजयते देवो विलासायुधः।।

अत्र 'यौवननिपीतशैशवया तन्वङ्ग्याऽनङ्गशृङ्गारवति सर्वाङ्गसङ्गमसखी सा काप्यभिनवा भङ्गिरङ्गीकृता यया निष्प्रयत्नपराक्रमः प्रभूततरारम्भसम्भारं विहाय त्रिभुवनसाम्राज्ये जयति देवो विलासायुध' इत्युक्ते कामस्य विलासायुध इति नामोपपन्नमेव, तन्वङ्गीभङ्ग्यैव सिद्धत्रैलोक्याधिपत्यविजिगीषायां कामसायकादीनां नैरर्थक्यात्।

Or, for instance, in my *Bauddhāvadānalatā*—

'Her childhood having vanished at the advent of youth the slender-bodied one has appropriated to herself fresh graces of blandishment, the very ornament of the god of love, a friend embracing all her limbs, the grace by which the god who has erotic pleasures as his missiles and whose onslaught knows no check, conquers the kingdom of the worlds, even without preparation on a large scale'.

Here, it has been said, 'the slender-bodied one, with her childhood being usurped by youth, has appropriated to herself a new indescribable grace which is her friend as it embraces all her limbs, and which is the very ornament of the god of Love, by which the god whose valour needs no effort to display itself and who has enjoyment as his missile, conquers the kingdom of the three words without preparation on any large scale'. In this statement the epithet, "he who has enjoyment as his missile" is proper for the god of Love, for in the desire to conquer the three worlds by means of the grace of a slender-limbed damsle, the other arrows and other (missiles) of the god of Love are useless.

न तु यथा कालिदासस्य–

क्रोधं प्रभो! संहर संहरेति यावद्गिरः खे मरुतां चरन्ति।
तावत्स वह्निर्भवनेत्रजन्मा भस्मावशेषं मदनं चकार।।

अत्र–पश्यतो भगवतस्त्रिनेत्रस्य स्मरशरनिपातक्षोभे वर्ण्यमाने तन्निकारकोपशमाय 'संहर संहर प्रभो क्रोधमि'ति यावद्वचः खे देवाना चरति तावद्भवनेत्रोद्भवः स वह्निर्मदनं भस्मराशिशेषमकार्षीत्–इत्युक्ते संहारावसरे रुद्रस्य भवाभिधानमनुचितमेव।। ३८।।

But not as in Kālidāsa's (verse)—

'O Lord, restrain, restrain thy wrath', while the voices of the gods in the air murmured thus, that fire born of the eye of the Auscipious One (i.e. Śiva) reduced the god of Love to ashes'.

Here, while describing the confusion caused by the shooting of arrows by the god of Love at the illustrious Śiva while he was seeing (all this), and the voices of the gods were moving in the air in order to pacity his anger, saying "Restrain O Lord, restrain thy wrath"; that fire born of Śiva's eye reduced the god of Love to a heap of ashes; the use of 'Bhava' (i.e. Creator) in place of Rudra (the terrific) is inappropriate.

आशीर्वचनौचित्यं दर्शयितुमाह–

पूर्णार्थदातुः काव्यस्य सन्तोषितमनीषिणीः।
उचिताशीर्नृपस्येव भवत्यभ्युदयावहा।। ३९।।

To show propriety of benedictory stanzas, (the author) says—

39. A proper benediction raises the value of a poem that gives a complete sense and satisfies the learned; just as a proper benediction increases the prosperity of a king who gives all his wealth (in charity) and appeases the learned men.

यथास्मदुपाध्यायगङ्गकस्य–

स कोऽपि प्रेमार्द्रः प्रणयपरिपाकप्रचलितो
विलासोऽक्ष्णां देयात्सुखमनुपमं वो मृगदृशाम्।
यदाकूतं दृष्ट्वा पिदधति मुखं तूणविवरे
निरस्तव्यापारा भुवनजयिनः पञ्च विशिखाः।।

अत्र 'स कोऽप्यसामान्यप्रेमप्रणयविश्रान्तिप्रगल्भकुरङ्गदृशा निरुवमो नयनविला सः सुखं वो देयात्, यदभिप्रायमालोक्य भुवनजयिनः कामस्य पञ्च सायकाः समाप्तव्यापारास्तूणीरविवरे लज्जयेव मुखं पिदधती'त्युक्ते सुखं वो देयादित्याशीःपदमुचितमेव, प्रियानयनविभ्रमस्य सुखार्पणयोग्यत्वात्।

As in my teacher Gaṅgaka's (verse)—

'May that indescribable play of the eyes of the fawn-eyed ladies grant you unparallelled joy—the play of the eyes which is steeped in love and throbbing with the intensity of affection and seeing whose wondrous (deeds), (love's) five arrows which conquered the world, relinquishing their work, hide their faces in the quiver'.

Here, is the staement "May that indescribable and unparalleled play of the eyes of the fawn-eyed lady, spirited with the intensity of love, grant you happiness; the play of the eyes, seeing whose valour (lit. object) love's five world-conquering arrows, giving up their work, hide their faces in the quiver as if out of shame"—the benedictory phrase 'may it grant you pleasure' is just proper, because the play of the beloved's eyes is capable of giving pleasure.

यथा वा मम वात्स्यायनसूत्रसारे–

कामः कामं कमलवदनानेत्रपर्यन्तवासी दासीभूतत्रिभुवनजनः प्रीतये जायतां वः।
दग्धस्यापि त्रिपुररिपुणा सर्वलोकस्पृहार्हा यस्याधिक्यं रुचिरतितराम ञ्जनस्येव याता।।

अत्र 'कामः प्रीयते वो जायतां यस्य दग्धस्याप्यञ्जनस्येवाधिक्यं रुचिर्यातिश्त्युक्ते प्रीयते जायतामित्युचितं, कामस्य प्रीत्यात्मत्वात्।

As also in my *Vātsyāyanasūtrasāra*—

'May the god of Love grant pleasure to you—the god of love, residing in the eye-corners of the lotus-faced ladies, who enslaves the people of the three worlds, and the grace of whom, though burnt by Śiva, has become clearer to (the people of) all the world, and who thus resembles the collyrium which is burnt black and resides in the eye-corners of lotus-faced ladies, and enslaves the people of three worlds, and is worthy of the longings of the people of all the worlds'.

Here, in the statement, 'May the god of Love, the grace of whom though burnt, like collyrium, has increased—(the benediction), 'may grant you pleasure' is proper because the god of Love is pleasure-incarnate.

न तु यथाऽमरुकस्य–

आलोलामलकावलीं विलुलितां बिभ्रच्चलत्कुण्डलं
किंचिन्मृष्टविशेषकं तनुतरैः स्वेदाम्भसां सीकरैः।

तन्वङ्ग्याः सुतरां रतान्तसमये वक्त्रं रतिव्यत्यये
तत्त्वां पातु चिराय किं हरिहरस्कन्दादिभिर्दैवतैः।।

अत्र 'तन्व्या रतिव्यत्यये लोलालकं चलत्कुण्डलं स्वेदसलिलेन किञ्चिदुन्मृष्टतिलकं न्यन्मुखं तत्त्वां पातु, किं हरिहरस्कन्दादिभिर्दैवतैरि'त्युक्ते पातु त्वामित्यनुचितम्, आनन्दयतु त्वामित्युचितं स्यात्।

अन्येषु काव्याङ्गेष्वनयैव दिशा स्वयमौचित्यमुत्प्रेक्षणीयम्। तदुदाहरणान्यानन्त्यान्न प्रदर्शितानीत्यलमतिप्रसङ्गेन।। ३९।।

But not as in Amaruka's (verse)—

'Away with gods like Hari, Hara and Skanda,—may the face of the fair limbed lady, at the end of the erotic pleasures when amorous play had ceased, protect you,—the damsel's face, which has beautiful tremulous tresses, unsteady ear-rings and the auspicious mark on the forehead washed off a little by the mild spray of sweat-drops'.

Here, the statement is—"May the damsel's face with tremulous locks and ear-rings and the mark of the forehead washed off by sweat at the end of amorous sport, protect you; talk no more of gods like Hari, Hara and Skanda". (Here, the expression) "may it protect you", is improper. "may it please you", should have been better. One should, in this very manner, see propriety in other parts of a composition. Their examples have not been cited for they are too numerous. Let me desist from prolixity.

आसीत्प्रकाशेन्द्र इति प्रकाशः काश्मीरदेशे त्रिदशेश्वरश्रीः।
अभूद्गृहे यस्य पवित्रसत्रमच्छिन्नमग्रासनमग्रजानाम्।।
यः श्रीस्वयम्भूभवने विचित्रे लेप्यप्रतिष्ठापितमातृचक्रः।
गोभूमिकृष्णाजिनवेश्मदाता तत्रैव काले तनुमुत्ससर्ज।।
तस्मात्मजः सर्वमनीषिशिष्यः श्रीव्यासदासापरपुण्यनामा।
क्षेमेन्द्र इत्यक्षयकाव्यकीर्तिश्चक्रे नवौचित्यविचारचर्चाम्।।
क्षीरत्नसिंहे सुहृदि प्रयाते शार्वं पुरं श्रीविजयेशराज्ञि।
तदात्मजस्योदयसिंहनाम्नः कृते कृतस्तेन गिरां विचारः।।
यस्यासिः परिवारकृत्त्रिभुवनप्रख्यातशीलश्रुतेः
सर्वस्यावनतेन येन नितरां प्राप्ता विशेषोन्नतिः।
आशाः शीतलतां नयत्यविरतं यस्य प्रतापानल-
स्तस्य श्रीमदनन्तराजनृपतेः काले किलाऽयं कृतः।।

There was Prakāśendra, the very light of the country of Kashmir. He (possessed) the glory of the lord of gods. In this house there were (always) going on a continuous sanctifying sacrifice inwhich the Brāhmaṇas obtained the foremost place. In the wonderful temple of great Svayambhu (Brahman) he installed the figure of (sixteen) mothers in painting. (In that very temple) in course of time he, the donor of cows, land, black deer skings and dwelling places, gave up his life (lit. left his body).

His son, Kṣemendra, also known by the blessed name of 'Vyāsadāsa' (follower of Vyāsa) and the pupil of all the learned men (of the age) and possessed of imperishable poetic fame, composed this new treatise on *"Propriety in Poetry"*.

When (his) honoured friend Ratanasiṁha had left for the heavenly abode in the reign of Śrī Vijayeśa,[1] these musings on speech were put together for the sake of his son, Udayasiṁha by name.

This work has been verily composed during the reign of the illustrious king Anantarāja, whose learning and good conduct are reputed in the three worlds, whose sword turns every one to be his follower, who has achieved unique exaltation by being modest to all, and the fire of whose glory keeps the quarters quite (lit. cool).

इति श्रीप्रकाशेन्द्रात्मजव्यासदासापराख्यश्रीक्षेमेन्द्रकृता औचित्यविचारचर्चा समाप्ता।

Thus ends A CRITICAL DISCOURSE ON THE THEORY OF PROPRIETY composed by Kṣemendra, alias Vyāsadāsa, son of reverted Prakāśendra.

—•—

1. विजयेशराज्ञि is incorrect according to Pāṇini; it is *mahākaviprayoga!* The names Vijayeśa and Ratanasiṁha do not occur is the Rājataraṅgiṇī. Thephrase शार्वं पुरं श्रीविजयेशराज्ञि may refer to a place of pilgrimage called Vijayeśvara or Vijayeśa, modern Bījabehārā between Anantanāga and Śīnagara, or शार्वं पुरम् may be modern Sopur and Vijayeśa may be a feudatory king.

महाकविश्रीक्षेमेन्द्रकृतं

सुवृत्ततिलकम्

Suvṛttatilaka or Forehead-Mark of Fine Metres

प्रथमो विन्यासः

Chapter I

गणपतिगुरोर्वक्रश्चूडाशशाङ्ककलाङ्कुरः
स्फुटफणिफणारत्नच्छयाछ्टाच्छुरणारुणः
गिरिपतिसुतासंसक्तेर्ष्याविलासकचग्रहः-
च्युतनखशिखालेखाकान्तस्तनोतु सुखानि वः।। १ ।।

1. May the crooked sporut-like digit of the moon on the head of Śiva (lit. Gaṇpati's father) grant you happiness;—the digit of the moon, which is red through the reflection of the lustre of shining jewels in the prominent hoods of the serpents, and which is as graceful as the bright (śikhā) mark of the nails made on Pārvatī's person at the time of catching her hair amorously in a fit of solicitous envy.

स्वच्छन्दलघुरूपाय त्रिजगद्गुरवे नमः।
स्पष्टवामनवृत्ताय मायावक्राय चक्रिणे।। २ ।।

2. (Our) homage to Viṣṇu, (lit. the discus-bearer) the preceptor of the three world, who can assume a small size at his will, whose exploits as a dwarf are well-know and who is crooked through his illusive power.

नमश्छन्दोनिधानायसुवृत्ताचारवेधसे ।
तपःसत्यनिवासाय व्यासायामिततेजसे।। ३ ।।

3. Salutation to Vyāsa of immnes lustre, the treasure house

of (different kinds of) metres, an authrotiy on good conduct and etiquette, and the very abode of asceticism and truth.

क्षेमेन्द्रेण सुशिष्याणां सरस्वत्याः प्रसाधनम्।
सुवृत्ततिलकं वर्णरुचिरं क्रियते मुखे।।४।।

4. Kṣemendra composes for his intelligent pupils, the 'Suvṛttatilaka' of chamring lttters, a decoration for the face of the Goddess of Learning, and a decorative mark of bright pigment on her forehead.

दृष्ट्वा छन्दांसि सौन्दर्यं विचार्यार्यप्रियः कृतः।
प्रसिद्धकाव्यकर्मण्यवृत्तानामेष संग्रहः।।५।।

5. Having examined the metres, and considered their (respective) charm, this collection is made (of metres) loved by eminent poets;—metres, which are chiefly used in the making of poerty.

दीर्घे संयोगपूर्वे च गुरुसंज्ञा प्रकीर्तिता।
असंयोगग्रहं ह्रस्वं लघुसंज्ञं प्रकीर्तितम्।।६।।

6. A vowel is said to be havey when it is long or occurs before a conjuct letter and it is said to be light when it is short and does not precede a conjunct letter.

त्रिगुरुःप्राग्गुरुर्मध्यगुरुरन्तगुरुस्तथा।
त्रिलघुःप्राग्लघुर्मध्यलघुरन्तलघुस्तथा।।७।।
मभजाः सनया रेफतकारौ चेति संज्ञिताः।
ज्ञेयो लघुर्लकारोऽत्र गकारश्च गुरुर्मतः।।८।।

7-8. (The groups of syllables having) three long (vowles), the initial as long, the middle as long, the final as long, the three as short, the initial as short, the middle as short, or the finalas short, have respectively been indicated by the letters : 'ma', 'bha', 'ja', 'sa', 'na', 'ya', 'ra' and 'ta'. The letter 'la' stands for a short vowel, while 'ga' designates a long one.

क्वचिद्विक्षिप्तसंस्थानैः क्वचिदेकपदस्थितैः।
क्व संयोगस्थैः क्वचिद् दत्तमुदाहरणमक्षरैः।।९।।

9. Examples have been given of consonants sometimes in the same foot, and sometimes occuring as conjuncts.

पूर्वाक्षरद्वयासक्तविरामेण षडक्षरा।
तकारेण यकारेण तनुमध्याऽभिधीयते।। १०।।

10. (The metre) having six letter, with the caesura after the first two letters, and having 'ta' and 'ya' (types of gaṇas), is called 'Tanumadhyā'.

As in my (verse)—

'Verily she has been so apportioned by her age that the slender-waisted[1] (Tanumadhyā) one acquires coquetry all the more'.

सप्ताक्षरसमायुक्तं जसाभ्यां गुरुणा तथा।
अविरामं विदुर्वृत्तं कुमारललिताभिधम्।। ११।।

11. (The metre) containing seven letters and comprising ja, sa, and one long syllalbe, and having no caesura is the well-known metre called 'Kumāralalita'.

As in my (verse)—

'These people, servile imitators, do not think of (lit. take pity on) the person who has been reduced to the state of memory (i.e. is dead). (Verily) this means frivolity of the young (Kumāralalita)'.

मकारयुगपर्यन्ते यत्संयुक्तगुरुद्वयम्।
विद्युन्मालाभिधं तद्धि वृत्तमष्टाक्षरं विदुः।। १२।।

12. The metre having eight syllables (consisting of) two long ones occurring after two *ma* combinations is called the 'Viyunmālā'.

As in my (verse)—

'At the time when the streaks of lightning (Vidynmālā) are busy dancing on the lap of clouds, the beloved (takes recourse to)

---

1. The names of the metres are so used as to give a relevant sense in the context. Most of the names of the metres signify attribute of young ladies. It shows that women took part in music and dance.

silence, meditation, sleeping on the ground, and her love-sickness becomes acute'.

लघोर्गुरोश्च विच्छित्त्यां यत्रानन्तर्यसङ्गतिः।
वृत्तप्रमाणनिपुणैः सा प्रमाणीति कीर्तिता।। १३।।

13. In which the short and logn syllables are used in close sequence (i.e. one after the other) in a charming manner, that is called the "Pramāṇī" by those who are authorities on metres.

As in my (verse)—

'A little knowledge flared up with arrogance means only labour for the teacher; and that power (Pramāṇī) which brings no good to others is also useless.'

पञ्चमं लघु सर्वेषु सप्तमं द्विचतुर्थयोः।
गुरु षष्ठं च सर्वेषामेतच्छ्लोकस्य लक्षणम्।। १४।।

14. The fifth (syllable) is short in all (the feet), while the seventh (is short) is the second and the fourth (foot); the sixth syllable is long in all (the feet). This is the scheme of a *śloka.*

असंख्यो भेदसंसर्गादनुष्टुप्छन्दसां गणः।
तत्र लक्ष्यानुसारेण श्रव्यतायाः प्रधानता।। १५।।

15. The varieties of Anuṣṭup metre, on account of its different combinations, are innumerable, *Appeal to the ear* accroding to the illustration in hand (in using the metre) is the main consideration.

As in the revered Vyāsa's (verse)—

'There the eastern quarter was adorned with the moon, the lord of white water-lilies, palish white like the cheeks of beautiful ladies, and a delight to the eyes'.

नवाक्षरापि ननमैरक्षरैरुपलक्षिता।
भुजगाग्रा शिशुसृता कथिता वृत्तकोविदैः।। १६।।

16. The metre having nine syllables of the combinations of 'na', 'na' and 'bha' groups, is called by those well-versed in prosody, Bhujaga-Śisusṛtā.

As in my (verse)—

'Why do not these dull people bow with devotion at Śiva's feet, which dispel the fear of births and rebirths, and which have a serpentine move (Bhujaga-Śiśusṛtā).

संयुक्तं भमसैरन्ते गुरुणा च दशाक्षरम्।
वृत्तं रुक्मवती नाम कथितं वृत्तशालिभिः।। १७।।

17. The metre called the "Rukmavatī" has been described by those engaged in (the science of) prosody as having ten syllables, comprising of goups 'bha', 'ma', 'sa' and a long vowel.

As in my (verse)—

'The great delusion of birth and rebirth full of illusion has been broken through thousands of unreal bodies. Alas! who can own this fortune, consisting of gold (Rukmavatī), coming and going, and as unreal as dealings in a dream'.

तकाराभ्यां जकारेण युक्तं गुरुयुगेन च।
इन्द्रवज्राभिधं प्राहुर्वृत्तमेकादशाक्षरम्।। १८।।

18. They call that metre 'Indravajrā', which contains eleven syllables comprising of two groups of 'ta' types joined to a 'ja' group and two long syllables.

As in my (vrse)—

'Oh him in whose heart dreadful greed and anger, invisible from their very inception have secured a foothold, befalls unbearable misfourtune resembing the fall of Indra's blazing thunderbolt and so on. (Indravajrā—a bolt from the blue)'.

जतजैर्गुरुयुग्मेन संसक्तैरुपलक्षितम्।
वदन्त्युपेन्द्रवज्राख्यं वृत्तमेकादशाक्षरम्।। १९।।

19. The metre 'Upendravajrā' is one that has eleven syllables comprising of the groups 'ja', 'ta', 'ja' in order and combined with two long vowels.

As in my (verse)—

'In this world those alone have conquered the worldly illusion who meditate as instructed by their preceptors on Śiva, who is worshipped by Brahamā and others, and Upendra, the thunderbolt-holder (Indra) and the lord of Waters (Varuṇa)'.

पदानन्तरविन्यासयोगैर्बहुभिरेतयोः ।
वैचित्र्यजातिरुचिरा भवन्त्येवोपजातयः ।। २० ।।

20. By means of various combinations of these two (i.e. the Indravajrā and the Upendravajrā) in alternate (feet of a verse) the metre becomes "Upajātiṅ charming through abundance of novelty.

भकारत्रयसंयुक्तमन्ते गुरुयुगान्वितम् ।
कथितं दोधकं नाम वृत्तमेकादशाक्षरम् ।। २१ ।।

21.The metre called the 'Dodhaka' has eleven syllalbes comprising three groups of 'bha' type follwed by two long syllalbes.

As in my (verse)—

'O ye wordly enjoyments, transitory like the worldly delusion, depart; now I have no more of infatuation; moreover there resides in (my) mind Śiva, bearing the digit of the moon and granting to his devotees immunity from fear'.[1]

पूर्वाक्षरचतुष्कान्तविरतिर्मततान्विता ।
गुरुद्वितययुक्ता च शालिन्येकादशाक्षरा ।। २२ ।।

22. (The metre called) Śāliṇi has eleven syllables comprising of 'ma', 'ta', and 'ta' in order, combined with two long syllalbes, and has caesura after the first four syllables.

As in my (verse)—

'Two whom is not dear the tremulous, intoxicated, and playful damsel (Śālinī) of sweet copper-coloured compact cheeks speaking irrelevant things in the middle of conversation, and closely embraced by youth.

---

1. The author had to labour to bring in *dodhaka,* which he could do only by splitting the word, and that quite inaccurately, viz. *do'dhaka.*

रनैरन्वितं युक्तं लघुना गुरुणा तथा।
ख्यातं रथोद्धता नाम वृत्तमेकादशाक्षरम्।। २३।।

23. The famous metre called 'Rathoddhatā' has eleven syllables comprising of the groups 'ra', 'na', 'ra' combined with a shoart and a long vowel—(all in the enumerated order).

As in my (verse)—

'O king, your banner, hoisted on your chariot (Rathoddhatā) facing (the enemies) in each battel looks like the creeper-like eye-brows of the fickle wives of (your) foes threatening the enjoyment of lovely pleasures'.

गुरुद्वययुतैरन्तेरनभैरुपलक्षिता ।
गदितं स्वागता नाम वृत्तमेकादशाक्षरम्।। २४।।

24. The metre called the 'Svāgatā' contains eleven syllables comprising two long syllables coming at the end of 'ra', 'na', and 'bha' groups.

As in my (verse)—

'It is only the good who really live in this world;—the good, who have heaps of virtues, spotles like the pieces of gems, busy in giving the desired obejct to those who supplicate, and who have their heads bent low in offering welcome (Svāgata) to those who approach them'.

सकारैरन्वितं वृत्तं चतुर्भिर्युगपत्स्थितैः।
उदितं तोटकं नाम वृत्तज्ञैर्द्वादशाक्षरम्।। २५।।

25. Those who know prosody name the metre having twelve syllables and consisting of four groups of 'sa' occurring consecutively as the 'Toṭaka'.

As in my (verse)—

'Reducing the great essence of love of th amorous age to mere memory, and attachment and infatuation having faded away, O wise one, taking an alms-bowl in hand, roam about in the wilderness all round'.[1]

1. The author had to labour hard to bring in the name of the metre in the stanza and that too in parts.

संलक्षितं जतजरैर्द्वादशाक्षरमक्षरैः।
छन्दोविचक्षणा वृत्तं वंशस्थाख्यं प्रचक्षते।। २६।।

26. The metre having twelve syllables with the scheme of 'ja', 'ta', 'ja' and 'ra' is called the 'Vaṁśastha by those well-versed in prosody.

As in my (verse)—

'Victorious are the prosperous good people possessed of proper merits, born of high family (Vaṁśastha) always removing the intense suffering of people due to inflammatoryh distress (ātapa) and thereby, they look like the high white umbrellas placed on huge bamboo sticks, warding of the intense heat of suffering from the humanity'.

अभिव्यक्तं नभभरैरक्षरैर्द्वादशाक्षरम् ।
वदन्ति वृत्तजातिज्ञा वृत्तं द्रुतविलम्बिनम्।। २७।।

27. Those who know the different kinds of metres call that metre the *'Drutavilambita'* which contains twelve syllables comprising of 'na', 'bha', 'bha' and 'ra', (in order).

As in my (verse)—

'The moon surrounded by clouds possessing the lustre of Śiva's neck and moving (both) quickly and slowly, sails in the sky, and (thereby) looks like a royal swan swimming admist the ripples of the Yamunā, and possessed of a beauty like that of Śiva's neck and moving both quickly and slowly (Drutavilambita)'.

समन्वितं मनजरैश्छिन्नं पूर्वाक्षरैस्त्रिभिः।
त्रयोदशाक्षरं नाम्ना कीर्तयन्ति प्रहर्षिणीम्।। २८।।

28. The metre having thirteen syllables comprising of 'ma', 'na', 'ja' and 'ra' (followd by a long syllable) and the caesura coming after the first three syllables is known as the 'Praharṣiṇī'.

As in my (verse)—

'The unpretended glory of those blissful people, who have become lustrous through their fame on account of charming virtues like self-respect and magnanimity, delights others (Praharṣiṇī);—the glory, which has been obtained by the growing prowess of their own arms and which serves as a menas of livelihood for each and every person devoted to them living in all directions.'

अभिज्ञातं तभजजैरन्तासक्तगुरुद्वयम्।
चतुर्दशाक्षरं वृत्तं वसन्ततिलकं विदुः।। २९।।

29. The metre having fourteen syllables comprising 'ta', 'bha', 'ja' and 'ja' (groups)(followed in the end by two long syllables, is known as the 'Vasantatilaka'.

As in my (verse)—

'On the arrival of his comrade, illustrious cupid, whose (associate) heredictory minister he was, the ornament of spirng (Vasantatilaka) whitish pale with blooming flowers, decorated his beloved, the beautiful earth, whose hair in the form of rows of bees were dressed in curls'.

अष्टाक्षरविरामेण युक्ता ननमयैः सयैः।
वदन्ति मालिनीनाम वृत्तं पञ्चदशाक्षरम्।। ३०।।

30. That metre is called the 'Mālinī' which has fiften syllables of the scheme 'na' 'na', 'ma', 'ya', combined with (another) 'ya', and the caesura resting on the eighth syllable.

As in my (verse)—

'To whom is not dear the wanton female-florist looking in every direction, getting started at the movement of even a blade of grass, saying, "No, No, No, No", at the time of loosening the girdle-string, and not letting of her upper garment for fear of laxity in her conduct?'

नज भैर्जजलैरन्तगुरुभिर्नर्कुटाभिधम्।
वृत्त चानष्टविच्छेदं विदुः सप्तदशाक्षरम्।। ३१।।

31. The 'Narkuṭa' is known as having seventeen syllables (of the scheme) of 'na', 'ja', 'bha', 'ja', 'ja' and a short and a long vowel in the end with the due caesura therein.

As in my (verse)—

'Tell me, how did you have your subjects attached (lit. reddened) to you while you rendered the kingdom white as lunar rays, by means of the heaps of fame of great virtue and prowess, secured by your own arm. To whom do your uncommon deeds not provide delight?'

जसजैः सयलैर्गेन युताष्टनवसंहृतिः ।
दशसप्ताक्षरा पृथ्वी कथिता वृत्तकोविदैः ।। ३२ ।।

32. The metre 'Pṛthvī' is defined by those versed in prosody as having seventeen syllables (of the scheme) of 'ja', 'sa', 'ja', 'sa', 'ya', a short syllable and a long one with the ceasura as eight and nine syllables.

As in my (verse)—

'That person destined to serve permanently, with his body covered with dust and his limbs tottering with fatigue, as he trudges towards his master's abode, a home of back-biters, thinks, infatuated as he is, that the entire earth is placed in his hands by the glances (of his master) that yield no reward'.

नसमैः रसलैर्गेन युक्ता सप्तदशाक्षरा ।
विच्छिन्ना हरिणी षड्भिश्चतुर्भिः सप्तभिस्तथा ।। ३३ ।।

33. The Hariṇī metre consisting of seventeen syllables (of the scheme) of 'na', 'sa', 'ma', 'ra', 'sa', a short vowel, and a long one, has its caesura as six, four and seven syllables.

As in my (verse)—

'As the time passes, pleasures cease to possess the same relish. Wealth and youth are transitory. Do meritorious deeds while this body does not perish. Some indescriable measurement of time runs quickly past like the frightened young fawns running in leaps and bounds'.

यमनैः सभलैर्गेन युक्ता सप्तदशाक्षरा ।
षडेकादशविच्छेदवती शिखरिणी मता ।। ३४ ।।

34. The Śikhariṇī is said to have seventeen syllables of the

scheme of 'ya', 'ma', 'na', 'sa', 'bha', a short vowel and a long one, with the caesura as six and eleven syllables.

As in my (verse)—

'Since anger has melted away, and with that has gone the pride of passion associated with prosperity. I think that ripeness agreeable to the ages of tranquillity has come. Now the mountain-land at its peak suits me most;—the land, which is lovely and hence fit for severe penance; and thus capable of ending this turmoil of births and rebirths'.

चतुःषट्सप्तविरति वृत्तं सप्तदशाक्षरम्।
मन्दाक्रान्ता मभनतैस्तगैश्चाभिधीयते।। ३५।।

35. The Mandākrāntā contains seventeen syllables (of the scheme) of 'ma', 'bha', 'na', 'ta', 'ta', and two long syllables with the caesura as four, six and seven syllables.

As in my (verse)—

'If one remembers those side-glances of your eyes of thick eye-lashes, accompanied by the big eye-corners, stealing away one's courage, then why in vain practise concentration in a forest by means of strict discipline? The venomous female serpent of slothful gait bites severely the hand it comes in contact with'.

मसजैः सततैर्गेन युक्तमेकोनविंशवत्।
शार्दूलक्रीडितं प्राहुश्छिन्नं द्वादशसप्तभिः।। ३६।।

36. The Sārdūlavikrīḍita is said to have nineteen syllables of the scheme of 'ma', 'sa', 'ja', 'sa', 'ta', 'ta' and a long syllable with the ceasura as twelve and seven letters.

As in my (verse)—

'Your sword does lion-like deeds on the battle-field against your foes—the sword, grown jagged with pearls sticking to it from the temples of elephants broken by terrible, infuriated and well-armoured warriors wafting vehemently its mane in the form of its fame and looked at by people frightened and confused at the beginning of its dreadful yawn'.

युक्तं मरभनैयैश्च त्रिभिः सप्ताक्षरैस्त्रिभिः।
छेदैश्च स्रग्धरा वृत्तमेकविंशाक्षरं विदुः॥ ३७॥

37. The Sragdharā is known to have twenty-one syllables of the scheme of 'ma', 'ra', 'bha', 'na' and three 'ya' groups, with caesura at every seventy syllable.

As in my (verse)—

'O Lord of the Earth, this world is adorned with your fame looks as if wearing garlands of perfume; —the fame, which possesses the lovely grace of intrinsic merit, which has reached the position of the ear-lotus of the celestial ladies on account of its immense virtues (similar to those of ear-lotus) ; and which has the lusture of sparkling pearls, of blooming *lavalī*, of the *kunda* flowers and of the moon'.

इति सरलतरत्वात्सर्वकाव्योचितत्वात्।
सुकविपरिचितत्वात्कीर्णकर्णामृतत्वात्।
परुषविषममात्रादुर्विरामोझ्झितेयं
प्रचुररुचिरवृत्तव्यक्तिरुक्ता हिताय॥ ३८॥

38. This exposition of numerous charming metres, devoid of difficult and uneven syllables and free from irregular caesura has been made for the benefit (of students) because (the metres in it) are easy, suited to all poetic needs, commonly used by great poets and which infuse ambrosia into the ear.

Here ends the first chapter called "THE CHOICE OF METRES" in the Suvṛttatilaka composed by Kṣemendra, also known as Vyāsadāsa, son of revered Prakāśendra.

—•—

द्वितीयो विन्यासः

Chapter II

कृते प्रसिद्धवृत्तानां लक्ष्यलक्षणसंग्रहे।
अधुना क्रियते तेषां गुणदोषप्रदर्शनम्॥ १॥

1. Having put together the definitions and illustrations of

popular metres, now the exposition of their merits and demerits is taken up.

न षट्सप्ताक्षरे वृत्ते विश्राम्यति सरस्वती।
भृङ्गीव मल्लिकाबालकलिकाकोटिसङ्कटे।।२।।

2. The goddess of speech does not rest comfortably on metres of six or seven syllables, just as a bee cannot rest on the narrow end of a tender bud of *mallikā* flowers.

समासैर्लघुवृत्तानामसमासैर्महीयसाम् ।
शोभा भवति भव्यानामुपयोगवशेन वा।।३।।

3. Lovely metres, if short, look charming with compounds and, if long, without compounds, or as the context suits them.

अनुष्टुप्छन्दसां भेदे कैश्चित्सामान्यलक्षणम्।
यदुक्तं पञ्चमं कुर्याल्लघु षष्ठं तथा गुरु।।४।।
तत्राप्यनियमो दृष्टः प्रबन्धे महतामपि।
तस्मादव्यभिचारेण श्रव्यतैव गरीयसी।।५।।

4-5. Some have generally defined the scheme of Anuṣṭup metres as 'the fifth syllable should be short and the sixth long'. But exceptions to his have been seen even in (the compositions of) the great. Thus, invariably appeal to the ear is of greater importance.

As in Kālidāsa's (verse)—

In that family of great purity was born Dilīpa of greater piety, who was a moon among kings, and was like the very moon born of the milky ocean'.

उपजातिविकल्पानां सिद्धो यद्यपि सङ्करः।
तथापि प्रथमं कुर्यात्पूर्वपादाक्षरं लघु।।६।।

6. Though the mixing up of various kinds of Upajāti metres is allowed, yet one should like the initial syllable of the first foot to be short.

As in revered Utpalarāja's (verse)—

'Why do these thick drops of your tears fall, dark on account of the collyrium (they have) washed away; and (thereby) looking like long strings of bees resting on the creeper like thick line of hair above the navel?'

सूत्रस्येवात्र तीक्ष्णाग्रं श्लोकस्य लघुना मुखम्।
कर्णं विशति निर्विघ्नं सरलत्वं च नोज्झति।।७।।

7. With the (one) short (syllable) at the beginning of the śloka, like the end of a thread, it becomes sharp and enters into the ear (of the listener) without difficulty and does not obstruct the cadence.

गुर्वक्षरेण संरुद्धं ग्रन्थियुक्तमिवाग्रतः।
करोति प्रथमं स्थूलं किञ्चित्कर्णकदर्थनाम्।।८।।

8. If obstructed by heavy syllables, as if possessed of a knot at the end, it causes some pain to the ear.

As in Kālidāsa's (verse)—

'There is in the northern direction the lord of mountains called Himālaya, possessed of divine spirit. With its extremities entering in the eastern and the western ocean, it stands like the measuring-rod of the Earth'.

त्र्यक्षरैस्त्र्यक्षरैरवच्छेदैराभाति दोधकम्।
अतोऽल्पैरधिकैर्वापि यतिं तालमिवोज्झति।।९।।

9. With the caesura falling after every three syllables does the Dodhaka look charming. (If the caesura be) on larger or lesser (number of syllables) than this, (the metre) seems to lost its noise as well as its rhythm.

As in my (verse)—

'Gather the grace arising from honouring and adoring the good; avoid the company of the evil. This is the means to avoid the danger of sinking in the furious ocean of existence which is difficult to cross'.

(With the ceasura) on larger or lesser syllables as in Tuṅjīra's (verse)—

'He, whose eyes have been well-curd (lit. cleared) by collyrium of seeing your moon-like face, does not see the strange path of the god of Death which presents itself before everyone'.

शालिनी श्लथबन्धैव स्वभावेन विभाव्यते।
उत्तेजयेत्तां यत्नेन मन्ददीपशिखामिव।। १०।।

10. Naturally a Śālinī looks charming with its joints loosely put together; (the poet) should increase its lustre with great effort, just as a dim flame of the lamp (has to be lit up with great effort).

Loose, as in my (verse)—

'The lustre of the moon seems to be a wicked man's treasure, since it causes a burning pain to those abroad, humiliating in the pride of the arrogant (ladies), and extremely busy in putting to shame all the good virtues.

शत्रन्ताक्षरसंयोगैः किञ्चित्कार्कश्यकारिभिः।
अन्ते विसर्जनीयैश्च शालिनी याति दीप्तताम्।। ११।।

11. A Śālinī becomes lustrous through the use of present participles, sounding a bit harsh, and with 'visargas' at the end.

As in my (verse)—

'When once immersed, from whose heart can be drawn out the side-long glances of ladies of thick eye lashes, beaming with love, beautiful with tremulous pupils, plunged in bashfulness and sharp like the ends of *ketakai* leaves, issuing forth slantingly?'

श्लथस्वभावान्माधुर्यं शालिन्याः परिवर्ज्यते।
रुचिः प्रयाति मन्दाग्नेः क्षीरेणात्यन्तमन्दताम्।। १२।।

12.Through looseness, a Śālinī gets devoid of sweetness, just as the appetite of one suffering from dyspepsia grows weaker by (taking) milk.

विसर्गयुक्तैः पादान्तैर्विराजति रथोद्धता।
कलापरिचयैर्जाता लटभेव प्रगल्भताम्।। १३।।

13. A Rathoddhatā shines with *visarga* at the end of its

feet, just as a beautiful girl becomes eloquent through her intimate knowledge of the art of love-making.

As in my (verse)—

'Here, in the spring season, blow constantly the breezes of the Malaya mountain—the breezes, unsteady like snakes, kindling fire in the hearts of ladies whose husbands are abroad, and captivating the hearts of lovers'.

अविसर्गैस्तु पादान्तैर्निष्प्रभैव रथोद्धता ।
अप्रार्थनाप्रणयिनी म्लानमानैवे मानिनी ।। १४ ।।

14. A Rathoddhatā having no *visarga* at the end of its feet lacks lustre like a proud woman, whose pride has been humbled and who shows attachment without being importuned.

As in Kalaśaka's (verse)—

'She of tremulous eyes uneasy to see her lover, let go from her palm the water (she had taken to) sprinkle her lover with; —the water, which was bespanged with the reflection of her eyes, which she took to be śaphara fish, and saying, "Oh I have it." I have it".

साकाराद्यैर्विसर्गान्तैः सर्वपादैः सविभ्रमा ।
स्वागता स्वागता भाति कविकर्मविलासिनी ।। १५ ।।

15. A Svāgatā displaying poet's power and playful with all its feet beginning with the letter 'ā' and ending in *visarga*, is really welcome and charming.

'The unsteady clouds during the rains, breaking down the firmness of travellers, beautiful with the streaks of lightning, looking like the border-line gems, or like the pearl-necklaces on bulky bosoms, are gathering round'.

But not as in my (verse)—

'O traveller! What a pitiful condition (of yours) must be as you have to wait at this time, when the sky (is overcast) with clouds heavy with the weight of water (in them), when the slopes of mountains are beautiful with intoxicated peacocks, and when the groves of 'kadamba' tress become the store-house of flowers'!

दुततालयैरेव व्यक्तं रुक्षाक्षरैः पदैः।
प्रवर्तयति यच्चित्तं तत्तोटकमभीप्सितम्।। १६।।

16. That kind of Taṭaka is desirable which makes the mind dance by its flowing rhythm and quick movement with feet containing harsh (lit. dry) letters.

As in my (verse)—

(It is only) the one who has done meritorious deeds that can enjoy (lit. drink or kiss) the face of (his) charming wife;—the face, whose bee-like eyes are rolling with infatuation, which exhibits great love, which is adorned with spring flowers, which possesses the lustre of a lotus, and which is the store-house of nectar'.

असमस्तपदैः पादसन्धिविच्छेदसुन्दरम्।
सर्वपादैर्विसर्गान्तैर्वंशस्थं यात्यनर्घताम्।। १७।।

17. A Vaṁśastha, beautiful when its words are not compounded and the 'sandhi' is not effected at the end of its feet, becomes highly valued if all its feet have no combined letters and end in 'visargas'.

As in Bhaṭṭa Bāṇa's (verse)—

'Victorious are the particles of dust of Tryambaka's feet,—the particles, which rest on Bāṇasura's head, which kiss the numerous crest-ornaments of the ten-headed demon, which lies on the ends of the top-knots of the lord of gods and demons, and which dispel darkenss (of ignorance)'.

Of different nature (is) another Vaṁśastha (verse) of his—

'I bow at Bharvu's lotus-like feet, which have been honoured by the descendants of the Maukharī family with the bow of their heads and whose red toes move on the prominent seat on the platform made by the crowns of all the feudatory chiefs'.

प्रारम्भे द्रुतविन्यासं पर्यन्तेषु विलम्बितम्।
विच्छित्त्या सर्वपादानां भाति द्रुतविलम्बितम्।। १८।।

18. A Drutavilambita looks charming if it begins with quick movement and ends with a slow one, and if all its feet are devoit of 'sandhis'.

As in my (vsere)—'

'Why do you always guard the wretched riches which are transitory like the water-drops on a lotus petal?? It is glory that lash longer and not life which is fickle like the moving scarf of a young elephant's ear'.

Lacking quick pace and having slow movement 'as in my (verse)—

'Great Śiva, is the only support of the people, who are fallen deluded, drowned and gone to the lowest depth with their hundred of kinsfolk in this frightful ocean-like world'.

आकारमन्थरैः प्रायः पादे पादेऽक्षरैस्त्रिभिः।
शेषाक्षरैर्द्रुततरैः प्रहर्षाय प्रहर्षिणी ।। १९ ।।

19. A Praharṣinī gladdens one if it has in each of its feet three syllables heavey with teh sound 'ā' and the rest having a quick movement.

As in Śrī Harṣadeva's (verse)—

'it is only the blessed in whose ears reach (lit. come within an earshot of) the words repeated by young parrots and sārikā birds—the worlds, which convey whatever has been said before her friends by the maiden bearing the irremediable pain of Cupid's arrow'.

Contrary to this (is) my (verse)—

'The evening twilight has for the moment sown on this earth the seed for the growth of intense darkness in that swarms of bees are darting forth, uneasy as they are because of the fear of being entrapped in the closing calyxes'.

वसन्ततिलकस्याग्रे साकारे प्रथमाक्षरे।
ओजसा जायते कान्तिः सविकासविलासिनी ।। २० ।।

20. With the intial letter having the sound 'ā', the splendour which becomes charming when developed, rises in the "Vasantatilaka" through its forcefulness.

As in Ratnākara alias Vidayādhipati's (verse)—

'May Śiva bestow happiness upon you,—Śiva, who bears a grandeuh of neck which has the dreadful lustre of poison resembling a beautiful wreath of blue lotuses clustered together; and which is of a dark colour as if by the smoke of incense which being presented (to Śiva) was drunk (by him)'.

आकारेऽपि कृते पूर्वं बन्धेऽल्पपदपेशले।
वसन्ततिलकं धत्ते निर्गन्धि रमणीयताम्॥ २१॥

21. If it is begin with the vowel 'ā' and if the joint (of the feet) is delicate through (employment of only) a few letters, Vasantatilaka, being free from knots, attains charm.

As in Parimala's (verse)—

'What king other than the lord of Avantī, has his heart set on the sweet and flavoury compositions of eminent poets, just as none but a swan (is keen) on bright, tender lotusstalks or a bee on fresh clusters of mango flowers?'

विसर्गहीनपर्यन्ता मालिनी न विराजते।
चमरी छिन्नपुच्छेव वल्लीवालूनपल्लवा॥ २२॥

22. A Mālinī with no 'visargas' at the end, does not look nice just as a yak (does not look nice) with its tail cut or a creeper with its sprouts lopped off.

As in Bhaṭṭa Bhallaṭa's (verse)—

'O Mālatī, why not better fade away in the sun, or be totally consumed in the bower in the forest fire, since you have been wreathed among ordinary flowers by numerous heartless people ignorant (of the qualities) of stems and leaves?'

It is perfect in Kālidāsa's (verse)—

'Then that flower-bannered god, approached Indra with folded hands, having placed his missile, the sprout of a mango-tree in his comrade Spring's hand, and having put on his shoulder, marked with the marks of bracelets of Rati, his bow whose ends were beautiful like the creeper-like eye-brows of lovely women'.

द्वितीयार्द्धे समस्ताभ्यां पादाभ्यां मालिनी वरा।
प्रथमार्द्धे समस्ताभ्यां पादाभ्यामवरा मता॥ २३॥

23. A Mālinī is thought to be charming with compounds in its latter half (i.e. third and fourth foot); it looks clumsy with compounds in the first hafl (i.e. first and second foot).

With compounds in the latter half, as in Gandinaka's (verse)—

'The copper-like flame of the lamp, being refelcted on the expansive breasts of the proud ladies, who are loosening the knots of their upper garment with their hands, forecasts the future playful writing of letters with nails'.

With compounds in the first half, as in Rājassekhara's (verse)—

''Here, at the advent of spring swarms of bees, with their bodies whitened when anointed with the pollen of clusters of flowrs, buzzing a sweet hum, sportively hover round and graceful, and unsteady Sinduvāra tree, which is dear to the bees on account of its pungent smell'.

अज्ञोऽप्यलक्ष्यं मालिन्यां वीणायामिव विश्वरम्।
श्रुत्वैवोद्वेगमायाति वाचा वक्तुं न वेत्ति तम्।। २४।।

24. Even an ignorant person feels disgusted, although he cannot express it, on listening to a jarring tone unexpected in the Mālinī, as in a lute (*vīṇā*).

As in Bhaṭṭendurāja's (verse)—

'Although getting prosperous on your account, the beloved of a ritualist accustomed to oil lamps, when her upper garment was removed in privacy, flings her petticoat at the jewelled lamp, striked at it with her lotuses adorning the ears and extinguishes it with the breeeze blown with her hands'.

गुरुलध्वादिनियमादविभ्रष्टेऽपि लक्षणात्।
दोषस्त्वदुपगतेत्यत्र श्रोत्रग्राह्योऽस्ति विस्वरः।। २५।।

25. Though (the metre) does not violate the scheme of long and short vowels, yet in the expression *tvadupaga* lies the defect to be perceived by hearing—namely, inharmoniousness.

प्रथमं द्व्यक्षरैश्छेदैस्ततस्त्रिचतुराक्षरैः।
पञ्चाक्षारैश्च पर्यन्ते नर्कुटं याति चारुताम्।। २६।।

26. With caesura after two syllables in the begining, after three and four later on, and after five in the end, the Narkuṭa becomes charming.

As in Vīradeva's (verse)—

'O mother, how has your foot placed impetuously at the head of the grat demon in the form of a buffalo become as heavy as the lord of mountains—your foot , which has a copper-coloured sole, is delicate like a lotus-petal and which resounds with the sound of anklets when moving in a gait similar to that of a royal swan'.

Different is (the following verse of) his—

'With the bright spear implanted in the body of the huge buffalo-demonyou look like a cave of collyrium filled with smoke and with a flame of fire blazing at its top, or like the reaised up rock in the Yamunā with white snake seated on it, or like the dark half of a month with clouds marked with streaks of lightning'.

असमासैः पदैर्भाति पृथ्वी पृथ्वी पृथक्स्थितैः।
समासग्रन्थिभिः सैव याति सङ्कोचखर्वताम्।। २७।।

27. The grand Pṛthvī metre becomes beautiful with words not in a compound and placed separately. The same (metre) becomes crippled on accouont of contraction and by containing knotty compounds.

Having separate words, as in Sāhila's (verse)—

'in playful battel of love, the fish-bannered god, in the case of impassioned people, renders the catching of hair a favour, biting with teeth an ornamentation, the curving of eyes as straighforwardness, the offering of mouthfuls of nectar as propitiation, scratching with nails as kindness, and embracing closely as causing no pain'.

Full of compouunds as in my (verse)—

'Victoroius are the coquettish movements of fawn-eyed ladies in the act of erotic play: the conquettish movements, which are adorned with the hissing sound uttered at the pain caused by the catching of the hair, and resembling the sweet buzzing of a bee unconcious on account of the pain of having been (trapped) in a lotus, and which abound in loving kisses imprinted in the ecstacy of joy'.

पृथ्वी साकारगम्भीरैरोजःसर्जिभिरक्षरैः ।
समासग्रन्थियुक्तापि याति प्रत्युतदीर्घताम् ।। २८ ।।

28. Containing letters full of vigour and the vowel 'a', the 'Pṛthvī' (metre), though knotty with compounds, becomes long.

As in Bhaṭṭa Nārāyaṇa's (verse)—

'Whence has this thundering roar, unheard of hitherto fore, dreadful to ears and coming from the ocean of battle has risen?— the roar, which has filled the vacuum of the earth and the heaven, and which imitates the terrible echoing and rumbling noise of clouds, the Puṣkaras and the Āvartakas, agitated by the winds on doomsday'.

त्वरातरलविच्छेदैर्विभाति हरिणीपदैः ।
मन्थरैर्ग्रन्थिबद्धेव याति निष्पन्दसङ्गताम् ।। २९ ।।

29. A Hariṇī shines withits feet separated by liquid and quick caesura. With slow caesura it becomes listless as if bound up with knots.

Having quick feet as in Dīpaka's (verse)—

'In pride of power and in the company of comrades, a person may pace quickly across the extremely dreadful wilderness made all the more terrible by pitiless robbers of trifling riches.But, O Traveller, the raod near the town in evidently hard to cross becaues it is full of soldiers in the form of the amorously dancing side-long glances of the city brides'.

Withthe slow-moving feet as in Bhaṭṭendurāja's (verse)—

'You my friend, fish-hook with your abode in a palce of pilgrimage, given to impartiality, gifted with an extremly strong body and a sound character, and possessed of great talent why do you deal a death blow to the life of one who wants to drink you in with winkless gaze—you, who are well stringed, an associate of river banks, firm at both knobs, quite strong and circular'.

त्रिषु पादेषु विश्रान्तविलासैर्ललिता पदैः।
अन्ते तरङ्गितगतिर्हरिणी हरिणीतराम्।। ३०।।

30. Beautiful with syllables lovely through the play of pauses in the (first) three feet, and in the end possessing the (quick) movements of ripples, the Hariṇī becomes all the more captivating.

As in the same (Bhaṭṭendurāja's) verse—

'O travellers, leave the road near the bank of the Godāvarī and seek another path, for there some accursed girl has made the red Aśoka tree (wear) a cloak of newly budding sprouts by striking her lotus-like foot against it'.

शिखरिण्याः समारोहात्सहजैवौजसः स्थितिः।
सैव लुप्तविसर्गान्तैः प्रयात्यन्यन्तमुन्नतिम्।। ३१।।

31. Through its ascendancy (samāroha) the Śikhariṇī has forcefulness inhrent in it; and the same (metre) becomes much more developed if the ends (of its feet) have the 'visargas' dropped.

As in Muktukana's (verse)

'As the smoky clouds, when moving cover the cavity of the sky; as the glow-worms appear like the parks of fire, and as the quarters get tawny by the flash of bright lightninig. So I feel as if the tree grove of travellers must have been caught in a woodland conflagration of love'.

Different in Bhaṭṭa Śyāmala's (verse)—

'How can the mouthful of wine, imparting lustre to her gaze acting as a friend of ripe 'Sahakāra' tree, anyhow reach the head of Madhu?—the mouthful of wine, which is retained in the expanse of cheeks, which is like the bee in the cavity of a lotus and which when rerleased by the playful lady makes the Bakula tree put forth blossoms'.

शिखरिण्याः पदैश्छिन्नैः स्वरूपं परिहीयते।
मुक्तालताया निःसूत्रमुक्तैर्मुक्ताफलैरिव।। ३२।।

32. With feet disjointed the Śikhariṇī loses its very form, just as a pearl necklace loses its very form when its pearls are scattered about.

As in Bhaṭṭa Bhavabhūti's (verse)—

'The world has no reality. The three worlds have been robbed of their jewel. The universe has lost its light. Kinsmen take refuge in death. Cupid is humiliated. The object of people's eyes is thwarted (now). Why are you busy making this world a wilderness?'

श्लोकेऽस्मिन् सचमत्कारसरसास्वादशालिनि।
केवलं शिखरिण्यैव स्वरूपमपहारितम्।। ३३।।

33. In this (above) verse which contains flavoury relish and charm, the form has been spoiled merely by the (metre) Śikhariṇī.

मन्थराक्रान्तविश्रब्धैश्चतुर्भिः प्रथमाक्षरैः।
मध्यषट्केऽतिचतुरे मन्दाक्रान्ता विराजते।। ३४।।

34. Mandākrāntā looks beautiful with the first four syllables in a slow movement and with the six in the middle also proceeding slowly in an extremely clever manner.

As in Kālidāsa's (verse)—

'With your shadow fording through the city of Brahmāvarta, you should honour the field of Kurus, notorious on account of the destruction of the Kṣatriyas, where the Wielder of Gāṇḍīva watered the faces of groups of kings by the rain of his sharp arrows just as you water lotuses with showers'.

Alike in the beginning and in the middle as, again, in his (verse)—

'A certain Yakṣa, neglacting his duties, with his powers (lit. greatness) fades, because of his master's curse lasing for a year and making the punishment heavier on account of his separation from his beloved, made his residence inthe hermitages on the Rāmagirī, where the trees have dense shade, and the waters have been purified by Sītā bathing in them'.

साकाराद्यक्षरैः पादपर्यन्तैः सविसर्गकैः।
शार्दूलक्रीडितं धत्ते तेजोजीवितमूर्जितम्।। ३५।।

35. With the long syllalbe 'ā' in the beginning and with 'visarga' at the end of its feet, a Śārdūlavikrīḍita comes to posses the high lusture which is its very life.

As in Bhaṭṭa Śyāmala's (verse)—

'O king, there shines your arm which brings widowhood to enemies' wives—the arm, which is the tying post for the elephant of victory, a bridge of rocks for crossing the ocean of distress, the eastern mountain for the dazzling glory of the sword, and the sportive pillow for the goddess of wealth, and the Mandara mountain for churning immortality out of the ocean of battle'.

Contrary is Lāṭa Ḍiṇḍīra's—

'It is indeed wonderful that a certain king, of great lusture, adorened this world, with the waters of the Ganges brought from the abode of the lord of gods. But is it not more wonderful, O you, the very milky ocean possessing the beauty of lunar rays, that you have filled the abode of Brahman with the greatness of your glory, even from (your position on) the earth?'

विसर्जनीयस्योत्वेन पदैर्निम्नोन्नतैरिव।
शार्दूलक्रीडितं याति पाठे सायासतामिव।। ३६।।

36. With the 'visargas' changing to '*o*' a Śārdūlavikrīḍita causes difficulty in reading, as if its feet wre falling high and low.

As in Muktākaṇa's (verse)—

'The treasses of the fawn-eyed lady loek victorious, dishevelled as they are at the end of amorous sport,—the tresses, which are the playful 'chaurie' of Cupid, which constitute series of clouds of black hair, which make theh peacocks restless with passion as they dispel all idea of darkness by means of the moonlike face (hidden under them), and which infatuate swarms to bees of pursue impetuously the sweet fragrance.'

विच्छिन्नपादं पूर्वार्द्धे द्वितीयार्द्धे समासवत्।
शार्दूलक्रीडितं भाति विपरीतमतोऽधमम्।। ३७।।

37. With words put separately in the first half, and full of compounds in the second half, a Śārdūlavikrīḍita looks nice; but if (the order is) reversed, (it is reduced to) a low type.

(With words put separately) in the first half as in Bhaṭṭa Bhavabhūti's (verse)—

'O wicked one, set at liberty Sītā in the hands of Marut's son, now, if you have, in our absence, taken her away out of ignorance or arrogance of sovereignty; otherwise accompanied by your son youwill go the kingdom of Death, (situated) at the end of the quarters and obscured by the canopy of blood oozing out of the wounds inflicted by murderous arrows shot by Lakṣmaṇa'.

Contrary is Rissu's (verse)—

'Why do you, in vain, want to bathe in the celestial Gangetic water, abounding in foam excelling the beauty of the foam of the milky ocean and extending up to the ends of quarters, when there is at hand the Ganges of your own fame pervading the seven regions at its will and capable of washing off the soot of sins of the Kali age?'

आद्यन्तयोर्गुणोत्कर्षकान्त्या सर्वातिशायिनोः।
शार्दूलक्रीडितं धत्ते मध्ये तद्गौरवोन्नतिम्।। ३८।।

38. By the excellence of merits in the first and the last (foot), excelling all others, a Śārdūlavikrīḍita attains exaltation in its middle because of them.

As in Kālidāsa's (verse)—

'May the buffaloes enter waters suitable for drinking and splashing under their horns. May the crowd of deer chew the cud in the dense shade of the Kadamba tree. May the lordly pigs destroy confidently the 'musta' grass in the pools. And may our bow take rest with its sring loosened'!

आद्यन्ताकारविरहात् पर्यन्ते चाविसर्गतः।
शार्दूलक्रीडितं स्वस्य रूपं नैवोपलभ्यते।। ३९।।

39. With the absence of 'a' in the beginning and at the end (of a foot) and with no 'visargas' at the end, a Śārdūlavikrīḍita does not gain its virtual form.

As in Śrī Yaśovarman's (verse)—

'The blue lotus which had the beauty of your eyes has sunk in water. O dea, the moon whichrmitated the beauty of your face has been obscured by clouds. The royal swans which imitated your gait have also left. Destiny does not bear my musing with things possessing similarity to you'.

सुकुमाररसस्यात्र रक्षायै वृत्तमुद्धतम्।
वाक्पाकेनैव गलितं कविना नीतमल्पताम्।। ४० ।।

40. In order to embody (lit. save) a delicate sentiment, a rough metre has been used; the beauty of the metre has been belittled and spoiled by the poet through his well-developed language.

आकारगुरुयुक्तादिपर्यन्तान्तविसर्गिणी।
असंस्यूतविरामा च स्रग्धरा राजतेतराम्।। ४१ ।।

41. A Sragdharā looks brighter if it has 'visargas' at the end (of every foot) beginnning with a long syllable or having the vowel 'ā' and with its pauses not mixed up.

As in Rājaśekhara's (verse)—

'May the ladies accompanying the battalions along with their beloveds, seated on stone slabs underneath the creepers and the 'Kramuka' trees sweetely encricled by 'Tāmbūlī' groves drinking unceasingly the jice of coconut fruits in the vessels of plantain leaves, enjoying the outskirts of forest which relieve them of perspiration of fatigue of flying in the air, and which are resonant with the sweet warbling produced in the playful moments of flocks of 'Dātyūha' birds'.

Reverse, as in Cakraka's (verse)—

'It is true, O Lord of waters (i.e. ocean), that your waters filled the cavities of caves of nether regions, in them sported the direction elephants, the firmament was pervaded by them, they bore Lakṣmī in them, their waves kissed the skies, and they were the abode of Viṣṇu no doubt. But they somehow could only fill the cavity of the palm of Agastya, when he was going to sip them'.

आद्यन्ताकारविरहाद् बन्धदोषः स्फुटोऽपि यः।
अविलुप्तैर्विसर्गान्तैः स्त्रग्धरायां समीहते।। ४२।।

42. In Sragdharā the cleademerit arising from the absence of 'ā' in the beginning and at the end, is compensated by the presence of 'visargas' at the end (of each foot).

As my (verse)—

'For whose delight is in his hand his sword, (which has a lustre) greater than (that of) a blue lotus, (which is) like the tresses of Glory of valour, which has its flowers displayed in the form of jewels obtained by crushing (the templs of) elephants, which is a gallant hero to protect the earth, which is the cloth of the banner of glory fluttering on the top of the family mountains, (which is) dreadful like the torrential showers of rain at the doomsday to extinguish the glory of hosts of enemies, and which (is beautiful) like the sidelong glances of the goddess of Glory'.

एवमुद्देशलेशेन वृत्तानां दर्शितः क्रमः।
अनयैव दिशा सर्वं ज्ञेयं तज्ज्ञैर्यथोचितम्।। ४३।।

43. Thus by a few examples, an order of the metres has been indicated. Those well-versed in metrics should, in the same manner, know it in detail according to propriety.

मन्द्राक्रान्ता भवेन्मध्ये शालिनी पूरिताक्षरा।
उपेन्द्रवज्रं वंशस्थं पर्यन्तैकाक्षराधिकम्।। ४४।।

44. Sālinī becomes Mandākrāntā with a few syllales filled up in the middle, while Vaṁśastha becomes an Upendravajrā with the difference of one syllable at the end.

इत्यादि दर्शितं नेह स्वतः सिद्धो ह्ययं क्रमः।
न वेत्ति तदवृत्तज्ञस्तज्ज्ञस्य क्वोपयुज्यते।। ४५।।

45.These and other things have not been shown here as the usage is quite well-known. One, ignorant of prosody, will not know them. Of what avail is (their enumeration) for one who knows them?

इदमतिशय सूक्ष्मैर्वृत्तचर्चाविचारै-
रभिहितमभिगम्यं योगितुल्याशयानाम्।। ४६ ।।

46. here has been said something by way of subtle discussion on metred to be apprehended by those with keen (and analytic) insight like 'yogins', who are familiar with the excellences of speech in various forms, and who have known the various defects (of poetry) even in their minute aspects.

Here ends the second chapter called the "ENUNCIATION OF MERITS AND DEMERITS" in the Suvṛttatilaka composed by Kṣemendra, also known as Vyāsadāsa, son of revered

—•—

तृतीयो विन्यासः
Chapter III

प्रबन्धः सुतरां भाति यथास्थानं निवेशितैः।
निर्दोषैर्गुणसंयुक्तैः सुवृत्तैर्मौक्तिकैरिव।। १ ।।

1. A composition looks bright with well-used metres, devoid of defects and full of merits, as if with gems.

शास्त्रं काव्यं शास्त्रकाव्यं काव्यशास्त्रं च भेदतः।
चतुः प्रकारः प्रसरः सतां सारस्वतो मतः।। २ ।।

2. The expansion of speech is stated by the wise to be four fold—science, poetry, poetry in science, and science in poetry.

शास्त्रं काव्यविदः प्राहुः सर्वकाव्याङ्गलक्षणम्।
काव्यं विशिष्टशब्दार्थसाहित्यसदलङ्कृतिः।। ३ ।।

3. Those who understand poety, call that to be science which is marked with all the requisites of poetry. Poetry is the beautiful ornamental setting of chosen words and meanings going together.

शास्त्रकाव्यं चतुर्वर्गप्रायं सर्वोपदेशकृत्।
भट्टिभौमककाव्यादि काव्यशास्त्रं प्रचक्षते।। ४ ।।

4. Poetry in scinece, pertaining to the four-fold pursuit of man, provided instruction to all; while the works of Bhaṭṭi and Bhaumaka are said to illustrate science in poetry.

तत्र केवलशास्त्रेऽपि केचित्काव्यं प्रयुञ्जते।
तिक्तौषधिरसोद्वेगे गुडलेशमिवोपरि ।। ५ ।।

5. Then there are some who use poetry (i.e. poetic form) in a work on science only; (it serves as) a bit of jaggery taken after the bitter taste of a distasteful medicine.

As in Vāgbhaṭa's (verse) on medical science—

'Wine with a lotus therein (is) like the face of my beloved. Sweet voice resembles the beloved reproaching. A bedding lovely with the setting of flowers is like a creeper putting forth sprouts and flowers'.

शास्त्रं कुर्यात्प्रयत्नेन प्रसन्नार्थमनुष्टुभा।
येन सर्वोपकाराय याति सुस्पष्टसेतुताम् ।। ६ ।।

6. One should write one's work on science (śāstra) in a clear style with great effor in the 'anuṣṭup' metre by which it will be of use to all and (thus resemble) a distinct bridge (over the difficulties).

काव्ये रसानुसारेण वर्णनानुगुणेन च।
कुर्वीत सर्ववृत्तानां विनियोगं विभागवित् ।। ७ ।।

7. One who knows the difference (in various metres) should make use of all the metres according to the sentiment or the theme of description.

शास्त्रकाव्येऽतिदीर्घाणां वृत्तानां न प्रयोजनम्।
काव्यशास्त्रेऽपि वृत्तानि रसायत्तानि काव्यवित् ।। ८ ।।
पुराणप्रतिविम्बेषु प्रसन्नोपायवर्त्मषु।
उपदेशप्रधानेषु कुर्यात्सर्वेष्वनुष्टुभम् ।। ९ ।।

8-9. In poetry admitting scinece, very long metres are of no use; in a work on science admitting poetry, the length of the metres (varies) with the sentiment. One well-versed in poetry (Kāvyavit) should use Anuṣṭup metre in all works which are of the type of the Purāṇas, or which are didactic in nature, and aim at clear exposition.

नानावृत्तविशेषास्तु कवेः शास्त्रस्य शासनात्।
यान्ति प्रभोरिवात्यन्तमयोग्या अपि योग्यताम्।। १०।।

10. On account of their employment by a great (lit. praised) poet, many metres, though extremely unsuitable, become suitable as, in the case of the powerful, even improper (acts) become proper.

उग्रगोग्रहसंग्रामे तत्कालसदृशोपमाः।
दृष्टास्त एव वैराटेस्त एवाश्वाः किरीटिनः।। ११।।

11. In the dealdy fight to catch the cows, the same horses (once) belonging to Virāṭa's son (and then) to Arjuna, are seen to be compared (differently) as suits the occasion.

तथाप्यवस्थासदृशैः साधुशब्दपदस्थिताः।
सुवृत्तैरेव शोभन्ते प्रबन्धाः सज्जना इव।। १२।।

12. Rendered in good metres, seeming proper throughtheir appropriateness to the situation, the composition shines like good people who look brigh with good conduct, appearing proper on account of its befitting the occasion.

वृत्तरत्नावली कामादस्थाने विनिवेशिता।
कथयत्यज्ञतामेव मेखलेव गले कृता।। १३।।

13. The pearl-necklace of metres, placed at a wrong place through infatuation, shows one's ignorance as in the case of girdle string worn round the neck.

न हि नाम नवोन्मेषिकुचायाश्चारुचक्षुषः।
चिरत्यक्तस्मराचारे जराजीर्णकचे रुचिः।। १४।।

14. Truly a woman of beautiful eyes,with breasts lately

developing does not like a person whose hair have dropped through age, and who has long given up the art of love-making.

तस्मादत्र यथास्थाने विनियोगाय सङ्गतिः।
उदाहरणदिङ्मात्रैर्दर्शिताऽभिमता सताम्।। १५।।

15. So, here, a collection of metres agreeable to the learned, has been made with just an index of illustrations (to show) the proper way to employ them.

आरम्भे सर्गबन्धस्य कथाविस्तरसंग्रहे।
शमोपदेशवृत्तान्ते सन्तः शंसन्त्यनुष्टुभम्।। १६।।

16. In the beginning of an epic poem, written in 'sargas' or where a long theme is summarised or where both instruction and story have an equal status, the wise ones like (to use) the Anuṣṭup.

As in the beginning (of) Bhartṛmeṇṭha's (work)—

'There was a demon called Hayagrīva, the valour of whosearms was spread in the palaces of his allies, by wealth smiling in the form of white royal umbrellas.'

In the course of the story, as in Abhinanda's (work)—

'In that (town) was a lustrous king Śūdraka by name, who had conquered the (entire) circle of his enemies by the valour of his arm, and who (thus) did resemble god Indra'.

In the advice for restraint, as in my (work)—

'What is the use of ruminating over (lit. chewing the cud of) the bundle of stories and sciences? Those who would know the reality ought to seek with effort the Inner Light'.

शृङ्गारालम्बनोदारनायिकारूपवर्णनम् ।
वसन्तादि तदङ्गञ्च सच्छायमुपजातिभिः।। १७।।

17. The description of the beauty of a noble heroine, acting as excitant of the Erotic Sentiment and (that of) spring or its concomitants, becomes grand when it is done in the Upajāti metres.

Description of beauty, as in Kālidāsa's (verse)—

'That girl whose middle-part (i.e. the waist) was (thin) like a raised platform bore the thre fold on her belly;—the folds, which had been provided by her fresh youth as a staircase for love to climb up'.

Description of spring, as in the same poet's (verse)—

'The still unblossomed deep red 'palāśa' flowers, crooked like the digit of the young moon looked like the fresh nail-marks on the woodland tracts coming in contact with spring'.

रथोद्धता विभावेषु भव्या चन्द्रोदयादिषु।
षड्गुण्यप्रगुणा नीतिर्वंशस्थेन विराजते।। १८ ।।

18. The Rathoddhatā looks divine (in the description of)_ excitants like the rise of the moon and others. (In the description) of six-fold policy, the Vaṁśastha is suitable.

Rise of the moon, as in the same poet's (verse)—

'By catching the mass of hair in the form of darkness by the fingers in the form of its rays, the moon as if kisses the face of the night in which the eyes in the form of lotuses have closed'.

Policy, as in Bhāravi's (verse)—

'That Kirāta (lit. roamer in the forest) who was dressed as a Brahmacārin, who had been employed to know the conduct of the lord of the Kurus towards the subjects, on which depended the stability of his royalty, came back to Yudhiṣṭhira in the Dvaita forest, having known (everything)'.

वसन्ततिलकं भाति सङ्करे वीररौद्रयोः।
कुर्यात्सर्गस्य पर्यन्ते मालिनी द्रुततालवत्।। १९ ।।

19. A Vasantatilaka shines in rendering the mingling up of the dreadful and the heroic sentiments. At the end of a canto, (the author) should use a Mālinī full of racy rhythm.

The combination of the heroic and the dreadful (sentiments) as in Ratnākara's (verse)—

'May that form of Hari purify you;—the form, in which the mouthbright with the yawn is reflected as another mouthin the looking-glass in the form of nails, which is full of great rage,which destroyes the enemies armies and which accomplishes the arrogant demon's slaughter.'[1]

At the end of a canto, as in Kālidāsa's (verse)—

'She of beautiful hair, plucking flowrs for offerings, clever in cleaning the altar, bringing water and Kuśa grass for auspicious rites, and with her fatigue dispelled by the rays of the moon on the crest, worshipped Śiva every day'.

उपपन्नपरिच्छेदकाले शिखरिणी मता।
औदार्यरुचिरौचित्यविचारे हरिणी वरा।। २०।।

20. A Śikhariṇī (is of special use) on the occasion of due discrimination. In the consideration of propriety rendered beautiful with a lofty sense, Hariṇī is better.

At the time of due discrimination as in Bhartṛhari's (verse)—

'You are the preceptors of those who have applied their mind to Vedānta, we also are the servants of poets who talk in a wonderful manner. Even then we say, there is no greater merit than doing good to others, and there is nothing more charming in this world than (ladies) who have eyes like blue lotuses'.

In the narration of a lofty idea also, as in the same poet's (verse)—

'Some brough to existence this world in primeval times; others protected it, while others having conqured it, gave it away to others, as if it were straw. In this world, other brave men enjoy the fourteen regions. What is this fever of pride in people who are owners of a few towns?'

साक्षेपक्रोधधिक्कारे परं पृथ्वी भरक्षमा।
प्रावृट्प्रवासव्यसने मन्दाक्रान्ता विराजते।। २१।।

21. Pṛthvī can bear excellently at the time of ridicule and

1. The poet has used the five Sandhis of a Sanskrit drama.

anger mixed with taunt. In describing the calamity of living abroad in the rainy season, Mandākrāntā excels others.

A tuant, as in Yaśovarman's (verse)—

'This is Aṅgada sent by Lakṣmaṇa, and the son of him whose evening-rites on the ocean remained clearly undisturbed (though he) went about with the ten-headed demon is'.

Living abroad in the rainy season, as in Kālidāsa's (verse)—

'Having spent some months on that mountain, that lover, separated from his beloved, and with his fore-arm bereft of the armlet which had dropped (because of its emaciation) saw on the first day of Āṣāḍha, a cloud clinging to the moutain-peak, which looked beautiful like a young elephant battering the ramparts'.

शौर्यस्तवे नृपादीनां शार्दूलक्रीडितं मतम्।
सावेगपवनादीनां वर्णने स्त्रग्धरा मता।।२२।।

22. The Śārdūlavikrīḍita is preferred in the praise of a king's valour, and the Sragdharā in the description of vehement winds.

Praise of valour, as in Śrī Cakra's (verse)—

'The elephants cannot be ferried by boats. How many horses can cross on skins? O Lord, there fore, make your army go across (the streams) while water reaches only up to the knees; otherwise the Irāvatī is about to rise quickly with both its banks up, being flooded with the water of gushing tears from the eyes of (your) enemies who have run away out of fear of being uprooted'.

A strong breeze, as in my Pavanapañcāśikā—

'The dragrant breezed blow in vehemence,—the breezed which are friendly towards ladies fatigued in loveosport, which inflate the entire universe, which are ear-ornaments for the directions,which consist of the moving waves of camphor, which waft over the entire kingdom of Cupid, and which resemble the clear gleam of boisterous laughter, and the shine of pearls bursting forth from sea shells as the rolling conch shells strike against them'.

दोधकतोटकनर्कुटयुक्तं मुक्तकमेव विराजति सूक्तम्।
निर्विषयस्तु रसादिषु तेषां निर्नियमश्च सदा विनियोगः ।। २३ ।।

23. A stanza in a Muktatka form of Kāvya looks beautiful in Dodhaka, Toṭaka, and Narkutā metres. Neither thie ruse for the display of particular sentiments is limited nor is regulation prescribed for their employment.

शेषाणामप्यनुक्तानां वृत्तानां विषयं विना।
वैचित्र्यमात्रपात्राणां विनियोगो न दर्शितः ।। २४ ।।

24. The use of other metres, that have not been mentioned here and have no particular field, and which are merely objects of curiosity, has not been described.

इत्येष वश्यवचसां सर्ववृत्तप्रसङ्गिनाम्।
उक्तो विभागः सद्वृत्तविनिवेशे विशेषवान्।। २५ ।।

25. This special classification in the use of metres has been described for those who can mould speech and can use all the metres.

एकस्मिन्नेव यैर्वृत्ते कृतो द्वित्रेषु वा श्रमः।
न नाम विनियोगार्हास्ते दरिद्रा इवोत्सवे।। २६ ।।

26. Those who have practised in just one, two or three metres, are not in a position to employ other metres like the port in a festival who have limited resources to enjoy.

वृत्ते यस्य भवेद् यस्मिन्नभ्यासेन प्रगल्भता।
स तेनैव विशेषेण स्वसन्दर्भं प्रदर्शयेत्।। २७ ।।

27. One who has obtained proficiency in the use of a particular metre through practice, should weave his composition in the same.

एकवृत्तादरः प्रायः पूर्वेषामपि दृश्यते।
तत्रैवातिचमत्कारादन्यत्रारब्धपूरणात् ।। २८ ।।

28. Regard for a spcial metre is seen even in the ealier

writers. They display extreme beauty in the use of that metre and finish a composition (in a metre) other than the one in which they started.

अनुष्टुप्-सततासक्ता साभिनन्दस्य नन्दिनी।
विद्याधरस्य वदने गुलिकेव प्रभावभूः।। २९।।

29. The diligence of Abhinanda is always focussed in the Anuṣṭup. In the mouth of Vidyādhara the same metre is very effective like a magic pill.

स्पृहणीयत्वचरितं पाणिनेरुपजातिभिः।
चमत्कारैकसाराभिरुद्यानस्येव जातिभिः।। ३०।।

30. Pāṇini is lovable by his charming Upajāti verses, just as a garden grows agrreable by its jasmine creepers which work unique wonder.

वृत्तच्छत्रस्य सा कापि वंशस्थस्य विचित्रता।
प्रतिभा भारवेर्येन सच्छायेनाधिकीकृता।। ३१।।

31. There is some indescribable beauty in the Vaṁśastha, the royal umbrella (i.e. best) of metres, of lustrous gleam by which the beauty of Bhāravi's poetic fancy has been enhanced.

वसन्ततिलकारूढा वाग्वल्ली गाढसङ्गिनी।
रत्नाकरस्योत्कलिका चकास्त्याननकानने।। ३२।।

32. The speech in the form of creeper, which climbs the vasantatilakā and embraces it closely and has buds coming forth, looks bright in the garden of Ratnākara's eloquence.

भवभूतेः शिखरिणी निरर्गलतरङ्गिणी।
रुचिरा घनसन्दर्भे या मयूरीव नृत्यति।। ३३।।

33. The charming Śikharṇī employed by Bhavabhūti and having its flow unimpeded, dances like a lovely pea-hen, at the advent of the rainy season.

सुवशा कालिदासस्य मन्दाक्रान्ता प्रवल्गति।
सदश्वदमकस्येव कम्बोजतुरगाङ्गना।। ३४।।

34. Kālidāsa's Mandākrāntā, weel in his hand, saunters like a mare of Kāmboja country in the hands of a good trainer of horses.

शार्दूलक्रीडितैरेव प्रख्यातो राजशेखरः।
शिखरीव परं वक्रैः सोल्लेखैरुच्चशेखरः।। ३५।।

35. Rājaśekhara is famous on account of his Śārdūlavikrīḍita like a high-peaked mountain with his extremely steep ranges.

इत्येवं पूर्वकवयः सर्ववृत्तकरा अपि।
अस्मिन् हार इवैकस्मिन् प्रायेणाभ्यधिकादराः।। ३६।।

36. Thus ancinet poets, though using all the metres, had regard for a special one, as if for a particular necklace.

सुवर्णार्हप्रबन्धेषु यथास्थाननिवेशिनाम्।
रत्नानामिव वृत्तानां भवत्यभ्यधिका रुचिः।। ३७।।

37. The charm of metres, used in their proper places in compositions containing beautiful words, increases like the beauty of gems placed appropriately in ornaments of gold.

तस्माद्यथायं विनियोगमार्गः प्रदर्शितो वृत्तनिवेशनेषु।
तथैव कार्यः कविभिः कृतज्ञैरवश्यवाचां नियमस्तु नायम्।। ३८।।

38. Thus, this plan in the use of metres should be followed in the manner indicated by poets, faithful to poetic tradition. This rule does not apply to those who cannot mould their speech.

इत्यारुरुक्षोः प्रथमोपयुक्तं प्रवृत्तवाचश्च विवेककारि।
महाकवेरप्यतिसूक्ष्मतत्त्वविचारहर्षप्रदमेतदुक्तम् ।। ३९।।

39. This exposition in metrics does good to him who wants to make progress in the art of peotry. It trains the judgment of those who have been initiated in that art, and causes delight to great poets as it deals with subtle and delicate topics.

इत्यौचित्यप्रचुररचनाविश्रुतश्रव्यवृत्त-
व्यक्तिः शक्तिप्रसृतवचसां दर्शिता संग्रहेण।

क्षेमेन्द्रेण प्रणयिविपदां हर्तुराश्चर्यकर्तु-
भूभृद्भर्तुर्भुवनजयिनोऽनन्तराजस्य राज्ये ।। ४० ।।

40. Thus in the reign of Anantarāja the sovereign lord and conqueror of the world, of wonderful deeds, and chastiser of the misery of those devoted to him. Kṣemendra by means of this treatise has expalined the use of metres agreeable to hear and employed by those who are well known for their writing full of propriety, and whose speech has spread far on account of their poetic power.

Here ends the third chpater **"THE USE OF THE METRES"**, by name, in the Suvṛttatilaka, composed by Kṣemendra Vyāsadāsa, son of Sri Prakāśendra.

HERE ENDS THE SUVṚTTATILAKA.

Index